P9-BYE-550

THE AGINCOURT WAR

THE
AGINCOURT WAR

❖

A MILITARY HISTORY OF THE LATTER PART OF
THE HUNDRED YEARS WAR
FROM 1369 TO 1453

Lieutentant-Colonel
Alfred H. Burne
D.S.O., F.R.HIST.S

"Agincourt! Agincourt! Know ye not Agincourt"

WORDSWORTH EDITIONS

TO JOHN PREST
who took me to Agincourt

First published in 1956
by Eyre & Spottiswoode

Copyright © 1956 Alfred H. Burne

This edition published 1999
by Wordsworth Editions Limited
Cumberland House, Crib Street, Ware,
Hertfordshire SG12 9ET

ISBN 1 84022 211 5

© Wordsworth Editions Limited 1999

Wordsworth® is a registered trade mark of
Wordsworth Editions Limited

All rights reserved. This publication may not be
reproduced, stored in a retrieval system, or
transmitted, in any form or by any means, electronic,
mechanical, photocopying, recording or otherwise,
without the prior permission of the publishers.

Printed and bound in Great Britain
by Mackays of Chatham plc, Chatham, Kent.

CONTENTS

LIST OF MAPS

PREFACE

MY previous book on the Hundred Years War, *The Crecy War*, carried the story from its outbreak in 1337 to the Treaty of Bretigny in 1360. The war broke out again in 1369 and lasted, with some intervening truces, till 1453. It is this second war, or portion of war, which, for want of a better title, I call *The Agincourt War*, that is described in the following pages. For all practical purposes it was two, if not three wars, for there was a truce from 1396 to 1415, while by the treaty of Troyes in 1422 the war changed its complexion, the governmental forces of both England and France combining to fight the forces of the Dauphin–"the King of Bourges".

Nevertheless, a central theme runs through the whole 116 years covered by the Hundred Years War–the struggle to maintain an English dominion within the borders of what is now metropolitan France.

The military power and reputation of England was at its height in 1369. We shall see it wane, wax, and wane again. Though the art and conditions of war changed but slightly during the course of this war, we shall see, at its beginning, knights in mail armour, and artillery in its infancy, at its end, knights in full plate armour, *cap-à-pie*, and artillery so powerful that it decided the issue in the last battle of the war.

Much of the campaign was spent in desultory siege operations, lacking in interest; by describing these operations briefly it has been possible to treat the battles in considerable detail.

Agincourt was the dominant battle of the wars, but there were several other battles so little less significant from a military aspect, that I have tried to rescue them from ever-increasing oblivion. In the same way, Henry V was the dominating personality on the stage, but while I have tried to do justice to his prowess and exploits I have tried to penetrate the blinding dazzle that surrounds him and which obscures the abilities

11

and achievements of his chief lieutenants. These men are unknown even by name to most educated persons–except where
Shakespeare comes to their help

"Harry the King, Bedford and Exeter, Warwick and Talbot,
Salisbury and Gloucester."

These names, and others, such as Huntingdon, Scales, Fastolf
and Kyriell, should be in our flowing cups freshly remembered.

For the rest, this volume is framed on the same lines as its
predecessor. That is to say, it is designed primarily for the
"lay" public rather than for the historian or historical student,
and since the average lay reader is repelled by a multitude of
footnotes I have reduced these to a minimum. On the other
hand I have added an appendix to most chapters which includes
a brief note on the sources,[1] and further notes on controversial
points. These can of course be skipped by the general reader.

The space devoted to political matters is kept to a minimum,
in order to admit greater space for military operations, bearing in mind the sub-title, "a military history". The political
side cannot however be completely omitted; for instance, the
effects of the shortage of money on the operations must be
mentioned, but not the causes of that shortage or the measures
taken to remedy it; again, the strength of armies must be
examined, but not the method of recruitment–except in outline.

The reconstruction of all history is largely conjectural, and
this applies more to military than to any other branch of
history. It should therefore never be forgotten that there is
this element of the conjectural in the reconstruction of all the
operations described in this book. It would however be wearisome to the reader were I to qualify almost every other sentence with such expressions as "It would seem that", "In all
probability", or "The evidence points to the fact that". When
in particular doubt or difficulty I have applied the test of what
I call "Inherent Military Probability" to the problem and
what I.M.P. tells me I usually accept. It is of course easy for

[1] In footnote references I have usually inserted the page number only in cases
of actual quotation.

the critic to pour ridicule on this method, and many critics have done so; but I know no other method.

No attempt has been made to keep chapters at a fairly uniform size. I see no merit in this, and have preferred to embody one operation or clear-cut phase of the war in a single chapter. This should enable the reader to find the section he wished to consult with a minimum of reference to the index.

The positions of all places mentioned, except very unimportant ones, are either shown on one of the maps or described in the text.

I am again indebted to Mr. Robin Jeffs of Trinity College Oxford for reading the MS. and endeavouring to keep me straight in political matters. If at times I have wandered from the narrow path of rectitude this must be accounted to me for waywardness, and not attributed to my mentor. In conclusion I should like to express my thanks to the officials of the London Library, who have invariably accorded me courteous attention and assistance.

ALFRED H. BURNE.

THE AGINCOURT WAR

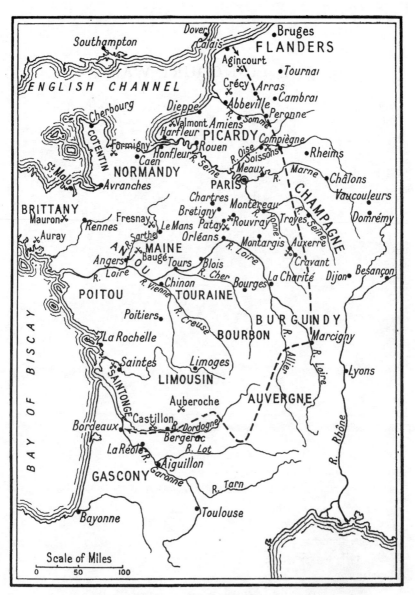

FRANCE DURING THE HUNDRED YEARS WAR
— — — → John of Gaunt's Grande Chevauchée

CHAPTER I

THE DUGUESCLIN WAR (1369–96)

"Overhead was the blue sky of heaven – but on the far horizon might be seen a little cloud, no bigger than a man's hand."

WITH the above words ended the book of which this volume is the sequel. The sky was blue, for the kings of England and France, after 22 years of warfare, had sworn eternal friendship: the little cloud indicated the uncertain state of health of the French monarch.

Throughout that period of 22 years, Edward III, king of England, pursued a single aim – the abolition of vassalage to the king of France for his French dominion; and now at last in the year 1360 the Treaty of Bretigny had brought it about.

By this treaty the king of England became the sovereign in his own absolute right of one third of the land of France. This abolition of the homage due by one king to another was calculated to remove the "running sore" that had poisoned the relations of the kings of two neighbouring countries for two centuries. It was all to the good. But it involved the transference by several provinces of France of liege loyalty from one over-lord to another. Although the idea of nationality was not as clear-cut as it was afterwards to become, this transference was bound to set up the sort of condition in a state that a surgical operation sets up in a body. It required a period of complete rest for the new limb to take root and thrive. A period of rest; that was the crux. The best, in fact the only, perceptible condition for this was that king John of France should hold the sceptre in his own country for several years; but his health failed and in 1364 he died, to be succeeded by his son Charles V.

"The death of king John sounded the knell of the Treaty of Bretigny."[1] The new king, Charles V was perhaps the least war-

---

[1] *The Genesis of Lancaster* by Sir James Ramsay, I, p. 460.

like of French kings, with the possible exception of Charles
VII. He had no desire for a new war, but on the other hand
he had every desire for revenge. And, being an astute man, he
worked patiently for the day when his desire might be fulfilled.

But in the meantime two events of importance occurred.
In Brittany "the War of Liberation" had dragged on with
alternating fortunes for over 20 years. Of the two claimants to
the Duchy, John de Montfort was sponsored by the English,
who by this time practically ruled the greater part of Brittany,
and Charles de Blois was the French nominee. . . . After a brief
truce the war had flared up again, and in 1364 it came to a
head. The rival armies met one mile to the north of the little
town of Auray, 60 miles south-west of Rennes. In the battle
that followed, the Anglo-Breton army, under Sir John Chandos,
utterly defeated the French under the count de Blois, who was
killed, and a Breton soldier named Bertrand Duguesclin, who
was captured. The battle ended the War of Liberation, and
ushered in the Golden Age for Brittany.

The second event of importance occurred in the far south.
King Pedro the Cruel (who has been maligned by his soubriquet almost as badly as "Butcher Cumberland") had been
ousted from the throne of Castile by his bastard half-brother
Henry of Trastamare. Pedro appealed for help to the Black
Prince, who had been created duke of Aquitaine by Edward III
and who held his court at Bordeaux the capital. Prince Edward
responded with alacrity to the appeal. Raising an army of
Anglo-Gascons–hereinafter called English for short–he crossed
the Pyrenees by the pass of Roncesvalles–rendered famous by
the epic story of Roland–and advanced through Pamplona to
Vittoria, along the same road that Wellington traversed in
1813. Prince Edward came up with the army of Henry of
Trastamare on a ridge six miles east of Najera, and gained a
signal victory over him. Bertrand Duguesclin, who commanded
a French contingent, was again captured. The English pursued
the enemy into Najera and rounded up the fugitives in a ravine
still called locally "The Ravine of the English".

The Spanish campaign, despite its victorious issue, had calamitous results. Not one penny of the war expenses was received from Pedro (who later was murdered by his half-brother) and it became necessary to impose heavy taxation on Aquitaine in consequence. Early in 1368 the Estates of Aquitaine granted the Black Prince the additional taxation that he asked for, but two of the chief nobles appealed to the king of England against it. Without awaiting his response they then appealed to the king of France. Now, by the Treaty of Bretigny Charles V had of course no jurisdiction in Aquitaine, but his jurists persuaded him, on the grounds that certain terms in the Treaty had not been carried out, that he had. After some hesitation therefore Charles "crossed the Rubicon" and received in audience the two appellants. After this action war became inevitable and on November 30, 1369 the king clinched the matter by confiscating Aquitaine—just as his grandfather had done a generation before.

Before taking this decisive step Charles had prepared for the coming war in various ways: the amassing of war supplies, the enrolling of allies and, most important of all, he cleverly "worked" the lesser landowners of Gascony through the medium of his brother, the duke of Anjou. All this time Edward III, totally unprepared for war, had made conciliatory overtures, but Charles with the bit in his teeth, passed them by unheeded, and even unanswered.

The Prince of Wales's attitude had not been so pacific. When the French king summoned him to Paris he made the famous reply "We shall go to Paris, but with helmets on and sixty thousand troops behind us"—a boast that it was not in his power to make good. To raise an army one tenth that size would have been about as much as was possible at that moment. The war was on!

THE DUGUESCLIN SUB-WAR (1369–96)

The war that ensued, lasting, with short intervals, from 1369 to 1396, has no name. We will call it the Duguesclin Sub-War,[1] after the soldier most closely associated with it. In this war nothing worthy of the name of battle was fought. This was because French armies refused to meet English armies in the field, acting under the strict orders of their king. English armies in consequence were able to roam the country at will, while the French confined themselves to sieges. The war is thus rather lacking in military interest, for there was remarkably little actual fighting.

In spite of the fact that the French had every advantage in war-stores, numbers, allies and surprise, and that they were invading a territory that was already on the verge of revolt, they were strangely hesitant. After over-running, without resistance, the outlying districts of Rouergue they resorted to sporadic assaults on isolated castles. This cautious behaviour may have been inspired by the knowledge that Sir John Chandos had been summoned south from his castle of St. Sauveur-le-Vicomte in Normandy and was soon on the war-path in Poitou.

For the first year of war the results were indeterminate. But a great blow befell the English in the death of the peerless John Chandos, "one of the purest glories of England",[2] before the gate of Lussac, in Poitou.[3] Sir Robert Knowles and Sir Hugh Calverley took up the mantle of Chandos.

LIMOGES

An event took place in the year 1370 which has been so distorted by subsequent writers that it deserves fairly detailed examination. In the course of the French advance the duke of Berry approached Limoges; but there was no reason to assault it for the bishop, who was in control, welcomed the French into the town. When the Black Prince heard of this treachery he was furious; the bishop had been one of his trusted friends, indeed he had stood as godfather to the Prince's son Richard of Bor-

[1] It was not a complete war, being terminated merely by a truce.
[2] The tribute of a Frenchman, B. Fillon, in a biography of *Jean Chandos.*
[3] The French still tend his monument at Lussac.

deaux, and there had been no suspicion of his disloyalty. The Prince of Wales vowed vengeance on the bishop, and together with his brother John of Gaunt who had now arrived at Bordeaux with reinforcements from home, he marched on Limoges: that is to say, the army marched; the Prince was too ill and weak, and had to be carried in a litter. The duke of Berry with his army prudently kept out of his way.[1] The English army laid siege to the city, mined it, and in six days carried it by storm.[2] There followed the famous "sack of Limoges".

Many writers–the worst offenders being, I am sorry to say, of English blood–have allowed their too fertile imaginations to run riot in describing the devilries committed by English troops egged on by the Black Prince himself. It may seem curious that a prince of chivalry, such as Edward of Woodstock was, should have descended to such depths of infamy on this one occasion–"the one blot on his escutcheon". But modern research has supplied the answer, and it is a simple one: there was no general massacre of Limoges. The too credulous followers of the recklessly irresponsible chronicler Froissart have seized upon his famous passage; "upwards of 3,000 men, women and children were put to death that day". This passage has been quoted *ad nauseam* by English writers, although Froissart discreetly deleted the number from his subsequent Amiens MS, which, never having been translated into English, was presumably unknown to the above-mentioned writers.

Roland Delachenal quotes Froissart's famous passage where the women and children fling themselves upon their knees before the Black Prince, crying for mercy, and he adds that this passage "is not negligible". Let us see. I once stood on the spot where the Prince's litter is reputed to have rested and tried hard to picture the scene as described by Froissart. I failed. In the first place, the women, in the confusion of the "massacre",

---

[1] "It is clear that the French feared the Prince of Wales, even though he had to be carried in a litter." *La Désolation des Eglises . . . pendant la Guerre de Cent Ans*, by H. Deniflé, Vol. II, p. 559.

[2] Prince Edward seems to have deliberately selected the anniversary of his victory at Poitiers, September 19, for the assault.

would not have been aware of the position of the Prince. Secondly, even if they had known it and had tried to approach him they would have failed. To reach him they would have had to pass up a narrow street, which would be barred by the Prince's escort; indeed, according to Froissart, they would have been struck down had they even attempted it for he states that they were killed wherever the attackers encountered them. Thirdly, the natural instinct of women in a confined town where murder is running riot is to slip out of the town, or to hide in a cellar, not to try to force their way, with their children, up a narrow street into the presence of the Prince. But it is a heart-rending scene, as painted by the shrewd old story-teller who knew well how to work upon the emotions of his readers. "Fut grant pitié"–it was a great pity–is an expression constantly flowing from his pen. In short, the passage *is* negligible: the whole scene was a figment of the chronicler's lurid imagination.

To sum up, the Prince of Wales made an example of the treacherous defenders of Limoges: on that the English chro-niclers are insistent and almost gleeful–but he did it by pillage and burning rather than by the taking of life. Even the bishop's life was spared–at the instance of John of Gaunt.[1]

THE GRANDE CHEVAUCHÉE

It would be tedious to recount in detail the many sieges and counter-sieges that took place in the next eight years, while the French slowly closed in on Bordeaux, nor to describe at length the *chevauchées* of the various English armies marching hither and thither through the land of France. There were no less than five of these *chevauchées*. The first, in 1369, was carried out by John of Gaunt, who landed at Calais and marched to Harfleur and back, without a real engagement with the enemy. The second, in 1370, was commanded by a commoner, Sir Robert Knowles. Also landing at Calais, he marched *via* Arras to Troyes, and thence passing Paris made for Brittany. Unfortu-

---

[1] The sources for the above account are listed in the Appendix to this chapter. For a detailed examination of the affair see an article in *The Fighting Forces* (February 1949), by Lt.-Col. A. H. Burne.

nately he quarrelled with the higher-born nobles, who eventually marched away and never rejoined him. Duguesclin took advantage of this dispersal of forces to pounce on isolated columns and completely break them up. The third campaign, in 1373 was the *Grande Chevauchée* of John of Gaunt, and deserves fuller treatment, for it captured the imagination of the civilized world of his day, and indeed in some respects was an epic resembling that of Christopher Columbus. Gaunt was provided with a huge army, 15,000 strong, and was ordered to take it to the relief of Gascony. Now the French had by this time attained the practical command of the sea and it was almost hopeless to try to go direct by sea. Gaunt accordingly landed at Calais, announcing that he would march right through the middle of France to Bordeaux. This was a map distance of nearly 600 miles through a hostile country. Everywhere he went the French armies evaded him, and hunger became his worst enemy, as, winter approaching, he entered the highlands of central France. Conditions got steadily worse, but Gaunt displayed the iron resolution of his father Edward III. On he marched over the mountains and at last down into the plain of the Dordogne, to reach Bordeaux at Christmas, nearly five months after setting out, having marched about 1,000 miles. He had with him just over half his army, the rest had perished by the wayside.

The result was regarded as rather disastrous by English chroniclers (and by other writers since then), but it was not—and is not—so regarded by the French. The *Grandes Chroniques* wrote that it was "most honourable to the English".

The expedition had in fact achieved considerable results; it had given Brittany a respite, for not only Duguesclin but the duke of Anjou had been hastily recalled from the duchy for the defence of France; it had brought a useful reinforcement to Aquitaine; it had raised the prestige and demonstrated the power of the English army and had brought loss and discouragement and indeed humiliation to its opponents, and had halted their advance into Aquitaine.

* * *

The fourth *chevauchée* was undertaken in 1375 by Edmund, earl of Cambridge, who landed in western Brittany and marched right through the duchy from end to end.

The final *chevauchée* was that of the earl of Buckingham, who practically followed in the tracks of Knowles's march into Maine, but continued right on to Rennes, the capital of Brittany, as he had contracted to do.

In the meantime the French were steadily pursuing their campaign of sieges in Gascony, and also operations on the sea, where Admiral de Vienne had considerable successes. Duguesclin was the predominant and most successful of the French generals, and at length Charles V made him Constable of France, probably the first commoner to receive this high honour. It was justified.

The decisive year of the war was 1377, when the French increased their efforts and brought the tide of war within 20 miles of Bordeaux. But it got no further. That same year both Edward III and the Black Prince died, to be followed three years later by Charles V and the Constable Duguesclin.

There was no land fighting of significance after 1380, and after a series of short truces a final truce was signed in 1396, recognizing the *status quo*, and leaving the vital question of the homage unsolved and indeed unmentioned.

* * *

What are we to make of this extraordinary war of 27 years in which no real battles were fought and scarcely any out-and-out sieges were carried out, in which however nearly one quarter of the land of France had changed hands? It would almost seem as if nature had asserted herself, and that the transfer of land had taken place by mutual consent, in the natural order of events. In the early stages and on the outer bounds of the newly acquired English territory this was not very far from being the case, for these old possessions of Henry II had long since been in French hands. But even when the fighting approached Bordeaux, in which French soldiers had not been seen for over 200 years, there had been astonishingly little fighting. The fundamental explanation is probably that propounded by Professor Perroy, that the French successes were won "more by diplomacy than by force of arms."[1] Whilst on the purely military side, we may quote with approval the words of that shrewd historian Professor T. F. Tout in *The Political History of England* (1906)–

"When the command of the sea passed to the French and their Spanish allies all hope of retaining Aquitaine was lost."[2]

With so little fighting, it is difficult to assess the military merits of the leadership on either side. One can but admire the spirit of enterprise–and indeed bravado–shown by the three great *chevauchées* of Lancaster, Knowles and Buckingham, whatever their strategical justification. On the French side there were of course a long succession of captures of towns and castles. And this brings us to the Constable of France, Bertrand Duguesclin. This almost incredibly ugly Breton commoner would not have risen to such dizzy heights unless he had possessed exceptional qualities, and yet his bare military record hardly seems to account for it. In both of the only really big battles in which he fought he was defeated and captured, and of his generalship in the field we know scarcely anything. This has probably led the latest French historian of the war to describe him as "a mediocre captain, incapable of winning a battle or being successful in a siege of any scope".[3] Yet this judgement seems altogether too sweeping. If only from the manner in which he swept down on one of Knowles's isolated columns, it is clear that he had the instincts of generalship; and there was more to it than that. Nevertheless, it is probably true to say that he was born at a lucky time; the pendulum was bound to swing against England in far-off Aquitaine once the command of the sea was lost, and whatever soldier happened at that time to be in command would find his cause successful

[1] *The Hundred Years War*, p. 164.   [2] Op. cit., p. 416.
[3] Edouard Perroy, op. cit., p. 148.

whether or not he engaged in any victories in the field or displayed any military genius. Thus the strategy of Duguesclin, whether imposed upon him by his master or not, would have led to ultimate success—as also in all probability would the opposite strategy of offensive action in the field.

Be this as it may, England did not consider herself vanquished in the field. For over ten years the French had evidently not risked a pitched battle. During the last two years England had arrested the French invasion of Gascony, and had herself taken the offensive, one of her armies roaming through France on its way to the succour of Brittany, whilst a second army had marched victoriously to the help of another ally in Spain. If she seemed resigned to writing off her outlying possessions in the south of France, she refused resolutely and obdurately to listen to any proposals to restore the homage that had been abolished at Bretigny or to hand back Calais. It was this obduracy that prevented a permanent peace being concluded; the truce of 1396 merely recognized the *status quo*, and it would require another war to decide the question for good and all.

APPENDIX

A NOTE ON GENERAL SOURCES

On the English side there could scarcely be less material than there is. Aquitaine was far distant, and sea communications were uncertain and infrequent. Rymer's *Foedera* is of course essential for details regarding expeditions and for dates. The standard chroniclers were Adam Murimuth (Continuation), Thomas Walsingham, and for the later part the *Chronicon Angliae* of which Walsingham was also the author. On the French side the *Grandes Chroniques* give by far the most information, though necessarily from the French point of view only. For nearly all the actual details of the fighting we must have recourse to Froissart, who is probably much more accurate here than he was of 1369-96 for the Crecy War.

The war has never been treated as a whole, but of modern

historians Roland Delachenal's *Histoire de Charles V*, Vols. IV
and V (1931), contains the most detailed account and is very
fair and reliable. A few facts not mentioned in Delachenal's
work are contained in *La Désolation des Eglises . . . pendant L
Guerre de Cent Ans*, by Henri Deniflé (1899). This French priest
is careful as to his facts but his military appraisals need not be
taken very seriously; he makes a travesty of the various invasions
of France by the English.

The English modern historians for the period are good as
far as they go, T. F. Tout and C. W. Oman in *The Political
History of England* and Sir James Ramsay in *The Genesis of
Lancaster*, Vol. II, are the main authors.

SOURCES FOR THE SACK OF LIMOGES

There are seven contemporary or near contemporary sources
as below, Nos. 1 to 4 are all of French origin and were written
within a very few years of the event.

Source No. 1 is contained in the *Catulaire du Consulat de
Limoges*. It states that the *Cité* (as opposed to the *Ville*[1]) was
taken by Prince Edward and destroyed. Prisoners were taken:
men, women and clergy, bishop and abbot. The city was then
pillaged.

Source No. 2.–An account by one P. Bermondet, notary of
Limoges. He states that Limoges was taken and destroyed by
the lord prince of Aquitaine and his brothers because it had
placed itself in obedience to the king of France.

Source No. 3.–In an *MS of the Abbey of St. Martial* (Limousin).
This states that Limoges was taken and burnt and more than
300 persons were put to death because of the rebellion which
they had made against Prince Edward, duke of Aquitaine.

Source No. 4.–*Written by a monk of the Abbey of Uzerches*
(Limousin), who writes that Limoges was captured by the
lord Prince, the town was burnt and almost destroyed, pillaged

---

[1] Limoges was in reality two towns: the *Cité* on the banks of the river was
mainly official and ecclesiastical, the cathedral being in the centre of it. Two
hundred yards separated it from the *Ville*, which was twice as large. Both were
fortified: the *Ville* remained always in English hands. Much of the *Cité* wall still
stands, but the gates have gone.

and became almost desolated: monastery and churches were spoiled and polluted (*depredata et polluta*).

* * *

Comparing these four sources together, we note several things. First, they are in essential agreement, and in no case contradict one another.

Second, none of them speak of a massacre.

Third, most of the indignation seems to have been caused by the conduct towards the church, its persons and property.

Fourth, such loss of life as occurred seems to have been regarded as military punishment, and no note of condemnation can be found in the account.

Beyond these four primary sources are three others, slightly later and not so reliable.

Source No. 5.—Le Petit Thalamus de Montpellier, merely records that the siege only lasted a few days (important because Froissart states that it lasted a month).

Source No. 6.—La Vie d'Auban V, relates that Limoges was captured and all persons within it. It was totally destroyed except for the cathedral, and the citizens were driven out.

Source No. 7.—Chronique des Quatre Premiers Valois (it was written by a clerk in Normandy several years after the event, and cannot be regarded as very reliable). The English mined the wall, and during the mining operations John of Gaunt [who was the real commander on the spot] met one of the French generals in the mine, and was wounded in a duel with him. [This has also been related of Henry V. It makes a good story.] Many citizens were put to death because they had surrendered to the French.

These last three sources fill in the story of the first four, adding the interesting fact that the citizens were driven out, which implicity denies that they were massacred. These sources were collected by M. Alfred Deroux and published by him in 1906 in his *Le Sac de la Cité de Limoges*.

THE ARMIES

Prior to the reign of Edward III, the English army, like the French, was constituted on a feudal basis, backed by the National Militia or Fyrd. But Edward revolutionized the system, substituting a paid army for foreign service raised by indenture. Certain persons, usually of the nobility, were appointed to recruit a specified number of soldiers, under specified proportions of men-at-arms and archers, with a specified rate of pay, for a specified period. This period seldom exceeded a year in length; at the end of the period the *indentee* (as modern jargon might call him) might be indentured for a further period or he took his discharge. The result of this was that England now possessed a paid, professional, short-service army for foreign service.

France, on the other hand, remained wedded to the feudal system till the closing years of the war. Her internal state had become, in comparison with that of England, primitive and almost anarchical. Thus the army was still a feudal host, of equal lords, with their retainers, over whom the Constable had the slenderest control. The knights and men-at-arms regarded themselves not merely as the backbone of the army: they *were* the army, although, in order to make up numbers, local levies of *les communes* were enrolled, and some foreign mercenaries who wielded the crossbow were recruited chiefly from Italy. But any conception of cooperation between the cavalry and the despised other arms was unheard of. The battle of Crecy had become the stock example of this conception, and France had not yet learnt the lesson, as had her rival many years before. Thus, in spite of her larger population, three or four times as great, France had up to this time never succeeded in putting in the field an army that could stand up to that of Edward III.

In the matter of arms and armament the two armies were not dissimilar. Men-at-arms were armed with a lance (or "spear"), sword, dagger and occasionally battle-mace. Mail armour was now giving place to plate armour, and by the end of the war knights were almost universally armoured *cap-à-pie*. The shield was gradually becoming obsolete, partly owing to the superior defence offered by plate armour and partly to its ineffectiveness against cannon balls. Each man-at-arms was attended by two archers, and often one swordsman, together with one or two pages or *valets aux armes*—an almost synonymous term—who were armed with daggers. The total outfit of four to six constituted a "lance". Herein lies a difficulty. The composition of a lance was always fluid in the English army, and only became standardized in the French army towards the end of the war, when it numbered six (including varlet and page). Moreover it is by no means always clear when the number of lances is given and also the number of archers whether the archers included in the lance are also included in the total number of archers indentured. I have made the rough assumption that in the case of the knighthood their archers are not included in the indentured archers, but that they are so included in the case of the ordinary men-at-arms. In the French army, however, right up to the end of the war, when lances are mentioned we must always multiply this number by four or by six, according to whether we regard pages as "combatants" or not. Ferdinand Lot regards them as non-combatants, but they seem to come under the same category as, for example, the drivers of modern guns, who are certainly combatants.

The English archer was by now usually mounted. Whether mounted or dismounted he carried long-bow, sword and dagger. The bow could be discharged six times a minute, and had an effective range of 250 yards and extreme range of over 350 yards. The French archer, on the other hand, carried a crossbow. Though more powerful than the long-bow it was four times as slow in its rate of discharge, and had less range. Generally the crossbowmen were Genoese mercenaries.

As for the third arm—the artillery—we hear little of its use in field operations on either side, but in siege operations it was steadily increasing in power and effect and in the last years of the Hundred Years War, as we shall see, it had a predominant effect in securing the surrender of defended towns and castles.

The infantry included in addition to the archers a number of foot spearmen (until their abolition by Henry V), though foreign mercenaries, Flemings, Germans, and also Gascons, etc., were included. Mercenaries also were not favoured by Henry V. As regards armour, archers wore steel helmets and breast-plates or padded hawberks, and spearmen were similarly attired except that they seldom wore breastplates.

DEVELOPMENT DURING THE WAR

In spite of the length of the Hundred Years War, develop-ment or change in arms, armament or method of fighting altered surprisingly little during its course. In two respects only was there a marked progress. The first was in the power and effectiveness of the artillery, of which mention had already been made, and will be again; the other was in the gradual intro-duction of plate armour. It was a very gradual process, and there is little direct evidence as to the rate of its progress. We are for the most part reduced to the evidence of brasses, effigies and stained-glass windows. But the progress was continuous, and at the end of the war body armour for knights was wholly plate. Its effect on the tactics was equally gradual. Its influence here was two-fold: it reduced the mobility of the dismounted men-at-arms, and it reduced the effectiveness of the arrow. As for the first, opinions still differ as to the amount of mobility and agility left to the plate-armoured knight. No doubt suits of armour themselves varied a good deal, there being no "sealed pattern" for them in either army. But generally speaking the tendency was to allow the horse to do the lion's share of the transport work of the knight. The effect of plate armour is easier to descry and define. It clearly rendered the dreaded long-bow less effective. Towards the end of the war we hear less than previously of the casualties caused by it, and instances occurred from time to time when mounted men-at-arms did succeed in breaking through the line of archers. Yet here also, the change was gradual and not well marked.

THE NAVY

Only two major actions took place during the period covered
by this book, and there is not much that can be said about the
rival fleets, though naval artillery was beginning to make its
effect felt. Both countries kept a small number of royal ships-of-
war under the direct pay of the king. The bulk of the fleet was
collected as occasion warranted, by the simple methods of
requisitioning, so many ships being required from each port. In
the case of the Cinque Ports there was a sort of standing order
or tally for each of them. The French in addition had a number
of war-galleys, usually stationed in the Mediterranean, but
rowed round to the Channel in the course of the war.

CHAPTER II

THE TRUCE OF 1396–1415

THREE years after the signing of the truce of 1396, Henry
IV wrested the throne from his cousin Richard II. The
change of sovereign had little effect upon the relations
between England and France or on the observance of the
truce. France was distracted by internal dissension, and
the new English king was at first too preoccupied with con-
solidating his position at home to make a resumption of the
war likely.

An involved political situation now developed, due to two
factions, in both England and France, in turn gaining the upper
hand and each in turn making commitments which the other
faction failed to honour. Thus suspicion between the two
countries increased and when in 1413 Henry IV died and was
succeeded by his eldest son Henry V, the seeds of open war
between France and England had been sown. England still
stood by the terms of the Treaty of Bretigny, and would hear of
no abatement; on the contrary, the divided state of France
seemed to offer a favourable chance of recovering the losses of
the previous war. The country rang with the duplicity of
France, and war fever began to rise.

This feeling was not discouraged by the young king. Though
only 25 years of age it might almost be said that he had been
born and brought up in the camp from the age of 12 years.

His attitude, and that of his country, is so well summarized
by that careful and profound historian C. L. Kingsford, that I
cannot do better than quote it here.

"The idea of war with France was not unpopular. The old traditional and commercial intercourse that bound England to Flanders
and Gascony favoured it. The long dispute between the two nations
was still unsettled, and the recent action of the French Government

had given the English good cause for complaint. To Henry himself, with his high belief in his own rights, the assertion of his claim to the throne of France must have appeared almost in the light of a duty. Possibly he may, even now, have had other motives and dreamed that, when Western Europe was united under his sway, he would restore the unity of the Church and become the leader of Christendom in a new Crusade."[1]

Though it is impossible to say at what precise moment the king "crossed the Rubicon" and decided definitely on war, it must have been sometime in the early spring of 1415. On March 22 he issued a proclamation ordering all soldiers who owed service by virtue of fiefs or wages to rendezvous at London. And yet more plainly and formally was the same announcement made at a great War Council held on April 16. The king also announced that he had appointed his second brother the duke of Bedford as regent in England during his absence. This was followed up by issuing indentures for his expeditionary force, and a general call-up of the shire levies; "embodiment of the militia" it would be called at a later date. The levies in the northern five counties were to remain there on guard against a possible invasion from Scotland (though as its king, James I, was a prisoner in England such an eventuality was unlikely). The remaining levies were to be grouped around the country, facing possible danger from Wales, where Owen Glendower was still antagonistic, or from landings on the coast.

As for the striking force; in recruiting, composition, equipment, organization and method of employment, it was substantially the same as it had been in the day of the king's great-grandfather.[2]

The only two changes since the earlier wars that need be noted are that mail had largely given place to plate armour on men-at-arms, and that the artillery had increased in weight and power. Henry had recently amassed a large force of cannon—some of large calibre—and of cannon balls.

The king's measures for the provision of the ancillary service

[1] *Henry V*, p. 110.
[2] See Appendix to Chapter I. The indenture system and description of the army is described in greater detail in *The Crecy War*.

and stores were of a far-seeing and far-reaching nature. Particulars of these are given principally in Rymer's collection of *Foedera*. No doubt the stored-up experience of the Edwardian wars was available. At any rate nothing seems to have been overlooked, either in the matter of *personnel* or *material*. For example, we hear of surgeons for the first time, 20[1] of them being included in the army. Then there were miners, masons, corderers, turners and carpenters (no less than 1,200 of these), farriers, chaplains, butchers, bakers, drovers, dyers, skinners, fishmongers, even minstrels and fiddlers. In addition to the large number of horses and draught oxen required, large herds of cattle were also embarked. Then there were of course carts, wagons and other vehicles, field-ovens and bakeries, corn-grinders, shovels, picks and saws. And what is most significant, large quantities of spares of all kinds.

To convey this vast expedition overseas required no less than 1,500 vessels, each of them nominally with over 20 tons portage. To collect such a number was a matter of some complexity. A few were specially constructed, and others were purchased in Flanders and the Netherlands. But the vast majority were requisitioned from the ports all round the coast.

Orders were issued that the whole force, army and fleet, was to be concentrated in the Southampton-Portsmouth area by July 1, 1415.

While the expeditionary force was assembling, the French sent a mission in a final attempt to avert the impending war. Henry received it in Wolvesey Palace at Winchester, and its proceedings have a curiously modern ring. It started with toasts and honeyed words, and ended some days later in anger and confusion.

*   *   *

On July 2, 1415, the king joined his army and fleet, and he busily engaged himself in the intricate problem of collecting, marshalling and supplying the great armada. All the creeks

---

[1] So Oman: but 13 according to Church.

and inlets along the coast facing the Isle of Wight were filled with shipping, while the interior was steadily filling up with soldiers and camp-followers. Anyone who witnessed the assembly in precisely the same area of the troops destined for a very similar venture 530 years later can perhaps envisage the scene. The task confronting Henry V and his staff was naturally less complicated than that of modern times, but, if less complex it was more difficult owing to the primitive nature of transport and of communications, especially between land and sea.

There is unusually little dispute as to the combatant strength of the army, thanks to what is known as the Agincourt Roll, but which might more accurately be called the Harfleur Roll. What it amounts to is that slightly over 2,000 men-at-arms, 8,000 archers, and 65 gunners, sailed with the expeditionary force. But as regards the numbers of the ancillary or non-combatant services we can but guess. They cannot even be roughly computed from the number of transport vessels, for these varied in size from 20 tons portage to 300 tons portage. But, by comparing the number of vessels required to transport this army with that for the Crecy campaign we realise how enormous and comprehensive these ancillary services must have been. Here are the approximate figures in parallel columns:

Campaign	Combatants	Ships
Crecy	15,000	700
Agincourt	10,000	1,500

On August 16 all was ready and the king took boat from Portchester Castle, where he had been residing, down Portsmouth Harbour, to his flagship the *Trinity Royal*, which was anchored at Spithead. This ship was the pride of the nation, being of the exceptional size of 500 tons portage, with the enormous crew of 300 sailors. Arrived on board, the king hoisted the sail to half-mast, signal for the fleet to concentrate on the flagship.

To carry out this apparently simple operation required four days. When collected they were so tightly packed together that when one ship caught fire the flames spread to its two neighbours. This was taken as an ill-omen, but when a flock of swans began to accompany the fleet as it set off, it was realized that Heaven smiled upon the venture after all.

The summer sun caught the sails, bunting and banners of the huge concourse and presented such a spectacle as might have brought Froissart from his grave to depict it.

At 3 p.m. on Sunday, August 11, 1415, the king gave the signal and, led by his uncle the earl of Dorset with two lanterns at his masthead, the great fleet slipped slowly down the Channel past the Isle of Wight and out to sea, sailing in a southerly direction.

CHAPTER III

THE INVASION OF FRANCE

THE French Government had long been aware that an invasion of their country was in preparation. But Henry made great efforts to preserve the secrecy of its destination. The only recorded statement made by him that I can discover stated that it might be Aquitaine or "the King of France", a sufficiently vague term. But the French Government was not to be hoodwinked into believing that it would be Aquitaine. Edward III, they recollected, had put out the same suggestion. Moreover, his wars had shown the hazards attaching to such an amphibious operation. No, the north coast of France was clearly indicated. It might be Brittany; Brest and St. Malo had in the past been favourite landing places for English armies. Or the king of England might emulate his ancestor and land near Cherbourg. Harfleur, on the estuary of the Seine, felt itself threatened and hastily strengthened its defences. Even Flanders was favoured by some. But the French Government believed that Boulogne was the actual point of invasion.[1]

The measures taken for defence were, however, singularly half-hearted. Of the two rival political parties, the Orleanists were lethargic, and the Burgundians on one pretext or another, refused to respond to the call for help. The Dauphin, Louis, a weak youth of 19, was made nominal commander-in-chief, and the Constable of France, Charles d'Albret, was made his lieutenant. D'Albret started to collect an army at Rouen, and stationed a force of 1,500 men under the joint command of himself and Marshal Boucicaut at Honfleur, on the south side of the Seine estuary opposite Harfleur. But the country as a whole was listless, being concerned more with the heavy taxation than with the threatened invasion.

[1] The parallel with 1944 when the Germans believed that the Boulogne area, not Normandy, was the destination, is inescapable.

Thus the prospects for the invasion were propitious when the English armada disappeared from view to the south of Bembridge, Isle of Wight. What was the destination of the king of England? If we study his recorded words and writings it becomes evident that he was more concerned to recover Normandy than to succour Aquitaine. Normandy was the older patrimony of the two. During a period of over a century it had been in Anglo-Norman hands but for some reason it had not been included in the Treaty of Bretigny. Henry resolved to rectify the omission, and therefore to make that province his first objective.

As for his ultimate aims and his plans for implementing them, not a word escaped his lips–still less his pen. We are in the region of conjecture, but we may obtain some insight into them by the method of what I call Inherent Military Probability. It is inherently probable that the young king had studied closely the successful campaigns of his great-grandfather and his generals–especially Henry of Lancaster, earl of Derby–indeed he may have had converse with some of them, and in particular with his great-uncle John of Gaunt.[1] Henry was 12 years of age when "time-honoured Gaunt" died and he would have eagerly sucked in any reminiscences and stories that he could glean from such a source. Henry V, then, imbibed and digested the lessons to be learnt from the previous wars. Four of these lessons were paramount. First, the difficulties inherent in maintaining a successful war in distant Aquitaine. The French were situated in what we call Interior Lines; they could mass a large army on its borders much more quickly and easily than England could send troops to defend it. Secondly, wide-flung operations on exterior lines were almost doomed to failure owing to shortcomings in communications. Thirdly, France was so well besprinkled with castles and fortified towns that, unless the invader was provided with a siege train, it was almost impossible to occupy effectively hostile territory, and so break the will to resistance of the enemy. Almost–but not quite–as Edward's last

[1] Charles VI had the advice of the Duke of Berri, who had fought at Poitiers.

successful campaign had shown. Fourthly, the value of a firmly established base in France from which to operate had been made manifest. Bordeaux provided one in the south and Calais in the north.

The logical corrollary of these lessons, combined with his own desire first and foremost to recover the ancient duchy of Normandy, was that Normandy should be the primary objective, that a base should be established there, that it should be a harbour analogous to Calais, and that to this end a siege train should be taken out.

Where should this base be established? The estuary of the Seine seemed indicated, and of the two fortresses guarding it, Harfleur on the north side was always regarded as "the key to Normandy", and was therefore the obvious objective. Considerations such as these must have disposed Henry V, as soon as his armada was under way, to issue orders that course was to be set for the mouth of the river Seine. And he followed this up by informing his captains that as a first step he intended to capture Harfleur.

*   *   *

After a smooth 50-hour passage, the fleet cast anchor at 5 p.m. on August 14, 1415, in the mouth of the Seine opposite a bare spit about three miles to the west of Harfleur, where now stands Havre. Though no enemy were visible on shore no one was allowed to disembark till next morning. Before dawn next day a reconnaissance party under the earl of Huntingdon and Sir Gilbert Umfraville landed and soon reported the coast clear. The king then ordered a general but methodical disembarkation, and was himself one of the first to land. His first act was to kneel down on the shore and utter a prayer that in the coming war he might do nothing which would not redound to the honour of God and the furtherance of justice.

The town of Harfleur was of ancient origin and the only harbour on the northern side of the estuary. It was defended by a wall and a wet moat with a perimeter of a little under two miles. Its position was strong by nature. It lay on the little river Lézarde, near its entry into the Seine. Consequently the southern face was protected by that river. On the east were salt marshes, crossed by a single road; to the north was the valley of the Lézarde. This had been dammed by the garrison, till the width of water was about 100 yards. All bridges for some miles to the north of the town had been destroyed. To the north-west and west the ground rose gently, and the summit was surmounted by trees and orchards. The river Lézarde flowed through the town from north-west to south and the harbour was in the centre of the town. Chains were stretched across the river at its exit from the town. The chief building was the church of St. Martin (which still stands). There were three gates, at the north-east, south-east and south-west respectively. Temporary barbicans of wood and earth had recently been thrown up outside the three gates, each surrounded by water.[1] A low earthen wall had been thrown up on the counterscarp of the moat. Entrenchments had also been dug along the shore to impede a landing, but the garrison was too small to man them. A number of guns were mounted on the walls and in emplacements and stores of quicklime and oil were placed on the ramparts to throw in the faces of stormers. When all is considered one is not surprised to learn that Harfleur was regarded as impregnable.

*   *   *

THE SIEGE OF HARFLEUR

It took three days to land men, guns and stores. A great camp was pitched on the hill to the north-west of the town, and about one mile distant. While the disembarkation was proceeding–always undisturbed–a welcome reinforcement to the garrison of 300 men-at-arms under lord de Gaucourt, reached the town by the south-eastern gate.

The first task facing the English army was obviously to complete the investment on the eastern side. But to reach this side

[1] Part of the eastern gate still stands.

a wide detour to the north was necessary owing to the river valley being flooded by the French. On August 17 the king despatched a column under his oldest brother and chief lieutenant, the duke of Clarence, to make this detour and established the blockade on the east of the town. This was successfully accomplished, and Clarence had the luck to fall in with a convoy intended for the garrison, consisting of guns, arms and ammunition. These were all captured although the garrison sallied out of the town to their rescue. After a sharp fight they were driven back into the town. Thus the "first blood" in the Agincourt War fell to the English.

Harfleur was now completely surrounded, and little help could be expected for it for some time to come. The Constable d'Albret was powerless to cross the estuary to its support, and the English fleet guarded the entrance to the river.

Henry V had now to consider by what means he should capture the town. To reduce it by starvation would take time, and time was precious. The other means were by direct assault, or by methodical breaching of the walls. This in turn could be effected in two ways, by mining or by the comparatively novel method of breaching the walls by artillery fire (for the ancient method, by rams, was rendered impracticable owing to the wide moat).

The king decided first to use his miners. But progress was difficult and slow. Moreover the English miners after the long peace appeared to have lost much of their efficiency and in addition the French possessed miners themselves, and enterprising ones too. They countermined and brought to nought this attempt at the breaching of the walls.

Consequently the king now turned to his artillery. We have no precise details as to its number or weight.[1] A letter written to a priest in Paris places the number of heavy guns at 12, but this was possibly an exaggeration. Three at least were abnormally heavy for they were given special names by the admiring troops–"London", "Messenger" and "The King's Daughter". These began a steady bombardment, aimed principally at

[1] It included some "engines of war" such as ballistas.

the walls and towers flanking the three gates and barbicans. But they also fired into the town, and "London" paid special attention to the tower of St. Martin's Church. (Church towers have at all ages had a special attraction to gunners.) When later the town was entered it was observed, that great damage had been done to the church steeple. The bombardment went on, according to one account, by night as well as by day. This, if true, is one of the earliest examples of "night firing" by guns, and one would be interested to have particulars regarding the methods of illuminations and laying employed. But the English gunners had another surprise up their sleeve, as will presently be seen.

The garrison replied with spirit to the bombardment, and damage to the walls and towers, of which there were no less than 26, was repaired by night (from which it would appear that the English night-firing was not very effective.) Meanwhile the weather remained unusually hot; so much so that the knights experienced acute discomfort merely standing up in their full armour. But armour, fortunately for them, was not much in demand at this stage of the siege for it was mainly an artillery combat on each side. The remainder of the army had but little to do—except to eat. There was an abundance of un-ripe fruit available, and the soldier, like Tommy Atkins in all ages, partook of it without discretion or moderation. The natural sequel was widespread trouble, accentuated by the un-healthy night atmosphere on the salt marshes, the lack of sanita-tion and possibly the absence of sufficient exercise. Soon dysen-tery was rife and one of its first victims was bishop Courtenay of Norwich, a close personal friend of the king. The earl of Suffolk was another victim as was also the earl of March but the latter two survived. The epidemic may also have been partly due to some food supplies having been damaged by sea water. The French also suffered from sickness, but it must have been due to other causes. At least one messenger escaped from the stricken town by night with an appeal to the Dauphin for help. But when urged by others to march on Harfleur at about this time he made the amazing reply that the town had already fallen into English hands.

For King Henry there was no rest. He attended to every little detail, being assiduous in all military duties, supervising everything and making constant personal reconnaissances by day, and visiting the watch by night. (The night scene in Shakespeare's play will come to mind.) After the siege had been in operation a fortnight he wrote a significant letter to Bordeaux. In it he asked for guns and wine to be sent, while at the same time he gave a confident, even jubilant account of the siege, and the estimate that it would only last another eight days; after that he would advance on Paris, and finally would march on to Bordeaux. It was soon after the despatch of this letter that the dysentery became serious, but it did not materially affect the course of the siege.

The English artillery concentrated mainly–and rightly–on the south-west gate and barbican (called "The Bulwark" by the attackers.)[1] The main effort of the miners had also been directed against this point, which was evidently regarded by the king as the decisive point of the defences. By September 16, 13 days after Henry's Bordeaux letter, the barbican was in ruins, and the gate behind it was hopelessly damaged. The moat flanking it had been partially filled up with fascines, in readiness for an assault.

In the afternoon of September 16, the day on which bishop Courtenay died, the French made a desperate sortie from the south-west gate. Taking the besiegers unawares they managed to reach the English trenches and to set the wooden palisade on fire. But the defenders rallied rapidly, drove out the French and extinguished the fire. Next day the garrison tried again, but this time the English were on their guard and made short work of the attempt. Then the young earl of Huntingdon, who was in command of that sector of the line, took the offensive himself. He directed his attack on the bulwark, first preparing the ground

[1] The Bulwark was circular in shape, about 50 yards in diameter and completely surrounded by a ditch or moat.

by a concentrated bombardment. Moreover he employed a new weapon, probably the invention of the king's chief engineer, "Master Giles". It took the form of what we should now call an incendiary shell; some form of combustible was attached to the stone cannon-balls and ignited and then discharged from the guns against the woodwork of the Bulwark. This was set alight and, the weather being dry, was soon burning furiously. Then the men-at-arms advanced to the attack; crossing the moat dry-shod over the fascines that had been thrown into it, and clambering over the ruined palisade. The defenders could offer no effective opposition and the English entered the blazing Bulwark in triumph. The French fell back across the town moat into the interior and closed the gate behind them before the attackers could pass through it.

The Bulwark was now firmly in English hands and the victorious troops turned their attention to extinguishing the flames. But so fierce was the blaze that it was nearly two days before it was got fully under control and for several days more it was smouldering.

This success was decisive; it put heart into the attackers and corresponding depression into the defenders. The state of these gallant men was now pitiable and hopeless. Of succour from without there was still no sign; they were weakened by disease; food and ammunition were running short, their strongest work had not sufficed to keep out the English, and they were indeed at their last gasp.

This was evident to King Henry, and he resolved to shorten the agony by a general assault unless the garrison immediately surrendered.

After some vague and ineffectual approaches by de Gaucourt next day, Henry issued orders for a general assault on the following morning. The bombardment was to be maintained all night, so that the defenders should get no rest, instructions were issued to each member of the storming party, and the French were left in no misapprehension as to the fate that awaited them next day.

But the threat was sufficient; in the course of the night emissaries slipped out of the town on the comparatively quiet side – the east – and requested the duke of Clarence to prevail on the king to grant them terms. Messages passed throughout the night, and the result was that the town promised to surrender if they were not relieved by the following Sunday, September 22, that is, in three days time.

The final negotiations had been conducted by the bishop of Bangor who assured the garrison "Fear not! The king of England has not come to waste your lands, we are good Christians and Harfleur is not Soissons." This was no empty promise.

The two armies then sat down, silently watching one another, all fighting being suspended. But no succour came to the beleaguered garrison, although the Dauphin had been informed of their plight, and when the stipulated period expired the king sent 500 troops to the gate to demand surrender.

The king's chaplain Thomas Elmham describes the scene that ensued.

"Our King, clothed in royal gold immediately ascended his royal throne, placed under a pavilion on the top of the hill; where his nobles and the principal persons were assembled in their best equipment, his crowned triumphal helmet being held on his right hand unpon a halberd by Sir Gilbert Umfreville. The Lord de Gaucourt came from the [waiting] tent into his presence accompanied by those persons who had sworn to keep the articles, and surrendering to him the keys of the town submitted themselves to his grace."

The chaplain discreetly omits to say that the unfortunate de Gaucourt and his 76 associates were obliged to appear with ropes round their necks; also that the king kept them waiting a good while in the waiting tent before deigning to receive them. All this was, without a doubt, copied from the procedure of his great-grandfather at the surrender of Calais, when the twelve burgesses had to approach him with halters round their necks. It was in both cases an elaborate piece of play-acting, designed to impress them with the might of the English king, and subsequently of his royal magnanimity.

In fact he eventually gave them all a sumptuous supper and

promised them fair and kindly treatment, the details of which he proceeded to enunciate.

His terms, again, were based on those taken by Edward III. That is to say, certain of the knights who seemed good for ransoms were either packed off to England or released on parole in order to allow them to raise the stipulated ransom. Of the remainder, those who were prepared to accept the lordship of the English king were allowed to remain in the town, together with their belongings, while those who were not so prepared were, a few days later, marched out of the town taking with them whatever they could carry, and duly handed over to the French authorities at Lillebonne. Advertisements were then circulated through England inviting merchants and others to come and settle in Harfleur, which Henry was resolved to make like Calais–an English town.

CHAPTER IV

THE MARCH TO AGINCOURT

HARFLEUR was now in English hands: the first stage of Henry V's grandiose plan was accomplished. The question now arose, should he continue with the second stage—an advance on Paris?

There were cogent reasons against it. The reduction of Harfleur had taken longer than had been expected (though five weeks was a reasonable time under the circumstances), and the season was getting late for campaigning. The king of France, it was known, was trying to assemble an army in the Paris-Rouen area, which though poor in quality (as hastily collected armies always are) would be formidable in numbers. But worst of all, the dysentry had made such ravages in the English army that little more than 7,500 fairly healthy troops were now available, the remainder having either died or been shipped back to England. Of the healthy troops 900 men-at-arms and 1,200 archers were allotted for the garrison of Harfleur, under the earl of Dorset. Thus only 900 men-at-arms and 5,000 archers, say 6,000 in all, were available for field operations. It followed that, should the French army challenge a battle, the disparity in numbers would be very great. Was it worth the risk? To march on Paris would mean striking at the enemy where he was strongest; it might have been just feasible with 12,000 men but with only half that number it was clearly inadvisable. When Edward III had invaded France he had taken steps to ensure that the French armed forces were scattered, a large proportion of them being in Gascony. Such was not the case now, and Henry reluctantly abandoned his design on Paris. There remained three possible courses: he might establish with his army a Harfleur Pale, on the lines of the Calais Pale; he could march on Calais, a *chevauchée* typical of his great-grandfather's strategy, or he could leave a garrison in Harfleur and ship the remainder of the army home for the winter.

The king held a war council which examined the matter. The first course does not seem to have had advocates, but on the second there was considerable discussion. As is the nature of war councils the various risks appertaining to a strategy of offence were pointed out by certain members, till a general atmosphere of what we should call "defeatism" was engendered, and in the outcome the council recommended the course which involved the least risk–in this case the return of the army to England.

Henry V stoutly opposed the recommendation of the war council. To do this required some moral courage, despite the prestige attaching to his rank. He was still a young man, and in going against the advice of his council he was taking a great risk; he might conceivably lose his whole army and himself be killed or captured, like the French king 60 years before. The immensity of the risk has impressed the historians of all ages. Their verdict may be summed up as follows: "The risk was unjustifiable; it was a rash, even a madcap, plan." Professor Wyllie himself seems overwhelmed by this impressive flood of opinion and is content to swim with the stream, describing the decision as "the most foolhardy and reckless adventure that ever an unreasoning pietist devised".[1] Only Professor Jacob has ventured to question Wyllie's verdict, and he somewhat mildly suggests that it is "perhaps an exaggeration".[2]

The risk was probably much less than appeared on the surface, for France was in a distracted and divided state: the embers of civil war were still smouldering; the chastening and unifying effect of a common danger–the invasion of their country–had had but little effect. The truth is, France did not possess that feeling of national unity and patriotism that was later engendered in her, largely by Joan of Arc. The duke of Burgundy was the stormy petrel, the incomputable factor. Whilst professing loyalty he made various excuses for not responding to his

---

[1] *Wyllie*, II, p. 76.   [2] *Henry V and the Invasion of England*, p. 93.

sovereign's summons to service; nor did he permit his son Philip, count of Flanders (later to be duke Philip the Good of Burgundy), to serve. All was confusion and disorder, and the national summons was obeyed only slowly and partially.

*　　　　*　　　　*

The concentration area for the French army was along the Seine, between Mantes, Vernon and Rouen. The Dauphin had reached Vernon on September 3, and on the 10th Charles VI, with befitting ceremony, took the Oriflamme–the national symbol for the repelling of invasion–from its receptuary in the cathedral at St. Denys and marched to Mantes, where he remained.

Meanwhile Boucicaut and D'Albret had moved from Honfleur to Rouen, where they were busy marshalling the advanced-guard of the national army. By the beginning of October this force was said to be 14,000 strong. No doubt this is an exaggeration, but it must have exceeded greatly the numbers the English could put into the field.

Let us presume that Henry was aware of the above, but was in total ignorance of the effective strength of the rival army at any given moment. From information gained during the previous two wars, if from no other source, he would have a fair idea of the relative positions of the localities in the area Harfleur-Paris-Calais. Now his objective was Calais, and to get there involved a march of a little over 160 miles. By marching light–that is, with all baggage and supplies carried on pack animals, he might just accomplish it in eight or nine days. The distance from Vernon to Calais is the same, but a French army of newly-formed troops, whose march-discipline would be weak, and whose army would be encumbered with carts and wagons, could scarcely do it in under 12 days. Thus, even if both armies started level, the French army would have little chance of catching up, still less of intercepting, the English army. But the two armies were not likely to start level; until the English actually set off, the French leaders at Vernon would have no knowledge of what was proceeding, nor would they get this news till at least 36 hours after the march had begun, for it is nearly 100 miles by road for a scout outside Harfleur to reach Vernon. Thus the French army would start off at least two days behind the English. Hence the danger of Henry being caught by the main French army, if his direct course to Calais was unimpeded, was negligible.

But there is an "if". Could he count on making good the direct route along the sea coast? There were two minor rivers to be crossed, the Béthune and the Bresle, but these would not constitute an obstacle to troops unencumbered with wheels. (The king purposed leaving all his guns behind). There was however the river Somme. Again following the example of his great-grandfather, Henry intended to make use of the Blanche Taque ford a few miles below Abbeville, which he hoped would be undefended. As a step to this end he had sent out a contingent to Calais at the outset of the campaign, with orders to operate in a southerly direction, thereby attracting to itself all local French forces, thus drawing them away from the vital ford.

There was however an unpleasant possibility. What of the troops in Rouen? Might they not intercept the march? On paper it looks as if they might. Rouen is 30 miles nearer Calais than Harfleur. But the chances of such an interception would seem to be small, unless previous knowledge of the direction of the march and its date leaked out. Moreover a sudden departure of the Rouen troops could hardly be undertaken without the permission of the Constable of France, who was then supposed to be in Honfleur, 30 miles away. As we have seen, both Boucicaut and D'Albret had in reality moved to Rouen, but the fact would not have been known to the English scouts, for the wide Seine estuary separated them from the road the Constable would take. Furthermore, Henry might well calculate that the Rouen troops would not dare attack his army in the field unsupported by the French main body. In this calculation, as we shall see, Henry was justified. There was a further contingency, namely that these Rouen troops might march to the Somme, cross it and take up positions on the far bank.

In short there were risks in the English plan, but no military operation is entirely devoid of risk, being dependent for its success on the human element, and frequently on natural elements too–the weather. In war if you risk nothing you gain nothing; and in this case there was a good deal to be gained. The alternative was a return to England. This would be construed as failure in both countries, the king's prestige would fall, there might even be a revolution and he might be supplanted by the legitimate heir to the throne, the earl of March; in any case conditions for a future invasion of France would be bad. On the other hand if Henry succeeded in his march, he would be reviving the memories of similar *chevauchées* which had done much to raise English prestige in the days of Edward III; he would show that an English army could apparently go where it liked in the lands he claimed as his own, and with two bases firmly established on the north coast of France the omens for a further invasion of the Promised Land would be propitious. All this might be accomplished by taking risks. As General Wolfe so truly said:

"In war something must be allowed to chance and fortune, seeing that it is in its nature hazardous and an option of difficulties."

To sum up, it seems to me that, with the information presumably at his disposal, Henry V took a justifiable and commendable risk.

*　　　　*　　　　*

The die was cast: the English army was to attempt to reach Calais overland. King Henry gave out his desire to meet the French army in battle during the operation; but the steps that he had taken to march "light" and as speedily as possible to Calais bear the impression of a directly contrary desire. How are we to account for this seeming contradiction? Up to a point his words seem supported by his deeds. That is to say, he had challenged the Dauphin to personal combat and had waited eight days at Harfleur in order to give time for the reply to arrive. This certainly does not look like the action of a man who wishes to slip away unperceived, yet his later actions do. I suggest that the explanation is that he made a slight change of plan, as a result of the opposition that he encountered from his war council. They had stressed the hazards of the proposed march to Calais, and in order to meet their arguments the king felt constrained to take all possible steps to minimize the chance of an actual encounter with the main French army in the field. This alone, in my opinion, explains the apparent anomaly.

The challenge referred to requires a word of exposition. In it King Henry challenged the Dauphin (his father being half demented) to a personal contest, in order to avoid effusion of blood, the winner to possess the kingdom of France after the death of Charles VI. It is hardly to be supposed that Henry expected the callow youth known as the Dauphin to accept this challenge. Indeed such a challenge strikes our modern minds as similar to the action of a school bully who challenges a smaller boy to a fight. But contemporaries did not take it like that; to them it was "ordeal by battle", and God would give the victory to the rightful claimant–perhaps to David rather than to Goliath–"God defend the right". King Henry was intensely religious, or perhaps we might now say, superstitious; he really believed in the justice of his claim to the crown of France, in a fanatical way and, whether by single combat or by the engagement of his whole army, he was convinced that the Almighty would give him the victory. Moreover he was only following the example of his revered ancestor, who more than once challenged the king of France to single combat, "to avoid useless effusion of blood"–and with the same negative result. The significance of the challenge is, as Ramsay observes, that it discloses the ultimate aim of Henry to be king of all France, a claim that he had never officially put forward.

THE MARCH BEGINS

The eight days having expired without reply being received from the Dauphin, the king gave his final orders for the march. Each man was to carry eight days rations with him, in order to be independent of the hazards of country supply during what was hoped would be only an eight-day march. All possible impedimenta (an apt word in this connection) was to be left behind, the army travelling "light".[1] Strict orders as to behaviour in the country had been issued on landing, and they were now emphasized and given more precision. No one was to fire buildings without orders; to maltreat priests, nuns, women or children; nothing was to be taken from churches or religious houses; no swearing was to be allowed. The king held his army in what for medieval times was an iron discipline. This does not mean that no excesses were committed; indeed the French chroniclers repeat the almost mechanical accusation of fire, robbery and pillage. One chronicler however, has the frankness to record that the English troops did not rob or rape, whereas the French troops in the area did both. Indeed, Joan of Arc, had she but known it, followed much the same line as Henry of Monmouth in her dealings with the troops.

Our sources differ as to the date of the march. Most historians give October 8 or 9, but Wyllie prefers October 6. This early date I doubt, on grounds of inherent military probability. If the army really set out on the 6th it marched only 10 miles on each of the first four days and 20 miles on the two ensuing days. Usually troops march furthest when they are freshest. True, there was slight delay before Montivilliers, and again to the south of Fécamp, but not enough to account for that great disparity. I prefer October 8 as the date.

The army marched in the usual three divisions: vanguard, main body and rearguard. Commanders of the vanguard were Sir Gilbert Umfraville and Sir John Cornwall, two highly trusted leaders. The king himself commanded the main body, being accompanied by his brother the duke of Gloucester and John Holland, later the earl of Huntingdon. The rearguard was under the king's uncle the duke of York with the earl of Oxford. (Shakespeare's earl of Westmorland was not present.) Arques was reached on the fourth day, an average of 15 miles per day (assuming the date of departure was October 8).

[1] But transport was provided for a portion (6 inches long) of the True Cross.

A curious thing happened at Arques. The famous Chateau commanded the bridge over the little river Béthune. It was blocked by the commander of the Chateau, who offered resistance.[1] But when Henry threatened to burn the town unless he gave passage, he not only did so but supplied the army with bread and wine. This stratagem Henry copied, as always, from his great-grandfather, who had adopted it with success in his campaign of 1359. Indeed, Henry continued to apply it with invariable success throughout his march.

Next day, October 12, the army marched a good 20 miles to Eu on the Bresle, where a smart skirmish took place with a strong body of troops. They were however repulsed and bread and wine were dutifully produced as on the previous day. Crossing the Bresle from Inchville to Beauchamps,[2] four miles south-east of the town, the army now set its course for the ford of Blanche Taque, five miles west of Abbeville, marching through Viriville.

But when within a few miles of the ford a prisoner taken at Eu reported that it was defended with stakes and that a strong force under marshal Boucicaut was stationed on the far side. After satisfying himself that the prisoner spoke true,[3] the king came to the reluctant conclusion that he must abandon the attempt to cross the Somme there and instead turned east and marched up the valley, hoping to find an unguarded crossing-place higher up-stream.

It was a nasty shock, and I expect the king was almost as surprised to discover the presence of Boucicaut as we are to read it. How had the French marshal, last heard of in Honfleur, got to the far side of the Somme? This we would all much like to know, but the sources do not give much help. One indeed asserts that he and the Constable d'Albret marched from Rouen *via* Amiens as soon as they heard that the English army had

---

[1] The extreme strength of the Chateau may account for the Castellan's contumacy.

[2] According to *La Bataille d'Azincourt* by René de Belleval, Vol. I (1865) but I cannot find the source.

[3] Waurin, who relates this story, asserts that the statement was not true and that the ford was unguarded, but modern writers discredit this. It is unthinkable that the English king should abandon his plan on the unchecked statement of a prisoner.

set out on its march. This seems impossible. The route *via* Amiens to Abbeville would be almost 100 miles and we must allow seven days for this. If they started the day after getting the news of the English march (which would be very quick action) they could not reach Abbeville *via* Amiens till October 15, two days *after* the English army had passed. But D'Albret evidently was there at least a full day before the English approach, for he seems to have made extensive and successful arrangements for the defence of all the passages over the Somme both above and below Abbeville, destroying the bridges wherever necessary.[1] Moreover, we now know that on the way to Abbeville he had detached Boucicaut to Eu, evidently to act as a delaying force. It was in fact Boucicaut who had opposed the English at Eu, subsequently falling back to Blanche Taque ford.

In the absence of reliable sources, there seem only two possible explanations of Boucicaut's operation. If he did not set out from Rouen till hearing of the departure of the English army, he must have marched light, probably with mounted troops only, followed later by dismounted troops and baggage. In this case, not wishing to become involved in a battle with the whole English army he would give them a wide berth, probably crossing the Somme at St. Remy (four miles east of Abbeville). The other alternative is that the news of the English king's plan leaked out and Boucicaut took the instant decision to forestall him by marching at once. In this case he probably took the direct road to Abbeville. Whether he had the permission of the Dauphin to split the French army in this way or not, his action was a brilliant one and stamps him as a fine commander. He has not been given sufficient credit for it either in England or his own country. His action might well have led to the undoing of the English army.[2]

---

[1] In this matter he seems to have been more prompt and effective than the Germans in their attempt to prevent the British army crossing in their advance from the Seine to the Somme in September 1944.

[2] We know that D'Albret was across the Somme a few days later, and it is probable that the two were acting in concert, so it may well be that D'Albret dispatched the Marshal to act as a rear-guard whilst he himself attended to the Somme crossings.

The English army, altering its course with a heavy heart and much foreboding, soon encountered its first rebuff. The bridge at Abbeville was guarded and Boucicaut's troops were in force on the far side. A few miles further up-stream the bridge at Pont Remy was also defended, and the army went into billets in Bailleul[1] and nearby villages. A 10-mile march.

Next day, the 14th, the search for a crossing was resumed, with the same result, and the army billeted at Hangest, midway between Abbeville and Amiens, a 14-mile march. On the 15th Amiens was given a wide berth and the night was spent at Pont de Metz, two miles south-west of the city. On the 16th they marched to Boves on the Aure.[2] The custodian of the château, after the usual persuasion, gave them bread and wine, the latter in profusion. The troops were tired and thirsty, and partook of the wine so freely that the king gave orders that no more should be served. When someone explained that the soldiers were only filling their water-bottles, the king replied sourly, "Their bottles indeed! They are making big bottles of their bellies and getting very drunk". Which was no doubt the truth.

The little English army was now very dispirited. It was also hungry; the rations carried had almost given out and local produce was hard to come by. For some days they had been living mainly on dried meat and walnuts. And there seemed no end to the march; it was the general opinion that they would have to march to the head-waters of the river, still 50 miles away, in order to get the other side.

On October 17 the army resumed its weary march, this time taking a north-east direction in order to regain the river and make a further attempt at a crossing. A six-mile march brought them opposite the walled town of Corbie, which lies on the northern bank of the river. The bridge was intact and a mounted party of the enemy made a spirited sortie, which for the moment took the English by surprise. But recovering, they

---

[1] The old home of the Balliols. Traces of their motte and bailey castle still exist.
[2] Another motte and bailey castle.

struck back with vigour, driving the French back into the town and taking several prisoners.[1]

Some of these prisoners stated that the French army intended to contest the passage of the invaders, and to make a dead set at the hated longbowmen by mounted attack. On hearing this, the king ordered that henceforth each archer should provide himself with a stake 6 ft. in length and pointed at each end. In case of mounted attack the stake was to be thrust into the ground, the upper end sloping towards the enemy. And so it was done.

It may be that these prisoners also gave the king some information of a valuable kind, namely some topographical particulars as to the course of the Somme up-stream. Whether this be so or not, Henry here made a sudden change in his direction of march, turning nearly 80 degrees to the right instead of continuing to follow the course of the river towards Peronne. It was a decision of great significance, as an examination of the map will show.

From Amiens, the river takes an easterly direction (facing up-stream) for 30 miles to Peronne. It then bends through a right angle to the right, and after going south for 15 miles about Ham it turns gradually to the north-east, as far as St. Quentin. Now the new course followed by the army cut across this great bend in the river, and formed a tangent to the Ham bend. Three advantages might be expected to be gained from this change of course. First, the river would be rejoined at a point considerably higher up where, even if no bridges were available, it might be possible to ford it. Second, if the French army which had been marching abreast of the English army on the northern bank continued to do so, it would, by taking the outside of the bend, have to march 12 to 14 miles further, and so would get one day's march behind. Third, any troops detailed to guard the crossing places in the Ham bend would not be expecting the early arrival of the enemy thus made possible, and might be taken off their

---

[1] The French would get good warning of the approach from the top of the lofty twin church-towers.

guard. It was in fact a brilliant step on the part of the English king, though it seems to have gone almost unrecognized and unappreciated.

So at Fouilly (south of Corbie) the army turned to its right and mounted the downlands, passing a little to the left of Villers Bretonneux. It is not known where they spent that night, though the implication usually is that it was opposite Corbie. I think this most unlikely and that Harbonnières for the main body and Caix for the advance-guard were the nights' billets.[1] In any case the English army was now entering upon the battlefield of the Somme of 1916 and of the 1918 retreat. For the next 60 miles of their march there will not be a village they passed through that did not see fighting by allied troops (in almost all cases British) during the 1914–18 war.

In either Harbonnières or Caix a soldier entered the church, seized the copper pyx, thinking it was gold, and hid it in his sleeve. When the loss was reported, the king ordered a hue and cry, the culprit was discovered, and by the king's orders hanged from a tree out of hand. There was no further trouble of this nature.

The following day's march brought them to Nesle. The inhabitants showed fight, but the simple threat to burn the fields brought about a change of attitude, and it is said that they informed the king that the fords over the river just ahead were unguarded. Whether or not they gave this information the fact would soon have been discovered, for the army was purposely heading that way with the object of crossing if feasible. At any rate scouts reported that the fords at Voyennes and Bethencourt, three miles north-west of the town, were unguarded, and the army marched off before dawn next day, the 19th, to cross by both simultaneously, the fighting troops making use of the one and the baggage the other.

But there were difficulties. The river valley was wide and marshy all along its course; and the causeways by which alone the army could cross had been destroyed by the defending

---

[1] The Fifth Army held up the German advance in 1918 for two days on this line.

troops. A small vanguard of 200 archers however managed to flounder across and drive off the few half-scared defenders in the vicinity. Thus a small bridge-head was formed whilst the causeways were repaired.

All day long the work of repair went on, the soldiers demolishing houses for timbers and toiling feverishly, for their lives might depend on the results. It was an anxious moment, for the enemy might appear in force before the passage was accomplished.[1]

At about noon on October 19, it became possible to start passing the army over, but it was a tricky business and required careful "traffic control". The king realised the importance of this and he himself supervised the crossing at the ford used by the fighting troops, and two trusted subordinates did the same at the other ford. At about 8 p.m, the last man was across, and the army marched on a few miles in the dark to billets at Athies and Monchy Lagache. "We spent a joyous night" wrote the king's chaplain, and one can well believe it.

Meanwhile, what was the French army doing? We have seen how its advanced-guard under marshal Boucicaut and the Constable d'Albret had set out from Rouen for Abbeville either before or just after the English army started on its march on October 8, also how King Charles VI and the Dauphin had taken up their quarters at Vernon whilst the main body of the French army was assembling at Rouen.

On October 12, while the king of England was approaching Eu the king of France entered Rouen in company with the Dauphin. They had the evident intention of placing themselves at the head of the army and advancing against the English. But no one in the French army relished the idea of being led by a madman or by a nincompoop, and the veteran duke of Berry was deputed to argue his sovereign out of the project. Berry had fought at Poitiers and retained vivid but bitter recollections of that battle and of the fate of the present king's grandfather

---

[1] The writer may be pardoned if he remarks that he himself experienced just such anxiety at a crossing a few miles down-stream during the Retreat of 1918.

John II. He therefore expostulated firmly with the king, summing up his argument in the words "Better to lose a battle and save the king than lose a battle and lose the king too". The logic of this was unanswerable and both the king and Dauphin consented to remain behind, and that the command should devolve on the dukes of Orleans and Bourbon, until the whole army could be re-united under the command of the Constable d'Albret.

The French army set out for Amiens on, I reckon, the 13th or 14th of October[1] while the English army was pushing its way up the Somme valley between Abbeville and Amiens. The French army must have reached Amiens on the 17th while its rival was passing Corbie. But cutting straight across the great bend traversed by the English army, the French had now almost caught it up. Indeed the fact that Corbie was so strongly garrisoned may indicate that the most advanced troops of the French army were already there. The prisoners taken there seemed to be in communication, at least, with the French main army. D'Albret with the vanguard may be pictured as only a few miles ahead, his face set for Peronne.

So we have this situation; whilst the English were marching across the curve of the Somme, the French, being north of the river, now had the longer route of the two—unless they decided to cross to the south bank, but this was not to be expected of them, for their obvious role was to defend the line of the river, keeping it between the enemy and themselves. Thus on October 18th and 19th, while the English were approaching and crossing the river to the east of Nesle, the French were marching along the north bank of the river to Peronne. There they arrived on the evening of the 19th while the English were in the act of making their hazardous crossing of the river. That night the two armies went to sleep a bare seven miles apart, and with no river dividing them. Decisive events might be expected to happen on the morrow.

[1] For a discussion of the march of the French army see the Appendix to this chapter.

But the English troops went to bed that night in high spirits and happy ignorance of the proximity of the enemy, and of the danger that now hung over their heads. For it must be recognized that the French, considering the size, hasty formation and heterogeneous composition of this army, had made remarkable progress and moreover had marched in exactly the right direction. How far this may have been due to accurate information of the English movements, how far to happy intuition and how far to pure luck it is impossible to say, for we do not know what information of their enemy the French possessed. Indeed their movements throughout this crucial campaign have been most inadequately recorded. Possibly this may be due to the unpleasant memories afterwards conjured up by the name Agincourt. (The French later changed the name to Azincourt.)

ACROSS THE SOMME

We now return to the English side. On Sunday, October 20, Henry V seems to have given his tired troops a rest after the exceptional exertions of the previous day. This was natural enough. Before deciding what route to take towards Calais it would be desirable to ascertain the situation of the hostile army; and while scouts were sent northward the king himself seems to have ridden forward. Meanwhile his soldiers fell to speculating as to how many marches it would take them to reach Calais. The "know-alls" declared that they would be there in eight days. Tommy Atkins, in his ignorance has ever been a born optimist.

The question of where lay the French army was soon solved— by the French themselves. For a deputation of three heralds arrived from the French headquarters at Peronne bearing a challenge from the dukes of Orleans and Bourbon. Titus Livius gives a graphic account of the scene. The heralds first approached the duke of York by whom they were led to the king's presence. They promptly fell on their knees, remaining silent until he gave permission for them to speak. They then gave out their message, opening humbly enough—

"Right puissant Prince, great and noble is thy Kingly power; as is reported among our lords. They have heard that thou labourest by thy forces to conquer towns, castles and cities of the realm of Franche, and of the Frenchmen whom thou hast destroyed."

But soon the tone changed, and they came to the point in these words –

"They inform thee by us that before thou comest to Calais they will meet thee to fight with thee."

King Henry, who evidently was now informed of the location of the French army, took this challenge to mean that he would be attacked next day somewhere between his present position and Peronne. He professed to be glad of the opportunity of crossing swords with his opponents. If Titus Livius's account is to be accepted, and I see no reason to doubt it, Henry's reply was a notable one, couched in terms of dignity and quiet pride and confidence.

"To which Henry, with a courageous spirit, a firm look, without anger or displeasure, and without his face changing colour, mildly replied that 'all would be done according to the will of God'. When the Heralds enquired what road he would take, he answered: 'Straight to Calais; and if our adversaries seek to disturb us on our journey, it shall be at their utmost peril, and not without harm to them. We seek them not, neither will the fear of them induce us to move out of our way, or the sight of them cause us to make the greater haste. We advise them, however, not to interrupt our journey nor to seek such an effusion of Christian blood.' "

The author of the *Vita* adds the interesting detail that the king was seated on horseback in the open country, surrounded by his staff when the heralds approached. Maybe he was making a personal reconnaissance to the front when the heralds approached.

Evidently expecting that the French army would advance to the attack when they received his uncompromising reply, King Henry issued a warning order to his army, and selected and started to occupy a position in which to accept battle. It would be interesting to know where this position lay. To anyone acquainted with the ground, it is not difficult to suggest the site of the position selected. The road from Athies to Peronne runs due north for one and a half miles, gradually ascending; it then crosses the great Roman road that runs straight as a die and due east-west right across the Somme battlefields of 1916 and 1918, linking Amiens to St. Quentin. Immediately to the north of the Roman road is a ridge, also running east-west. The Athies-Peronne road crosses this ridge and then sinks gently into the valley of the little river Cologne, and so on into Peronne. This ridge, I make no doubt, was the position selected by the English king.[1]

Throughout the day anxious eyes were strained in the direction of Peronne, four miles ahead; but not a sign of the enemy could be seen, either advancing or taking up a position to the east of the town, barring their own advance. With a sigh of relief the army went to sleep that night: evidently there would be no battle on the morrow.

Meanwhile what had happened to the French army after the sending forth of its challenge? Not one word has come down to us in explanation of the curious course adopted by the French leaders. If as they said, they really intended to bar the Calais road to the English they could not have found a better position in which to do so than that in which they now lay. Peronne itself, combined with the ridge on its eastern side, formed a cork to the bottle in which the English army now found itself. To their left lay the broad marshy valley of the Somme, which they had just, with so great labour, traversed. To their front lay the defended town of Peronne, and to their right front was a ridge, just to the north of, and covered by the river Cologne. There was little chance of circumventing it, for if they attempted a turning movement to the east, the French men-at-arms, who were of course all mounted and who formed the greater part of the army, could sidestep to their left quicker than the English army could move, for the pace of an army is its slowest unit, and the slowest English units were on foot.

[1] Five hundred years later it was occupied by the artillery (in which the writer was serving) of the rear-guard of the Fifth Army during its retreat towards Amiens. It is as unlikely that anyone was aware of the significance of that ridge as that anyone fighting in the Battle of Vittoria was aware that the Black Prince's troops had fought there 450 years before.

The reason why the French, instead of this, marched 13 miles due north, as they did, to Bapaume, is baffling. It may be that the Constable D'Albret, the nominal commander, had contacted the main army in person, after the issue of the challenge, and that he was opposed to risking battle with the English.

Another possibility is that the main body of the army fell back to Bapaume in order to join up with d'Albret's column. If this were so, it would go far to explain the inactivity of the combined French army next day, for a halt would be required in which to amalgamate the two forces which had never seen each other before. This seems the most likely of the two explanations. On October 21 the English army was far from motionless. Pursuant to his stated intention, King Henry gave the order to resume the march on the direct road to Calais.[1] This took the army close past the walls of Peronne. A few French horsemen emerged from its gates and a skirmish took place, but it was devoid of significance. The direct road to Calais lay through Albert, nearly 20 miles to the north-west of Peronne. One mile to the north of Peronne the road crossed the Peronne-Bapaume road up which the French army had marched 24 hours before, leaving unmistakable tracks behind them, a sure indication of the direction of their destination. The English king cannot have failed to be surprised by this, for Bapaume lay a good 10 miles to the right of his own line of march. Did the enemy really intend to bar his road? Or did they intend to attack him on the march from a flank? It was obviously desirable to guard against such an eventuality, and he therefore sent out a right flank-guard, along the high ground to the south-west of Bapaume, from whence any hostile approach would be visible. This ridge-road runs through Combles, Ginchy and Martinpuich, names that became familiar during the 1916 battle of the Somme. The flank-guard observed no motion on the part of

---

[1] The Duke of York now commanded the vanguard. *The Brut* (*Continuation H*) explains this by stating that for some time the king had lost confidence in York, and that the duke, being aware of the fact, requested to be given the vanguard in order to prove his worth.

the enemy and may be presumed to have spent the night in the Grandcourt-Miraumont area in the valley of the Ancre.[1]

Meanwhile the main body was plodding its way along the direct road to Albert buffeted by rain and wind, and halting for the night probably in the Mametz-Fricourt area, after a march of about 16 miles.

Next day, Oct 22, it resumed its march (the flank-guard rejoining it on the march), passed through Albert and Bouzincourt, and halted for the night at Forceville, Acheux, and Beauquesne. The last-named place was rather far to the left, and I suspect the advance-guard had missed their way. Such mistakes are easy, even today, when accurate maps are available. The same day the French army, which had been resting at Bapaume the previous day, set off. It had good reason for rest, having marched rapidly and without respite all the way from Rouen, paying little heed to the common foot-soldiers of its company who must have been well-nigh worn out. At Bapaume it had been abreast of the English army, and 10 miles to its flank, but this day it marched, as I reckon it, 16 miles to its opponent's 14 miles and ended up in the Coullemont area about three miles ahead and eight miles on the right flank of the English. In short, the routes were gently approaching one another, the French being always slightly in the lead.

On October 23, the English made a long march of 18 miles, passing three miles to the right of Doullens, through Lucheux, to Bonnières, with advanced-guard, now led by the duke of York, at Frévent. Bonnières was a good two miles to the left of the direct road, and it again looks as if the column had mistaken its way. But as several villages were utilised as billets it may be that the others were on the more direct road.

On the same day the French made a slightly shorter march, to St. Pol or its environs, where it was still nearly three miles ahead, but the distance to the flank had narrowed to three miles. All this time the two armies were said to be out of touch with

[1] The area reached by the Ulster Division on the first day of the battle of the Somme.

one another as no music was being played. At this distance
music would have no effect either way, but it is unlikely that
mounted patrols from the two armies were not fully apprised of
the motions of the other army.

Whether or not the main body lost its way, the king certainly
did, and found himself at nightfall two miles in advance of

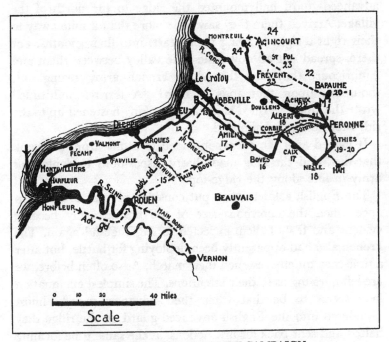

Sketch Map 1; THE AGINCOURT CAMPAIGN

12, 13, etc.	Dates in October	Adv. gd.	Advance-guard
→	Route of English army	M.	Miraumont
-▸--→	Routes of French army	B.	Blanche Taque Ford

the village allotted to him for a billet by the harbingers. But
Henry would not withdraw; the billet must advance to him.
He gave the curious reason that, "God would not have me now
go back and forage, for I have my coat-armour on".

From Frévent on October 24 the advanced-guard after a
12-mile march entered the little village of Blangy, in the valley

of the Fernoise. French patrols had recently been seen in the village; evidently the enemy was closing on them at last. Indeed scouts had already reported sighting them three miles to the right. But the king held on his way, refusing to diverge to the left. The river valley at Blangy was crossed by a narrow causeway and the operation was a lengthy one. Meanwhile the advanced-guard had mounted the ridge to the north of the village. Arrived there they saw little more than a mile away to their right a sight to bring their hearts into their mouths. For there, spread out all down the little valley between them and Ambricourt they saw the whole French army strung out, thousands upon thousands of men! "A terrific multitude" wrote the king's terrified chaplain. The king hastened up to the ridge-top to see for himself.[1]

It looked as if the enemy intended to attack from the flank that day, and the king made hasty dispositions to deploy his army in line along the ridge-top.

The English soldiers were put considerably out of countenance when the enormous size of the hostile army became evident and few of them expected to see England again. The French also had apparently been deploying for battle, but after a time they quietly resumed their march. As so often before, we are left guessing as to their intentions. The simplest explanation here seems to be that when their advanced-guard almost blundered into the English advanced-guard on the ridge they halted and sent back for instructions, at the same time forming line to face the enemy. This no doubt resulted in prolonged and excited discussions among the French leaders, ere they decided to resume the march, and take up position a couple of miles further on, barring the road to the English. Thus the march was resumed and at nightfall the French host bivouacked on the open ground astride the road to Calais, just short of the little village of Agincourt. The English army also resumed its march, halting in and around the village of Maisoncelles, one mile short of the enemy, who now completely barred their line

[1] The approximate spot is still easy to identify.

of retreat. A battle on the morrow, the Feast of St. Crispin, seemed inevitable.

APPENDIX

THE ENGLISH MARCH

The course of the march of the English army is not hard to establish within fairly narrow limits. Nor is the speed of the march difficult to compute, if we are agreed on the date of departure. I have accepted the date given by the contemporary *Chronicle of London*—October 8.

I agree with the map in Ramsay's *Lancaster and York* except that it shows the route going through Tréport after passing Eu, and places Tréport on the coast between the estuary of the Bresle and that of the Somme, whereas it is actually on the Bresle estuary. But Ramsay's script does not always agree with his map; he writes that the English army passed to the *left* of Peronne, whereas his map (correctly) shows it as passing to the *right*. His map makes the English pass through Albert, whereas he writes that they passed through "Encre", the medieval name for Albert, but states that it is "on the Miraumont". There is no such river as Miraumont, but there *is* a village Miraumont (famous in the 1914-18 war), which lies on the river Ancre. Ramsay must have misread the map. The fact is that he has jumbled two conflicting accounts: one states that the road passed through Albert, the other through Miraumont, both on the river Ancre. As they are a good seven miles apart, and it is desirable to establish which of the two routes is the correct one, I have conjecturally solved the problem by the test of inherent military probability, and have sent a flank-guard *via* Miraumont, and the main body through Albert. I have not seen this problem discussed by any of the historians, some of whom select one and some the other, without giving their reasons. Wyllie favours Miraumont, but to travel through both Miraumont and Forceville would involve an almost right-angle turn at the former place and would add a good four miles to the march. Professor Jacob also gives Miraumont, but his map seems to indicate Albert. Moreover St. Remy (who gives Miraumont) who might be supposed to have his geographical facts correct, seeing he was with the English army, makes a big geographical error in the very sentence in which he mentions Miraumont. He writes "King Henry passed the river Somme at Esclusier", six miles below Peronne, and 15 miles from the actual crossing place. Waurin and Momstrelet on the other hand make Henry march "straight" to Forceville from near Peronne, which would take him through Albert. I accept this. For the remainder of the march there is no dispute as to the route.

We can now construct a march-table for the English army, with tolerable certainty. It is of course impossible to measure distances with precision, but in the following table I have made ample allowance for twists and turns in the road, but not of course for counter-marches when the wrong turning was taken –a thing that must have often occurred.

THE ENGLISH MARCH

Date	Approx. billets	Miles	Total	Average m.p.d.
Oct.				
8	Depart Harfleur			
11	Arques	60		
12	Eu	21		
13	Bailleul	23	104	17
14	Hangest	15		
15	Pont de Metz	17		
16	Boves	9		
17	Harbonnières	18		
18	Nesle	18		
19	Athies	9	190	14
20	Rest			
21	Mametz	18		
22	Acheux	16		
23	Frévent	20		
24	Agincourt	16	260	17½

From the above table we note that, taking the march in three stages, the march to the Somme was done at 17 miles per day, the march along the Somme at 14 miles per day and the march thence to Agincourt at 17½ miles per day. Including the rest day the whole march of 260 miles was accomplished in 17 days at an average speed of just over 15 miles per day. This was not bad going for hungry men, though of course for the mounted men it was child's play.

The route of the English army was remarkably direct. If a straight line be drawn from Peronne to Calais, a distance of just 100 miles, it will be found that Agincourt lies a bare 10 miles to the left of this line, and that nowhere does the lateral error exceed 12 miles. It is true that the first two days march was 15 degrees to the left of the direct line. But on reaching Acheux this error was largely corrected and from there to Calais the route followed the direct line very closely, the biggest lateral divergence being at Agincourt itself where it was about four miles. This raised the question, did the army possess maps? And if not, how did it estimate the direction of a place 100 miles away? This directness of route had been still more striking in the campaigns of Edward III, and it has led me to the tentative conclusion that some sort of map must have been in the possession of the army. If Edward III had a map of this region of France it is not impossible that Henry V also had one—possibly the identical one used by his great-grandfather.

THE FRENCH MARCH

The route and timing of the French army presents much greater difficulties than does the English, as has been hinted at in the text. Also there is the complication that there are two forces, not one, to consider–the advanced-guard under the Constable Charles D'Albret, and the main body under the dukes of Orleans and Bourbon–at least as far as Peronne. We will take the advanced-guard first. Waurin is our chief source for this. He records that d'Albret, Arthur of Richemont, the duke of Alençon and others were present on the Somme in the Abbeville region when the English army advanced. From the *Chronique de Percival de Cagny* we learn that the Duke of Alençon, "by his diligence managed to reach Abbeville before Henry could reach Blanche Taque", which seems to imply that he marched straight into Abbeville, and not *via* Rouen, as Oman asserts. Now Alençon was Cagny's master and was in the company of D'Albret, which would explain why Alençon rather than the Constable is mentioned; but it is clear that the advanced-guard is indicated. Waurin takes up the tale, telling us that D'Albret "went to Corbie and thence to Peronne, keeping their men always pretty near them on the road". After Peronne, according to him, they moved on to Bapaume. Unfortunately he does not say whether this was before or after joining forces with the main body of the French army. I will revert to this point in due course.

Now let us try to trace the march of the French main body. The date it departed from Rouen where it had been assembling is unknown, but we get an indication from the date of the arrival of the king at Rouen. Various dates are given. The monk of St. Denys, a reliable source, states that Charles VI arrived in Rouen early in October at the head of some of his troops. The exact date was the 12th, and the army would require at least one day to amalgamate the new arrivals with those already collected at Rouen before marching out. Thus the march could hardly have started earlier than October 14 or 15; if it had started earlier it would probably have bumped into the English army in the act of passing Amiens; on the other hand it could hardly have started later as it was in or near Peronne on the 19th. The distance from Rouen to Amiens is just over 50 miles; thus by starting on the 14th or 15th the army might be in Amiens on the 17th. Thence to Peronne is 25 miles: a full day's march on the 18th and a short march on the 19th would take the army there. If the above is what happened the French army must have crossed the tracks of the English army near Pont de Metz about 48 hours later, and reached Amiens on the day that the rival army was passing Corbie 10 miles away. The French were catching up, and the long detour then made by the English army allowed the

French to get right across their path at Peronne as we have seen. And thus it came about that on the 21st the English in their turn crossed the tracks of the French, as we have also seen. All the known facts now seem to fall into a clear pattern.

I do not think there can be much doubt that the above is approximately what happened, but commentators give us little assistance in the elucidation of a real problem. Wyllie is silent on the subject, contenting himself with remarking (in a footnote) that Ramsay shows the French army on his map as marching, "by Beauvais and Montdidier to Amiens and thence round to Ham and Bapaume without touching Peronne", without indicating whether he himself agrees with this astonishing route. As a matter of fact Ramsay's map does not show the French as marching through Amiens at all; from Montdidier it goes to Ham and thence north to Bapaume.

Ramsay gives no authority or reasons for the route he shows; nor does he even refer to his map in the text. His route is of course preposterous, the act of a madman – and the mad king was not present. Beauvais is due east of Rouen; what should induce a French army to take that direction, when its object was to prevent the English army reaching Calais? Its own advanced-guard was busily engaged in this task when the French army left Rouen; the last information it could have had from the front before setting off was that D'Albret was somewhere in the neighbourhood of Abbeville, that is, to the north-east of Rouen, 45 degrees to the left of a line to Beauvais. Moreover in order to prevent the English army reaching Calais the French would try to get to the north of them – not the south. Beauvais is 30 miles south of the Somme, and to wander into that region when the English were trying to cross the Somme would be, as I say, the act of a mad general. The surprising thing is that the French army did not march direct to Abbeville, instead of to Amiens. Presumably the reason was that, knowing or believing D'Albret to be guarding the Somme in the Abbeville area, Orleans and Bourbon rightly judged that the English would be obliged to march up the southern bank of the river

Somme, and might be encountered at Amiens. If this be so, it was a pretty shrewd appreciation and a good mark should be accorded to the French dukes. Reverting to Ramsay's map, if the French had taken the route shown on it their journey to Peronne would have been over 30 miles longer than *via* Amiens, and they could hardly have overtaken the English. Indeed the route from Ham to Bapaume would have taken them through Monchy Lagache, where they might well have bumped into Henry in his billet! A clear indication that the main body marched *via* Amiens is the fact that the duke of Brittany halted in that city, leaving the army to go on without him.

Let us get back to the French army marching along the northern bank of the Somme on October 19, through Corbie, Bray, Clery and under Mont St. Quentin—all localities that figured prominently in the final British advance in 1918. The question to resolve is where did the French army join forces with its advanced-guard? I can find no direct evidence on the point and doubt if there is any. I am reduced to deducing it from a single indication. When the three heralds approached King Henry they were hardly likely to have come from a place so distant as Bapaume, for the English army had only reached its billets in the middle of the preceding night and their billeting area could not have been located till next morning. Bapaume is over 20 miles from Monchy, and to get the news there, prepare the challenge and send off the heralds, and for them to cover the 20 miles, and return with the answer the same day seems unlikely, to say the least. No, I think the challenge must have come from Peronne. Now it was issued by the dukes of Orleans and Bourbon, not by the official commander-in-chief, the Constable D'Albret. Though the dukes are said to have had little regard for him they would hardly have gone to this length, and yet consented to fight under him at Agincourt a few days later. The explanation, I suggest, is that while the main body under the dukes was at Peronne, the advanced-guard had already moved on to Bapaume, as reported by Waurin. If this be so, it is easy to see how the dukes, having issued their challenge continued their march in order to concentrate the whole army at Bapaume before risking an engagement with their opponents.

From Bapaume to Agincourt, there seems no debatable point; in the absence of precise information I have indicated a purely conjectural route, compiled after study of the map.

N.B.–For the sources for the march, see the appendix to the next chapter.

CHAPTER V

AGINCOURT

THE rival armies went to rest, but few to sleep, on the eve of that fateful day of St. Crispin, in very different physical and mental states. The English had marched for 17 days with only one day's rest and had covered 260 miles, an average of 15 miles per day. The greater part of the army, it is true, was mounted, but there remained an appreciable portion of archers on foot. The French had not experienced such a trying and exhausting time. They had certainly marched with speed, covering about 180 miles in ten days, but all save a tiny portion of the combatants were mounted.

The mental state of the two armies was even more dissimilar. The English as a whole believed that they would most of them lose their lives in the inevitable battle next day. The idea of surrender does not seem to have entered the heads of any of them. It was to be literally a case of "do or die". They prepared solemnly for the contest, saw to their weapons, confessed and were shriven, and laid themselves down to rest on the rain-soaked open field. Well might they despair of victory. They had seen the enormous French army, over four times as numerous as their own,[1] which was under 6,000 strong, of whom less than 1,000 were men-at-arms, the rest being archers (for they had no artillery.) It was a small army, but it was homogeneous and it possessed a degree of discipline that was quite unique for that epoch. Let a French contemporary, whose sympathies were French, testify on this score. The monk of St. Denys declared:

"They considered it a crime to have bad women in their camp. They paid more regard than the French themselves for the welfare of the inhabitants, who (consequently) declared themselves in their favour. They closely observed the rules of military discipline and obeyed scrupulously the orders of their King. His words were

---

[1] See Appendix to this chapter for the numbers.

received with enthusiasm, and not only by the leading men; for the common soldiers also promised to fight to the death."

The king had strictly enjoined complete silence in the lines that night, and his orders were obeyed. Such was the silence that the French outposts suspected that the English were preparing to slip away. St. Remy adds picturesquely, "Not a horse neighed". Henry V worked up his troops to a pitch of fervour and camaraderie akin to that produced by Joan of Arc in the French army marching to the relief of Orleans.

"We few, we happy few, we band of brothers." Shakespeare hit it off perfectly.

In the opposite camp things were vastly different. On the one hand the French lords, at least, were "cock-a-hoop", wagering as to which of them should capture the English king, and so on. It is even stated by Polydore Vergil that they had a cart specially painted in which to promenade their royal captive through the streets of Paris. The other contrast was that in the French camp all was clamour and confusion, attaining almost to chaos. The noise of shouting lords, grooms and servants, reached even to the English lines over half a mile away; the rain was falling steadily most of the night, and the lords were shouting for their varlets, and sending them in all directions in search of straw to lay on the sodden churned-up ground (recently sown with autumn wheat) on which they had to lie. On the one hand was the ordered discipline of a regular trained army of selected soldiers; on the other, a vast rabble-like horde of hastily-raised troops, of a heterogeneous nature, brought together from all parts of France, and even from further afield, and lacking one single undisputed head to whom they could look with reverence and confidence in the ordering of the battle. Indeed there could scarcely have been a greater contrast, except in the arms and armour carried, between two medieval armies.

The English king had billets in the village of Maisoncelles but there could be little sleep for him that night. He must have been in a state of mental excitement. What his inmost feelings were it is difficult to say. Until quite recently he had affected to welcome a battle, and it is generally held that he spoke the truth. But the sight that had greeted him that afternoon, of the vast French army, surely removed any desire that he still retained for a battle. Yet if he felt any misgivings he kept them strictly to himself. The story is well attested, and is not a figment of Shakespeare's imagination, that when the impossibility of avoiding a battle became manifest and Sir Walter Hungerford exclaimed:

"I would that we had 10,000 more good English archers, who would gladly be here with us to-day,"

the king replied:

"Thou speakest as a fool! By the God of Heaven on whose grace I lean, I would not have one more even if I could. This people is God's people, he has entrusted them to me to-day and he can bring down the pride of these Frenchmen who so boast of their numbers and their strength."

But whatever his secret feelings, he had others thing to occupy his mind and attention during the hours of darkness. He was prepared, whatever he might say, to strike a bargain for the possibility of reaching Calais without a battle, and negotiations to that end passed to and fro between the two headquarters, just as they had done in the night before Poitiers. The price he was prepared to pay was the return of Harfleur to its old owners; but the French, confident in their own strength, would not agree to this and the price they proposed was beyond what Henry's pride allowed him to concede. The negotiations thus fell through and a battle next day became inevitable.

At dawn on October 25, 1415, the feast day of St. Crispin and St. Crispianus, the two martyr-cobblers of Soissons, the rain had stopped and the two weary armies roused themselves and were deployed by their respective marshalls in order of battle. The English king, having attended Mass, donned his armour and surcoat, resplendent with leopards of England and the fleur-de-lys of France, his helmet encircled by a golden crown, studded with pearls, sapphires and rubies. He then mounted his grey palfrey, having for some reason removed his spurs; and thus he rode down the line, stopping frequently to harangue the troops and to receive their acclamations.

He then placed himself at the head of the centre division, the duke of York being in command of the right division and the Lord Camoys in command of the left division. The French however appeared not to be ready for battle, and a long and doubtless painful pause ensued, during which we may describe the ground about to be fought over.

It is easily described for it is beautifully symmetrical. If the two contestants really desired a field that would give no advantage to either side as they declared, they certainly found it at Agincourt. As my sketch-map shows, the arena formed a rectangle, the two sides being formed by the woods surrounding the villages of Agincourt[1] and Tramecourt, the open space being 940 yards wide at the narrowest point, and the two ends being formed by the two armies in line, just over 1,000 yards apart. There was a barely perceptible dip between the two armies, but the two flanks fell away appreciably, a surprising discovery to the visitor, for no account mentions the fact. Owing to the slight dip between them the two armies were in full view of one another. Each army filled the open space, a newly-sown wheat-field, and as the arena was slightly wider on the French side it follows that their line was slightly longer than the English, about 1,200 yards to 950. But the French being many times more numerous their line had a similar proportion of extra depth. The English men-at-arms in fact were only four deep, and the archers about seven to the yard. The numbers were so small that the king could not afford a reserve, bar a minute baggage-guard. In this he took a profound risk, but a desperate malady requires a desperate remedy.

There is wide divergence of opinion as to the exact formation of the English army, but I believe it to have been as follows. It consisted in the main of three divisions, each division having

---

[1] The French called it Agincourt at the time; it was at a subsequent date that they changed it to Azincourt.

its men-at-arms in the centre and its archers on the wings. In addition there was a strong force of what we should now call "army archers" attached to no division but formed in two bodies one on each wing. The archers of the centre division would thus be in contact with the archers of the inner wings of the flank divisions; likewise the outside archers of the flank divisions would be in contact with the "army" archers. Thus, looked at from the front at a distance as the French would see them (and this is important for my argument) the English army would appear to have men-at-arms in the centre, divided by two small clumps of archers, while the main archer force would be on the wings. I suggest that the army archers were about 3,100 strong and the divisional archers 1,850. Thus the biggest clumps, viewed from the front, would be on the wings, each nearly 1,900 strong. A simple calculation shows that such a formation should just fill the space of 940 yards between the woods.

The French army, unlike the English, was mainly composed of men-at-arms. These were formed in three lines, all being dismounted except the rear one and two bodies of cavalry, each 600 strong stationed on the two wings. The latter were detailed to open the battle by a mounted attack on the English archers who could be seen grouped on the wings. The French army being practically an undisciplined rabble, when I speak of three lines, I mean in theory only. In practice there was a deal of jostling, squeezing and intermingling of men-at-arms and archers, while the guns seem to have been pushed out of line altogether; it is doubtful if they fired more than a few rounds at the most. For simplicity the sketch map shows only two lines.

*   *   *

Thus the two armies formed up at dawn on October 25, 1415, and for the next four hours they stood motionless, eyeing each other closely, each waiting upon the other to advance. But a battle cannot take place if neither side will advance, and at

11 o'clock the king of England decided to take the offensive himself. "Advance banner," rang out the famous order, on which everyone "knelt down and made a cross on the ground and kissed it".[1] The whole army then began to advance in line.

The French front was, I reckon, 470 yards north of the Agin-court-Tramecourt road and the English army moved steadily forward till it was 170 yards north of the cross-road, 50 yards south of the present coppice wherein lies the main French grave pit. It moved slowly, frequently halting for the heavily-armoured knights to take breath. At extreme bowshot range the army came to a halt, the archers planted their stakes in front of their front rank thus making a sort of fence,[2] and opened fire.

This fire was probably calculated to provoke the French into advancing, for they had few archers with whom to return the fire. It had the desired effect. The mounted cavalry essayed to charge the flank archers according to plan, and as they started to advance, the front line of dismounted men-at-arms also moved forwards, probably without explicit orders from the Constable d'Albret, their nominal commander-in-chief.

The mounted attack of the two flanks was to be made by parties each about 600 strong, (there is much contradiction about the numbers) but owing to the confusion and lack of discipline in the French ranks only a mere 150 or so on each wing actually took part in the attack. That on the Agincourt side was led by Sir William de Savense, whose party in the words of St. Remy:

"threw themselves on the English archers, who had their sharp stakes fixed before them; but the ground was so soft that the said stakes fell. And the French all retreated excepting three men, of whom Sir William was one; to whom it unluckily happened that by their horses falling on the stakes they were thrown to the ground, among the archers and were immediately killed. The remainder, or the greater part of them, with all their horses, from fear of the arrows retreated into the French advanced-guard in which they caused great confusion, breaking and exposing it in many places,

[1] *The Brut* (*Continuation H*), (ed. Brie), p. 554.
[2] Monstrelet says, "Each archer placed before himself a stake", which makes nonsense of it.

6

and caused them to retire to some new-sown ground for their horses were so wounded by the arrows that they were unmanageable. And thus the advanced-guard being thrown into disorder, the men-at-arms fell in great numbers and their horses took to flight behind the lines, following which example numbers of the French fled."

Up to this point I think the story is quite clear and straight-forward. But now comes the crucial point. Before quoting it, however, we must glance at the French main body which was now advancing in the centre.

All the authorities agree that when they came into contact with the English they were in such close formation that they could scarcely raise their arms to make use of their weapons. How came this about? Surely they would not form up in such ridiculously close order? I believe two causes conspired to produce this unfortunate and fatal result. Look at the map and you will notice that the width of open space in the French position was about 150 yards wider than in that of the English, and that as the French advanced their frontage would diminish owing to the funnel-shape of the open ground made by the two woods. This was bound to have the effect of compressing the French lines somewhat as they advanced.

But I think there was another and more decisive cause than this. I have described the English men-at-arms as being in three groups, separated by clumps of archers. These archers were formed in wedges (cuneos) which I take to mean the same formation that proved so effective at Crecy, namely bastion-like projections in front of the line of men-at-arms. As the French army advanced they would instinctively, if not by order, concentrate against the English men-at-arms, whom they considered their rightful opponents – not the despised common breed of archers. Indeed one account specifically states that they did so. Moreover the nearer they approached and the more they were goaded by the arrows of the English archers, the more they would tend to flinch away from these archers as they pushed forward into the three ominous re-entrants that the English line in effect comprised.

It should be noted that there is no mention in the above

English account of the horses or men being made immobile
by the mud. After all, the English experienced the same mud,

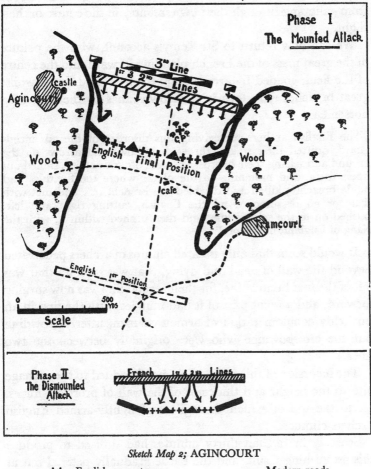

Sketch Map 2; AGINCOURT

+ + English men-at-arms   **- - -** Modern roads
  ▲ English archers   G.P. Grave pits
  ▨ French dismounted men
  ◨ French mounted men

for the rain raineth on the just and the unjust alike, and though
the English had had plenty of rain in the night they advanced

further through the mud than did their opponents. No, it was arrows not mud, that turned back the French horsemen and started the rot. Nor did the mud prevent the French horsemen from galloping through their own infantry in the course of their flight.

We can now return to St. Remy's account, with the picture of the great mass of the French plodding forward into the centre of the field, goaded by arrows from the front and flanks whilst great breaches were torn in their own ranks by the panicking horsemen.

"The English archers, perceiving this disorder of the advanced-guard, quitted their stakes, threw their bows and arrows on the ground and seizing their swords, axes and other weapons, sallied out upon them, and hastening to the places where the fugitives had made breaches, killed and disabled the French, . . . and met with little or no resistance. And the English, cutting right and left, pushed on to the second line, and then pushed within it, with the King of England in person."

It would seem that only isolated clumps of archers penetrated beyond the wall of dead and dying, that was soon all that was left of the first French line, for their second line was now surging forward, and a great part of it had mingled with the first in an unwieldy conglomeration of armoured men, utterly crowding out the crossbowmen who were originally between the two lines.

The incursion of this second line merely added to the carnage and to the height and thickness of the wall of prostrate forms, on to the top of which the agile and lightly-armed English archers climbed.

Scarcely more than thirty minutes had sufficed to produce this astonishing result, and the battle gradually petered out as fewer and fewer Frenchmen remained on their feet. The contest had been for them a kind of nightmare: the more they pressed forward into the fight the more impossible it became for any of them to fight at all. They could not wield their arms and one man falling would bring down those next to him—and there was no getting up; the pages, one of whose duties it was to help their lords to their feet, were not at hand. It was said that the weight of two men in armour falling on top of a third would take away the breath of the man underneath. Some Englishmen indeed fell victims to this disaster. The duke of York at one period pushed forward into the front line. He over-balanced or was pushed over, and others fell on top of him. When, after the battle was over, his body was pulled out from the shambles he was found to be unwounded but stone dead. He had been suffocated to death. Thus perished the last re-maining grandson of Edward III.

Large numbers of the French men-at-arms met the same fate. Indeed John Hardyng, who was present, declares in his rhymed Chronicle, "More were dead through press than our men might have slain."[1]

Thus in a remarkably short space of time the first two French lines, outnumbering their opponents by at least three to one, had been vanquished. There remained the third line who, it will be remembered, were mounted. They did not advance; to do so would have been quite fruitless; neither did they retire as a body, but there was considerable confusion, and many fainter-hearted men quietly slipped away to the rear. Those who stood fast became visible to King Henry, over the wall of dead. One glance showed him that for the moment at least, no danger need be expected from them, and he allowed the victors to take up the congenial task of taking prisoners and arranging for ransoms. But it was a slow task, and a rather gruesome one, disentangling the living from the dead, prising open helmets, unriveting plate-armour and collecting and marshalling those of the living who could walk. The work had gone on for over two hours when suddenly two disturbing events occurred, one in front, the other in the rear.

Only a small baggage-guard had been provided, and it was quite inadequate to ward off a serious attack. Such an attack was now delivered by an armed marauding body, who broke

[1] This is confirmed by *The Brut* (*Continuation H*): "Great people of them were slain without any stroke". (*The Brut*, ed. Brie, p. 555.)

into the camp, and made havoc therein. Not only were the royal beds carried off but the king's chief crown and his seals. At the same time danger suddenly appeared in front. Strenuous efforts had been made by the leaders of the French third line, who were now joined by the duke of Brabant (youngest brother of the duke of Burgundy), with a small body of men. The force thus collecting in his front by itself outnumbered the English army; the English troops were completely off their guard, absorbed in prisoner-taking. Moreover the prisoners had not yet, for the most part, been divested of their armour. The archers thus had their hands full; if they let go of their captives and moved off to repel the impending attack their captives would have been free to pick up weapons that sprinkled the ground and attack them in the rear, possibly in conjunction with their comrades who were still running amok in the English camp. It was an ugly situation; anything might happen. Something had to be done at once, and there seemed only one thing to do: it must be a case of "No quarter" after all: the prisoners must be killed. Sternly the king gave the order, and reluctantly and hesitantly his soldiers obeyed, for it meant to them the loss of ransom. How many were killed is not known, but presently the threat of attack died away and the throat-cutting was stopped.

Some modern English writers have condemned this measure in unmeasured terms: "a cruel butchery" it is dubbed by Ramsay. But needless to say, such things should be judged by the context and customs of the time, and no contemporary chronicler seems to have condemned it, not even the French ones. Indeed one contemporary Frenchman blames his own countrymen for it, on the grounds that their useless rally made this slaughter inevitable. It is also tolerably certain that the French would have done the same under similar circumstances. Indeed 20 years previously on the eve of the Battle of Nicopolis the French commander had cut the throats of 1,000 prisoners, so as not to be encumbered with them next day.[1]

---

[1] Yet the latest French biographer of Joan of Arc seldom mentions the name of Henry V without the elegant soubriquet "The Cut-throat".

A feature of the battle was the enormous number of Frenchmen killed. The total cannot have been far short of 10,000 and it included three dukes—Alençon, Brabant and Bar—the Constable of France and commander-in-chief Charles D'Albret, together with no less than 90 other lords and 1,560 knights. Indeed it was said that more than half the nobility of France were casualties. The prisoners included both the leading dukes, Orleans and Bourbon, the count Arthur of Richmont and marshal Boucicaut, in fact a "clean sweep" was made of the higher commanders in the French host, which thus became a scattered flock without a shepherd.

The English casualties were at the most a few hundred, mainly wounded; it is impossible to give closer figures than this. The chief victim was of course the duke of York, to whom the credit must go for the provision of double-pointed stakes for the archers. The young earl of Suffolk, whose father had died at Harfleur, also perished.

Of the actions of the French leaders in the battle there is no reliable information, but two stories about King Henry are well attested. At one period of the battle he entered the fray, and at that moment his young brother Humphrey of Gloucester was slightly wounded and fell at his feet. The king stood over his prostrate body till the duke could be dragged away. The other story is that 18 French knights swore that they would hack their way to the king of England and strike down his crown, or perish in the attempt. They perished in the attempt, but not before one of them had got within reach of the king of England and struck him on the helmet, lopping off one of the fleurons of the crown and denting the helmet. The dented helmet now hangs high up on the wall above the tomb of the king in the chapel of Edward the Confessor in Westminster Abbey—surely the most dramatic piece of medieval armour in existence!

In contrast to Crecy and Poitiers, the issue of the Battle of Agincourt was decided in the first half hour. This is the more striking when we remember that the odds were even greater against the victor at Agincourt than at the former two battles, and historians have spilt much ink in trying to find the explanation for the overwhelming success. But I think the answer is not far to seek. Battles can be likened to a tug-of-war. On each side there are a number of factors, all pulling the same way–towards victory. The resultant force of all these factors is the measure of the "pull to victory", and the side which produces the biggest resultant is the winner. It is as simple as that.

In the case of Agincourt, there is no need to label and examine each of these factors in detail, for all the factors except one–relative numbers–were, as far as can be seen, in favour of the English army. Hence the English victory. The result can however be summarized in a single sentence: a regular, trained and disciplined army defeated one that possessed none of these military virtues.

THE RETURN MARCH

On the morrow of the battle of Agincourt the English army resumed its march to Calais. It seems always to be taken for granted that such was the right course; but it is interesting to speculate as to the upshot if King Henry had suddenly reversed his plan, and marched in the opposite direction–on Paris. It is interesting to note that in very similar circumstances Edward III had declined to change his plan after his victory at Crecy, and that both monarchs–though for different reasons–continued their march on Calais. The matter deserves a brief examination.

Consider first the sad plight that France found herself in on the morrow of Agincourt. Her sole army had dissolved overnight. For the time being she was practically defenceless. All her leading men except the old duke of Berry and the duke of Burgundy (and his loyalty was suspect), were out of action. The court seated at Rouen, or what was left of it, was distraught at the news. The king wept and cried, "We be all dead and overthrown!" According to Juvenal des Ursins, he had but few troops with him at Rouen, which is very likely. It is true that the distance from Rouen to Paris was a four-day march whereas from Agincourt it was about eight. But the English army would have had a big start, and might well have reached the French capital first. Of course the citizens might have shut the gates in his face as they had done to Edward III 55 years before. On the other hand, it is at least possible that, faced with the prospect of further chaos, with a demented king, and a dying Dauphin (he died a few weeks later) they might have preferred to embrace the chance of getting some firm and ordered government after the miseries of the present reign. And the Treaty of Troyes might have been anticipated by five years. However that may be, the English army resumed its march on Calais next day, early in the morning, according to one chronicler; which seems hard to credit, for there must have been much to do. Prisoners had to be sorted out, escorts provided and also food, for the captives could not forage for themselves and would have no money. The English dead had to be seen to; eventually they were cremated by placing them in a nearby barn and setting fire to it. A tally had to be taken, so far as possible, of the high-born dead on the French side; the body of the Duke of York, and also that of the earl of Suffolk had to be parboiled, in order to reduce the weight (the duke had grown corpulent, and heavy) in order that their bones might be taken home. The captured armour that was not required had to be disposed of, and so on.

Eventually the army set out, taking the most direct route to Calais. The 45 miles was covered in four days, without incident. It must have looked a curious sight as the prisoners (there were about 2,000 of them) trudged alongside their captors, who themselves were laden with booty, each with as much as the man could carry, strung all over his horse. They must have looked like an army of "White Knights" as described in "Alice in Wonderland".

On arrival in the Calais Pale the army was met by the earl of Warwick, the captain of Calais, and conducted into the town in state. Here a rude awakening met the tired soldiers. The food which had been sent for their use from England had not arrived and for some days, owing to bad staff work, they were in a sorry state. Food and lodgings were hard to come by and there were not enough ships to take them home. In fact it was some time before all got back to England.

The king rode with his two captive dukes beside him, discussing the battle with them. To their enquiry whether he was not now ready for peace he replied that nothing was nearer to his heart. On that Orleans sent a herald to Rouen with the news—but nothing came of it.

After a short stay in Calais King Henry took ship for Dover, and from thence by easy stages he made his way to London, stopping two days in the abbey of St. Augustine at Canterbury. He arrived at Eltham Palace exactly four weeks after the battle. Hither next day came the mayor of London, with 24 aldermen in his train, and followed by no less than 15,000 to 20,000 craftsmen of the City, all mounted on horseback and carrying their trade devices.

The reception in London was worthy of the capital, and was on a scale and magnificence never before witnessed. The culminating scene was in St. Paul's where the king was welcomed by 18 bishops and a solemn Te Deum was sung. It was England's greatest hour of triumph.

APPENDIX

THE NUMBERS

The English army. There is no problem here. Everyone is agreed that the English army numbered about 6,000 – Elmham's figure. It had set out with 900 men-at-arms and 5,000 archers. To this must be added the archers in the ranks of those high-born knights who were not included in the regular ranks of the archers – say 100. This would bring the total to exactly 6,000. From this must be deducted the wastage during the march – sick, wounded, prisoners and possible deserters. Of these numbers we have absolutely no information. That there were some walking sick is evident because they were included in the baggage-guard during the battle. As for wounded and prisoners, casualties were incurred in the skirmishes at Eu and

Corbie, especially the latter, and possibly at other places too. If we allow 5 per cent. for wastage we shall probably not be far wrong. This would bring the effective total at Agincourt to 5,700, and we may feel pretty sure that the correct figure is within 200 of this total.

The French army. To estimate the strength of the French army is a very different proposition. Throughout the Hundred Years War chroniclers show that they have no exact figures and this is not surprising for, as it appears, no exact tallies of dismounted levies, or "Communes", were ever made, and no-one, not even their own commanders, knew what the figures were. The chroniclers were thus reduced to guessing, and the wildness of their guesses may be realized when we note that they varied between 10,000 and 200,000. Clearly it is a waste of time to try to establish the true or even the approximate total from an examination of these figures. We must have recourse to the known factors that may have a bearing on the subject. Of these there are four. The first is that the French largely outnumbered the English. On this point practically all the chroniclers, English, Burgundian and French, are in agreement. Two modern professors have attempted to dispute this fact. Fifty years ago the German Delbrück, flying in the face of all the evidence, asserted that the English outnumbered the French, and in our own day Ferdinand Lot has done the same.[1] Their arguments, if they can be called arguments, are derisory, but since the French professor is widely and rightly revered as a historian, and as his thesis has received no notice or reply on this side of the Channel, his argument must be examined. It occurs on p. 14, vol. II of his *L'art Militaire et les Armées au Moyen Age* (Paris, 1946). His salient point is comprised in a single sentence which must be quoted:

"Sur 800 mètres de front – au maximum – étant donné que la cavalerie se deploie alors sur trois rangs, separés par un espace de 50 mètres environ on ne peut engager plus de 1800 cavalerie au maximum."

[1] This need occasion no great surprise when we hear that he made the same assertion for Crecy.

He assesses the archers at 3,600, making a total of 5,400. His assessment of men-at-arms is 600 men in each line, on a frontage of two men to three yards. He assumes that each division of men-at-arms was in a single rank, whereas the English were in four ranks (and would no doubt have been in still deeper formation had they had the men). On what grounds does he assume that the French men-at-arms advanced in single rank? It would be a singular and almost unheard-of formation. Moreover, only two French divisions were engaged, so the total of men-at-arms that came to grips with the English was only 1,200, *i.e.*, one-and-a-third men per yard of frontage. Whence then came the corpses that we know built up a formidable wall of dead? Even if every single man-at-arms was killed that would be insufficient to make a wall of any dimension; but we know that by no means every man-at-arms was killed in the engagement. Apart from the unknown number who were despatched after the fighting was over, about 2,000 prisoners were marched away? Whence came these prisoners, if less than that number of men-at-arms were engaged in the fighting? No doubt a few would be crossbowmen, but only a few, for they were scarcely engaged in the battle, being shouldered out by their men-at-arms.

In short it is impossible to reconcile Lot's figures with the general agreed course of the battle.

As opposed to the French professor I may cite the most recent English professor to describe the battle—Professor E. F. Jacob. He contents himself by stating that the French army was "notably superior in size".[1] (Dr. Wyllie estimated that the French army outnumbered the English ten times, but does not give his reasoning in the text; this he reserved for an appendix which most unfortunately he never lived to write.)

Coming now to the second known factor, the battle formation of the two armies. It is known that the English army was formed up in one line, while the French was in three lines or divisions, the rear one being mounted. But there was also an

[1] *Henry V and the Invasion of France*, p. 102.

intermediate line between the first and second lines, composed of crossbowmen, archers and guns. If we assume that the depth of each line in both armies was the same, that would make the French nearly four times the number of the English. But the French divisions were probably in deeper formation.

The third known factor is the ground. The width between the two woods is believed not to have altered appreciably. At the place where the French army drew up it is about 1,200 yards wide. As to how many ranks there were in each line, Ferdinand Lot could not know, for no-one knew. If the truth be told, I doubt if there was so regular a formation that anyone could have counted the ranks: I envisage the formation as three conglomerations rather than three neatly formed ranks and lines in dressing so many metres apart, and such evidence as there is tends to show that the lines were densely packed from the start: the wretched archers and cannons were "shouldered" out of the line: there was no space for them to ply their weapons. On the whole an average depth at the outset of five to six per line, would seem reasonable and bring the total (including archers, etc.) to at least 24,000, over four times the English army. Incidentally this figure agrees with the best and most reliable French chronicler, the monk of St. Denys, who states that the French outnumbered the English by four times. Why does professor Lot ignore his own chronicler?

The fourth known factor is the number of casualties, if one may accept it as "known", in view of the usual disagreement among the sources. Dr. Wyllie estimates the number as 10,000. Much the most reliable source for this, I consider, is the MS. of Chateau Ruisseauville. This document was composed locally, and where it gives local topographical information should be worthy of credence. It states that after the battle the bishop of Terouannem accompanied by the abbot of Blangy visited the stricken field of battle, blessed the ground on which the dead still lay and gave orders for grave-pits to be dug for their bodies. It adds that five grave-pits were dug all close together, and upwards of 1,200 bodies buried in each. That would mean upwards of 6,000 burials in that place. Allowing for bodies of knights removed for burial, etc., and remembering that most of the casualties were incurred by the first line, and none by the rear line, it would put the total number engaged in the region of say 20,000 to 30,000.

From several points of view, therefore, the total would appear to lie about 25,000, and I purposely select this round figure in order to show that my estimate is a "round" conjecture.

*　　　*　　　*

SOURCES

The sources for the history of Henry V's reign are at first rather confusing, for two reasons. First, their titles are very much alike, and second, the authorship of one of them was in error attributed by Thomas Hearne 200 years ago to Thomas Elmham, whereas he was the author of another of these histories. Consequently when one reads the name Elmham one must know the date of the work in question. The three chief histories are as follows:—

1. *Henrici Quinti Angliae regis gesta.*
2. *Vita et gesta Henrici quinti.*
3. *Vita Henrici Quinti.*

No. 1 is now known to have been written by Thomas Elmham, the king's chaplain, and is sometimes called "The Chaplain's" Account, and sometimes *Gesta*, for short, in order to distinguish it from No. 2 which is sometimes called *Vita* for short, and is by an unknown author, and in Hearne's edition, Thomas Elmham, nowadays described as "Pseudo-Elmham". No. 3 is by an Italian, Titus Livius, and is mainly compiled from Nos. 1 and 2. Of the three the *Gesta* is much the best for our purpose as the chaplain took part in the Agincourt campaign, and wrote his account only two years later; indeed, it is our chief source for the march to Agincourt.

The most important English chronicle of the reign is that of Thomas Walsingham, *Historia Anglicana*, written only a few years after Agincourt.

Three Burgundians also wrote contemporary accounts of the Agincourt campaign, Enguerrand Monstrelet, Le Fèvre, Lord of St. Remy, and Jean de Waurin. Waurin fought in the battle on the French side, St. Remy on the English side; Monstrelet fought on neither but he lived close to the battlefield, and his *Chronique* was published before that of either of the other two. From internal evidence one would say that all three copied from the others in various passages, which at first sight seems absurd. It is indeed an interesting puzzle to unravel, reminding one of the "Synoptic Problem", but whereas we know that Matthew and Luke copied from Mark copiously and Mark copied from neither, Dr. Wyllie asserts that Monstrelet wrote first and that the other two made use of his account. But by comparing carefully the three accounts it would seem that Monstrelet must have written after the other two, although his account was published first and therefore that he copied from them. The other puzzle is to decide whether St. Remy or Waurin copied the other, and strange though it may appear they seem to have copied each other simultaneously. The only possible explanation is that before writing they exchanged experiences and also showed each other their own rough drafts or notes before writing their complete works. It further seems that St. Remy imparted rather more than he borrowed from Waurin. Hence St. Remy's account of the battle must be accounted as the most reliable and informative. The chaplain is undoubtedly reliable as far as he goes (except for his estimate of the French numbers, but this worthy priest witnessed the battle from afar, namely from the baggage lines at Maisoncelles). Still we are much more fortunate in our sources than for Crecy or Poitiers, where no combatant wrote about it,[1] whereas at Agincourt we have three combatants (including John Hardyng, whose rhymed account is however disappointingly short). Thus the battle is exceptionally well documented.

Of the French chroniclers, by far the most reliable is the

---

[1] The two priests who recorded it were out of sight of the battle in the baggage park.

monk of St. Denys who was scrupulously careful with his facts, and even dared to criticize the French high command although he was in essence the Court official historian.

There are several other French chroniclers who add items here and there but who scarcely come within the limits of this short note on sources. The most complete bibliography is contained in Wyllie's *Henry V*, volume III, which cites nearly 3,000 printed books, but it covers the whole reign, not merely the military operations.

Modern accounts of the Agincourt campaign (as opposed to the battle), are disappointingly meagre, especially concerning the French army, which in most books pops up on the eve of the battle out of the blue, so to speak, without any explanation of how it got there. *The Reign of Henry V*, by Dr. J. H. Wyllie, is the most detailed. Next comes *Lancaster and York* by Sir James Ramsay. The account by Sir Charles Oman in his *Art of War in the Middle Ages*, volume II, is good, but shorter still. Ferdinand Lot in his *L'Art Militaire des Armées au Moyen Age* is chiefly concerned to prove that the English outnumbered the French in the battle, and the most recent of all (1951), *La Guerre de Cent Ans* by Edouard Perroy, dismisses the battle in a couple of sentences. Probably the best French account is *La Bataille d'Azincourt* by René de Belleval, published in 1865.

CHAPTER VI

VALMONT AND HARFLEUR

AT the news of how a tiny English army had vanquished a great French army at Agincourt all the world wondered – not least the Emperor Sigismund of Luxemburg (younger brother of "Good King Wenceslas" and more correctly called king of the Romans). This monarch had been foremost in trying to heal the Great Schism of 1378, whereby, to the scandal of the church, two rival popes reigned, one at Rome the other at Avignon. Now the French recognized the Avignon pope and the English the Roman pope. Sigismund realized that England was now such an important power in Europe that no settlement of the problem could be reached without her cooperation. He therefore took upon himself the office of peacemaker. To this end he visited France in 1416, arriving in Paris in mid-March. After a fruitless stay of six weeks he passed on to England.

The duke of Gloucester went down to Dover to meet him. With his retinue he rode into the water, all with drawn swords, as the emperor's boat approached the beach and declared that he could not be allowed to land unless he disclaimed all pretentions to exercise any jurisdiction in England. This the emperor duly disclaimed and he was then permitted to land. On Sigismund's arrival in London the king made amends for any lack of warmth in his welcome at Dover by entertaining him magnificently, and by bestowing upon him the Order of the Garter. Sigismund was thus the first foreign potentate to receive this honour. Possibly the fact that he brought with him what purported to be the heart of St. George had something to do with it.

Under the stimulus of Sigismund, peace negotiations were carried on, though in a desultory fashion, throughout the summer. But King Henry took his stand firmly on the Treaty of Bretigny (which gave back to England all her Aquitaine empire, whilst the English king gave up his claim to the French throne). The French might have agreed to these terms but they would not agree to Henry retaining Harfleur. This was the rock upon which the negotiations broke.

Eventually on August 15 Sigismund and Henry signed at Canterbury the Treaty of Canterbury whereby they swore "eternal friendship" between their countries, and undertook to support one another in any war, whether offensive or defensive.

When the news leaked out the French government were naturally indignant, and declared that Sigismund was a weak creature who had been seduced by the stronger English king. There may be some truth in this.

But the emperor had no military means of rendering effective military support to England, even if he really wished to do so. For one thing, there was what may be loosely described as a buffer state between the two, namely the Flemish territories of the duke of Burgundy. If Burgundy could be drawn into the alliance, thus forming what Professor Jacob calls "The Big Three", the situation would be entirely altered. Henry decided to try to bring this about. He seems to have again been following the example of his great-grandfather in building up a great anti-French alliance in Europe, for he was also making overtures to the Flemish provinces.

Early in October the Big Three met in Calais. John the Fearless, duke of Burgundy, son of Philip the Good, had been enticed to Calais with great difficulty. He was a suspicious man and had demanded that if he came to Calais one of the king's brothers should be handed over as a hostage for his personal safety the while. An elaborate ceremony was therefore enacted on the frontier near Gravelines, which vividly illustrates the degree of insecurity and suspicion that reigned between contiguous states in that era. The duke of Gloucester had been selected as hostage. The meeting was fixed near the mouth of the river Aa, which was tidal. At low water the retinues of the two dukes crossed the stream simultaneously. That done, the two dukes entered the water mounted, met in midstream, shook hands and then passed on–Burgundy to Calais, Gloucester to St. Omer.

Arrived at Calais, Burgundy went into most secret talks with the English king, the details of which were never committed to paper. Henry tried to persuade his guest to sign a paper recognizing him as king of France, and promising him all support. Burgundy would not sign but gave Henry orally to understand that he agreed with it and would give all possible aid when the time came.

*   *   *

The interest now shifts to Harfleur. It will be remembered that King Henry had left there a small garrison under the earl of Dorset to repair the defences and hold it for the king. Artisans and merchants were also enticed thither, the king's aim being to make it a second Calais. In order to secure food and fodder, constant raids into the surrounding country were necessary, and in this connection we meet for the first time one captain John Fastolf, whom we find leading such a raid, in late November, to within six miles of Rouen.

In January, 1416 the garrison was relieved by a new and enlarged one, consisting of 900 men-at-arms and 1,500 archers. This new garrison soon made its presence felt, carrying out a number of successful raids on both sides of the estuary. At the beginning of March the earl of Dorset returned from leave in England, and he soon took action. On March 9, he set out with a force of 1,000 men, all mounted, on a three-day raid to the north-east. All went well, and it reached and set fire to Cany, a little town seven miles south of St. Valery. He then turned for home. His route took him through the villages of Ouainville and Valmont. At the former, three miles west of Cany, and five miles short of Valmont, French patrols spotted the English army, which however continued on its way, suspecting nothing. When near Valmont it suddenly found its way barred by a superior French force, estimated at about 5,000.[1]

[1] This is the chaplain's figure and Wyllie accepts it, but 3–4,000 seems a more probable estimate. See below.

It was trapped! This French army was led by Bernard, count
d'Armagnac, who had recently been recalled to Paris from
the south, and created Constable of France. He had brought
with him to Paris an army of 6,000 Gascons. Hearing of the
increased English activity at Harfleur, he had marched north
with 3,000 of his army to deal with it. In addition he picked
up some local garrisons on his arrival in Normandy including
650 men of Rouen, so the total can have been but little short
of 4,000.

The earl of Dorset, seeing that he was about to be attacked,
dismounted his whole force, and sent the horses to the rear, in
the approved English fashion. Then he hastily formed up his tiny
army, in a single line, stretched to the utmost in order not to be
outflanked by the enemy. But it was dangerously thin, and when
the French cavalry threw in one mounted charge after another,
weak places began to appear in what we might call "the Thin
Red Line". Some gaps were made, and excited and exultant
French knights plunged through. Then instead of wheeling
about and finishing off their dismounted opponents, they charged
straight forward against the horses and baggage. To cut down
the grooms and pages tending the horses was a simple matter,
and then the victorious horsemen fell to looting the baggage, in
a fashion typical of cavalry in all countries and all ages.

This misguided action gave a brief respite to the battered
English line, and the earl of Dorset, though grievously wounded
himself, was quick to make use of it. Abandoning his horses
except the handful that he had with him, he reformed his
troops and led them off to a flank where he saw a large garden
surrounded by a tall hedge and ditch. This he lined with his
men, facing all directions. It formed what we might term a
zariba or small "hedgehog" (considering the big part played
by the hedge the latter is "le mot juste"). But his force was
reduced to some 850 fighting men.

Up to now the English, in spite of their surprise and dis-
comfiture, had acquitted themselves well. The fair-minded
monk of St. Denys pays them a handsome tribute:

"In spite of the surprise which an unexpected attack always causes even the most intrepid hearts, the English resisted stoutly. There was a furious mêlée in which the English infantry wounded the greater part of the horses of our auxiliaries (the Gascons?) and put them out of action."

The count d'Armagnac reconnoitred the new position occupied by the English, and the more he looked at it the less he relished the idea of attacking it. Nor were his enemies in a happy position. Outnumbered and practically surrounded, and with their road to Harfleur firmly blocked, they must have felt like King Henry's troops on the eve of Agincourt. As on that occasion, negotiations were set on foot, but, as at Agincourt, nothing came of them. Dorset was anxious to secure some terms by which he would be allowed to continue his homeward march, but the terms offered by the Constable were too high. "Tell your master", declared the earl to the French emissary "that Englishmen do not surrender!"[1]

By this time darkness had fallen, and the bulk of the French army had withdrawn into Valmont to obtain food and rest. The opportunity that had thus arisen did not escape Dorset, and he set about making plans for escape. The details we do not know, but the result is clear: his whole remaining force managed under cover of darkness to creep silently away to the West, without apparent detection.[2] Marching probably through Fécamp and then turning south-west, the little army plodded on another seven miles (making 14 in all) and took cover at about dawn in the wood at Les Loges, four miles east of Etretat. Here they evidently laid up during the hours of daylight, no doubt sleeping most of the day. The French had completely lost track of their opponents. When daylight appeared and it was discovered that the enemy had vanished, Armagnac sent out a force under Marshal Louis de Loigny, his second-in-command, to discover their whereabouts and to bar their road to Harfleur but not to attack them till he himself could come

---

[1] The details of the negotiations are obscure, as they were in the case of Poitiers and Agincourt; no doubt they were kept as secret as possible.

[2] Wyllie says it was with the connivance of Armagnac but the general sense of the Chronicles does not support this.

up. He was taking no risks, "for he knew that they still could sting".

Darkness fell on the second day of this remarkable but little-known operation,[1] and still the English were "lost". Hope of seeing Harfleur again rose, as the column left the shelter of the wood and set its face for the sea-shore. At or near Etretat they reached the coast. It was Dorset's intention to march along the beach the whole of the distance to Harfleur, his reasoning being that by hugging the sea he had at least one secure flank, besides having thus the best chance of avoiding detection.

It was an arduous march, and the troops became footsore from the rough going over the shingle, for nearly 30 miles in all had to be covered. But on they marched, mile after mile, urged forward by the spur of desperation. After plodding along for 20 miles in this fashion, they rounded the Cap de la Heve just as dawn was breaking and the estuary of the River Seine hove into view. They had almost reached their goal and still they had not been discovered. Spirits rose accordingly; but, alas! one mile further on, when they had reached the foot of the cliffs of St. Andress, they saw on the summit on their left hand a body of French troops. They had been found after all. It was the mounted column of the Marshal de Loigny who, either by shrewd calculation, or from information received from inhabitants during the night, had posted his men in an almost ideal ambuscade. Gleefully the Frenchmen sprang off their horses, and plunged down the hill, regardless of their orders from Armagnac. The prey was too easy to be missed; it could not escape, it would be annihilated or be driven into the sea. It was veritably a case of "Twixt devil and deep sea". Or so it seemed.

But the English remnant, weary, footsore, taken unawares, and undeployed for battle, had still to be reckoned with. Like Sir Richard Grenville and his company "they still could sting".

The shouting Frenchmen, charging down the steep hill by a number of goat-tracks, necessarily lost all semblance of order.

---

[1] Most accounts make it appear that only one night was involved, but a study of the map shows this to be impossible.

Consequently they arrived at the bottom of the cliff piecemeal. The brief period that had elapsed since they had been spotted from the beach had allowed the English to form up in some sort of line. Probably orders were few; indeed Dorset himself cannot have been present with them, for owing to his wound he was being brought round in a boat. Perhaps young John Fastolf took charge; we do not know. But we know the upshot of a desperate and apparently one-sided fight. The French were utterly routed, the English making great play with their axes. Though the numbers killed and captured are in dispute, the Chroniclers, both French and English, are practically unanimous in declaring that the French were completely cut up. One source avers that they were only saved from practical annihilation by the timely arrival of Armagnac with the main body. But even if we had no other evidence this would be hard to believe, for the English had time and opportunity to strip the bodies of the dead French soldiers and coolly cast them into the sea, a procedure they would hardly have engaged in, instead of hurrying on to Harfleur, if the French main body had been in the neighbourhood. Moreover, if Armagnac did arrive in time why did he not attack, instead of waiting to be attacked.

That Armagnac did eventually arrive on the scene is however clear, and here comes the most remarkable episode of the engagement. For when the English, engaged in stripping the corpses, perceived a new enemy, these astonishing troops picked up their arms again and charged straight up the cliff against their new opponents, attacked them, and put them to rout. Armagnac's column fled from the field, making for Rouen. Now the road to Rouen took the fugitives past Harfleur. The garrison of this town were already on the *qui vive*, for the sound of the fighting at Chef de Caux had been wafted to them by the breeze blowing in from the sea. From the top of the walls and towers, or at least from the Church tower they would witness the fight on the cliff-top and the flight of the French across their front. The opportunity was too good to be lost. Mounting their horses in haste they sallied forth and engaged in a hot pursuit for some distance, taking many prisoners. Then they drew rein, and returned in triumph to Harfleur bringing their prisoners and spoils with them. Indeed the unique spectacle may well have been witnessed of the simultaneous entry into Harfleur of two victorious forces, each laden with the spoils of war; the one on horseback from the east, the other on foot from the west.

The deeper I study it the more am I impressed by the achievment of this devoted little band of English soldiers. For pluck, endurance and sheer doggedness, for coolness, discipline, and hitting power when cornered–in short, for all those military virtues that made the reputation of the English army in the Hundred Years War–and has kept it ever since–this epic of Valmont stands with scarcely a rival in the whole of the Hundred Years War.

*   *   *

BATTLE OF THE SEINE

Harfleur was saved from danger of attack by land, but its trials were not over–they were scarcely begun.

Henry V was trying to make of his Norman acquisition a base in France as firmly established as that of Calais. But he had overlooked the geographical factors. At Calais the English Channel is at its narrowest: at the Seine estuary it is four times as wide. While it was possible to maintain a constant command of the sea at the former this proved impossible at the latter. The French had been quick to sense the inherent weakness of the English position: if a local command of the sea could be obtained in the Seine estuary and maintained, a blockade could be established and Harfleur starved into submission.

Her own maritime resources were not sufficient for the purpose, so she had recourse to Navarre (as had Charles V) and also to Genoa. The Genoese sailors were then accounted the finest in Europe and their warships the most powerful: neither England or France had anything to compete with the Genoese carracks, which out-classed them in size and power. Moreover

France possessed a number of galleys – also emanating from the Mediterranean, which could of course manoeuvre against the wind, whereas the sailing ships of the English could not. Thus by the Spring of 1416, while Henry V was concerned mainly with the visit of the Emperor Sigismund, France had accumulated a powerful fleet and had concentrated it in the Seine area. The blockade of Harfleur by sea as well as by land was now complete.

After the Valmont raid few supply ships could get through the blockade and the garrison soon began to feel the pinch. The rejoicings in England over the Valmont victory were rudely interrupted by an alarming letter from Dorset setting out the dangers of the situation and the dire need for supplies of all sorts, especially horses and guns. A convoy of supplies was collected at Southampton under the earl of Hungerford, but it does not appear that it was able to deliver its cargoes. At any rate the shortage and privations in Harfleur continued, and Dorset's pleas for help increased in intensity.

But the difficulty of running the blockade steadily increased, and it became apparent that the French had secured the command of the sea in the central sector of the Channel.

It was thus borne in upon the king that if Harfleur was to be saved a major effort would be required. He therefore gave instructions for a great fleet to be collected on the south coast, and he planned to lead it in person to the relief of his Norman possessions. He even got as far as Southampton with this object but the peace negotiations became so urgent that he was obliged to hand over the command to one of his brothers. He selected John, duke of Bedford, his second brother, no doubt as a "consolation prize" for having missed the glories of Agincourt.

Bedford assembled one portion of his fleet at Southampton, while the other collected at Winchelsea; and he fixed the rendezvous for them off Beachy Head.

It was not till the end of July that the two squadrons were ready for action, and Bedford went down to Southampton to take command. Meanwhile tension and excitement was steadily rising in England as fresh messages – possibly of an unduly alarmist nature – kept arriving from the stricken town. The relief operation was complicated by the fact that a portion of the French fleet was in the act of raiding the south-west between Portland and Portsmouth, and when Bedford was ready to set sail to his rendezvous he found his course blocked by enemy ships at Spithead.

Early in August the coast however became clear and Bedford after a stormy passage united his whole fleet at Beachy Head. The Earl of Hungerford was Admiral of the Winchelsea Squadron, and the grand total of the fleet probably exceeded 100, though a German resident in England at the time puts it as low as 70.

The French fleet may be assessed at 150 all told, but in addition to numbers it had, as we have seen, the superiority in big ships. Its Admiral was one Guillaume de Montenay.

By August 14, the fleet was fully assembled and moored off Beachy Head, and early that morning it weighed anchor, and with a fair wind set sail for France. A beacon announcing the fact was lit on Beachy Head, and by a chain of beacons the good news was conveyed to the king who sat awaiting it at Westminster. Immediately he hastened off to his confessor and besought him to pray for divine aid on the operation.

The wind was fair and the fleet made a remarkably rapid crossing and in the evening of that same day they dropped anchor in the mouth of the Seine estuary, the French fleet being further in-shore.

During the night, which was stormy, Bedford sent out rowing-boats to reconnoitre the French dispositions. They came back with the report that the enemy had anchored in mid-stream, and when morning dawned – the wind having abated – the French ships could be seen, drawn up in close order in the centre of the estuary, between Honfleur and Harfleur.

The duke of Bedford then held a war council in his flag-ship. The plan it decided on was a simple one – as all such plans should be. That plan was to drive straight ahead with sails full-set and engage the enemy at close quarters.

The normal procedure of an attacker of that period was to attempt to ram the enemy, ship for ship, or, failing that, to grapple; then to drive the hostile missile-throwers from the shrouds and bulwarks, and finally to board and engage in a hand-to-hand mêlée. Such had been the procedure in general at the battle of Sluys 65 years previously, and such was the procedure adopted now.

We have no specific information as to the dispositions of the French fleet: it seems to have been a dense formation, and it probably was drawn up in no clearly defined lines, as had been the case at Sluys. For though an attack had been foreseen for some weeks, when the English fleet actually hove in sight on the previous evening it had taken the French by surprise. Many of the personnel were on shore and they had to return in haste to their ships and put out into the Channel. Little time was available for it would be dangerous to attempt to manoeuvre in darkness in those constricted waters, and there was a heavy swell on that evening. We can therefore picture the French fleet as drawn up in a serried mass, with a minimum of water-space between each ship.

As the English fleet bore down on them, evidently running before the wind, there can have been little more order in their array than in the French, for Bedford's signal for the advance was a simultaneous one – the blowing of trumpets throughout the fleet, and the fastest sailors would – whether advertently or not – soon take the lead.

Thus as the leading ships got within range of the hostile fleet they must have drawn upon themselves the concentrated fire of their opponents – arrows and crossbow shafts from the nearest, cannon balls and ballista balls from those further off. Thus ere ever they had succeeded in ramming or grappling their opponents the English ships' crews suffered heavy casualties. This was particularly so among those that found themselves opposed by the huge Genoese carracks (probably eight in number) with their towering castle-like poops and prows, from which the defenders could rain down upon the unprotected decks of their attackers darts, stones and iron bolts as well as arrows.

Despite the losses thus caused, the English persevered in their efforts to grapple their opponents, and having grappled, to hold on grimly until their archers had mastered the missile throwers on the decks, in the shrouds and even in the fighting tops of the French, Spanish and Genoese ships.

In a contest of such a nature the details are necessarily swallowed up in the confusion and carnage, and it would be fruitless to attempt to unravel them. There is indeed a statement that a portion at least of the English fleet made a turning movement and attacked the enemy flank. This is hard to credit, for it is doubtful if a squadron not trained to manoeuvre and work together could in those days—whatever the wind conditions—have operated together in such confined waters with effect.

What however seems certain is that the fight lasted for about seven hours—an astonishingly long period under the circumstances, and we can picture the complement of one ship after another succeeding in boarding their "opposite number", and then, by sheer physical strength—in which the English at that period were pre-eminent—either killing their opponents or pushing them into the water, to be drowned. They even succeeded in boarding a number of the lofty carracks by one means or another, and no less than four of them were captured, while a fifth ran aground and was lost. On their side the English lost heavily, 20 of their smaller ships being sunk and their complements drowned.

The issue hung in the balance for a long time; what seems to have decided it was the capture of the four carracks, and the flight of the remainder. Their example was followed by the smaller ships which still remained afloat and navigable—in short the allied fleet disintegrated, dispersed and fled for the shelter of Honfleur harbour. Thus the English fleet was left master of the sea, and the passage to Harfleur was open. It was a victory almost as notable as that of Sluys. But the cost had, this time, been very high. It is useless to attempt to estimate the respective numbers of casualties. The French chroniclers not unnaturally placed the English losses higher than their own, which seems inherently unlikely, whilst on the other side the preposterously low figure of 100 killed given by the *Gesta* (so reliable in everything except in numbers), can be ignored. Amongst the wounded on the English side was the duke of Bedford himself.

When the last French ship had quit the scene of the action the English fleet did not immediately put into Harfleur. For one thing there would not have been room for the whole fleet in such a small harbour. For another the earl of Hungerford, who presumably assumed control on the wounding of Bedford, would be anxious to get the duke home for treatment as speedily as possible, and it would be dangerous to send a single unescorted ship with its valuable cargo, across the Channel.[1] The wounded men were therefore collected into a portion of the fleet on the spot, and while they set sail for Southampton, taking their prizes with them (the wind presumably having conveniently veered) the remainder continued on its way, and sailed in triumph up the river Lézarde into the beleaguered town, amid the acclamations of its inhabitants.

The relief and rejoicings in England when the great news arrived, were scarcely less marked than those of Harfleur itself. The king, when he heard it, was near Hythe. He sprang to the saddle and galloped to Canterbury, where a solemn *Te Deum* was sung in the cathedral in the presence of the king and the Emperor Sigismund.

Finally, the Genoese carracks were taken over by the English navy, which thus emerged from the operation rather stronger in power than it had entered it.

---

[1] Also, if the wind was fair for the French making for Honfleur it was probably foul for the English sailing in the opposite direction.

APPENDIX

STRECCHE'S ACCOUNT OF VALMONT

This was the only pitched battle fought in the reign of
Henry V after Agincourt. It therefore claims particular attention. The sources for it contain the usual crop of discrepancies
and contradictions which have to be elucidated, and as a
result of this elucidation my account of the battle differs in
some important respects from that usually given. The reason is
that I have based it mainly on the chronicle of John Strecche,
which is ignored by most historians (though used by Ramsay
and Wyllie). It is possible that very few historians of the battle
have read it, for it has only been printed of recent years, and
both Ramsay and Wyllie worked from the MS. But it would
appear that neither of them placed much credence in it. I must
therefore give the reasons why I have followed it as closely as I
have.

John Strecche was a canon of Kenilworth in the reign of
Henry V. It was the king's favourite abode during his brief
visits to England during the war, and Strecche would come into
contact with members of the royal household who had fought
in the wars; thus he would pick up at first- or second-hand a
number of stories of the war. As he wrote his chronicle not very
long after the death of the king these stories would be fresh in
his memory, though they may have been jumbled and distorted in the telling. The account that he gives of Valmont is so
markedly different from the others and is so full of circumstantial detail of a kind that one would not expect him to invent,
that it is obviously deserving of closer examination than it
appears to have received. It hangs together as a story in a
convincing way, and in the most important phase of the
operations is implicitly and unexpectedly endorsed by a French
participant in the battle, as we shall presently see.

As the chronicle has never been translated and as the original
appears in a volume not easily come by (*Bulletin of the John
Rylands Library, Manchester, Vol.* 16, 1932), I will give a resumé of

my own rough translation of the salient passages (square brackets enclose my own comments).

At the outset Strecche gives the numbers of the English army as "1,080 men-at-arms and archers", which is more specific than the "1,000 horsemen" of the *Gesta*, which is the usually accepted figure. On the other hand he gives Armagnac 50,000 men; such absurd exaggerations of the French numbers disfigure his narrative and may have induced Ramsay and Wyllie to treat Strecche's narrative with excessive caution. Here then is a précis of his narrative.

"Before the battle opens Armagnac offers terms of surrender which Dorset declines with disdain. Armagnac then attacks. [The other sources place these palavers after, not before the opening action. Strecche might easily get the order of events wrong from his informants.] In the action that ensues the English lose 400 and the French 3,000. Then the English march towards Harfleur having lost their baggage and all their horses. They march "the whole day" very fatigued, and are followed to a flank by the French. [This is quite different from all the other accounts which place the march in the night, and represent the French as having lost track of them. Probably Strecche confused this march, which took them to Les Loges Wood, with the following one along the sea-shore.] At about vespers the French again attack and the fight goes on till dark. During the night Dorset holds a war council at which Sir Thomas Carew and a Gascon knight urge that in view of their state of fatigue and shortage of food and drink, having already marched a day and a night, they could, without affront to their honour hasten to their refuge (Harfleur). [This is important as showing that the retreat to Harfleur took two marches, not one – as usually stated. I had been driven to this conclusion from a study of the map before reading Strecche's account. I have however followed the other chroniclers in making the marches entirely by night, as I consider this course more in accordance with inherent military probability.] Dorset follows the advice of the two knights and the march is resumed. This time it takes place

along the seashore [as in the other sources]. The French follow
along the cliffs on the left flank and at dawn take up position on
top of the cliffs at Chef de Caux, the modern St. Adresse. The
French charge exultantly and carelessly down the steep slope
but with unsteady steps, and thus are precipitated over the
rocks into the marsh below. "The English, seeing them falling
about in this way, attacked and killed them with their axes,
stripped their armour off and cast their bodies into the sea.
Directly after this they climbed up from the marsh against the
army of the count [Armagnac], and fought with their enemy
in such a way that the sound reached the inhabitants of
Harfleur; and the count and his army were thus forced to turn
bridle and quit the field speedily." [All this is utterly at variance
with the usually accepted account of Juvenal des Ursins, "If
Armagnac had not come up in time Longwy would have been
badly mauled". We shall see presently what value to place on
Juvenal's statement.] "Which seeing, they who were in the
town of Harfleur, mounting their horses, sallied forth at once.
And the said count with his troops fled with all their might, and
the English captured and killed with the edge of the sword
several thousands of them, and then they returned into the
town with much booty, heated with the chase, and all refreshed themselves."

Now all this is so very different from the recognized French
chroniclers that we turn to the two Frenchmen who took part
in the operation and wrote about it afterwards. The first of
them, Guillaume de Meuillon, has practically nothing to say;
he evidently finds the whole affair distasteful, and passes on as
quickly as possible to more pleasant topics. If Armagnac had
indeed come up in the nick of time and saved the situation
Meuillon might well be expected to mention the fact. The other,
Jean Raoulet, is more explicit. He does not give details of the
action, though he states that 22 English were killed and 200
taken in the first action (a likely enough figure, the majority
probably being in the horse lines); of the action on the Chef
de Caux he says, the English defeated the French, many of

whom were killed or captured, and then comes the vital sentence, "But D'Armagnac escaped, and hanged many captains and men at Caudebec for running away". Thus the French soldier corroborates in essentials the story told to the English chronicler at the time: the French Constable of France, so far from saving the situation, fled with his army to Caudebec, when he vented his exasperation on his unfortunate officers.

SOURCES FOR VALMONT

There are three main sources for the whole operation, which it is difficult to differentiate in value. Elmham's *Gesta* is usually quoted (at least by English writers) for the respective numbers at the outset, but he exaggerates later on in his narrative. From the Burgundians comes the *Chronique de Normandie* by Sire Georges Chastelain (bound up with Benjamin Williams's edition of the *Gesta*, 1850, with an English translation). This seems to be unbiassed, but was written a good many years after the battle. The virtues of the chronicle of John Strecche have already been referred to. The fourth most useful source, though short, is the *Chronique de Jean Raoulet* (to be found at the end of J. Chartier's *Chronique de Charles VII* (Ed. Viviville). The monk of St. Denys does not seem as unbiassed as he appears in his account of Agincourt, and is full of excuses for the French (though he gives the all-important fact of the English repairing to Les Loges Wood). The same holds good for Pierre Cagny's *Chronique des ducs d'Alençon*, and Juvenal des Ursin's *History of Charles VI*. Little of material value is to be gleaned from the Burgundians Le Fèvre, Waurin and Monstrelet, and the same applies to the English chronicler Thomas Walsingham.

8

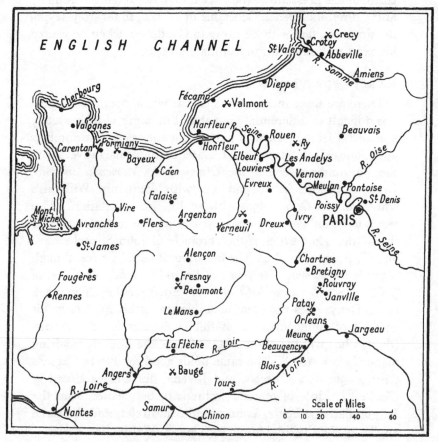

Sketch Map 3; NORTHERN FRANCE

CHAPTER VII

THE CONQUEST OF NORMANDY

W E return to England. Whilst peace negotiations were in train King Henry was steadily building up the military resources of the country with a view to a further campaign in France. This action gave occasion for the French to tax him with duplicity and for the English to praise his foresight. For however sincere he might have been in his desire for a peaceful attainment of his ends, he realized that it was better to negotiate from strength rather than from weakness, and further, that should the negotiations come to naught he would be in a position to pursue his aim without undue delay. For even in those days an overseas military expedition could not be created overnight.

By the end of the year 1416 King Henry had come to the conclusion, rightly or wrongly, that he could not achieve his main aim–the recovery of the old dominion of Aquitaine and the duchy of Normandy–without recourse to arms. He therefore pursued his warlike preparations apace. Every little detail was taken into account. The accumulated experience of past campaigns was made use of; nothing was overlooked that was within the bounds of human perspicacity. In particular, his own painful experiences of the difficulties of river-crossing were not forgotten: for example provision was made for pontoons made of leather stretched on wooden frames. He also built up a royal navy; indeed his reign marks the beginning of the continuous history of the Royal Navy. He realized that the command of the sea was a *sine qua non*.

By April 15, 1417, a number of ships and troops had assembled at Southampton, but there ensued a series of exasperating delays – an almost invariable feature of our medieval amphibious undertakings. One of the pre-essentials for a successful invasion was as we have seen, that the local command of the sea should be assured and maintained. Now, in spite of the great naval victory of Harfleur, Genoese carracks still abounded off the south coast, and in order to sweep a clear channel–to use a modern mine-sweeping term–the earl of Huntingdon was despatched with a fleet in the month of June to do so. On the 29th of the month, near the mouth of the Seine, he came across a strong Genoese fleet, which included nine great carracks and a numerous force of Genoese crossbowmen. There ensued a sea fight that followed the main lines of that of Harfleur. The English ships drove straight ahead into action at close quarters. In so doing they lost heavily at the expert hands of the crossbowmen; but not swerving from their course, they closed with their opponents, grappled and then boarded them. The upshot of a stiff battle lasting three hours was a complete victory for the English. No less than four of the carracks were captured and the rest of the Franco-Genoese fleet dispersed and fled.[1]

The coast was now clear for the invasion. But still there were unforeseen delays and it was not until the end of July that the expeditionary force set sail from Southampton. We know more about the strength and composition of this force than of any other that set out from England in medieval times, thanks to an extant roll sometimes, but wrongly, called the Agincourt Roll. This roll gives the names of 7,839 combatants, but it has two sets of omissions. In the first place, the royal retinues and several others have been omitted. These may amount to as much as 2,800, bringing the total to well over 10,000. Secondly the ancillary services–gunners, sappers, miners and smiths–are omitted, which would bring the grand total to possibly over 11,000.[2] Titus Livius gives a total of 16,400. If this figure is based on exact information it probably includes pages and grooms, all of whom would carry a weapon of personal defence.

[1] The French Chroniclers found it convenient when describing these naval defeats to speak of "the Genoese Fleet" not the Franco-Genoese Fleet.

[2] Professor Waugh deals with the matter in detail in a footnote on p. 52 of Wyllie's third volume, his calculations being based on the unpublished researches of Professor Newhall. He concludes that the total "cannot have reached 11,000". But it seems that he does not include the ancillary services.

By July 30 the whole army was aboard ship and ready to set out for the conquest of Normandy. But few of those on board were aware of their destination. As in the case of Edward III, the king had kept his destination a dead secret. In France the mystification was still greater; the fact that an invasion was imminent had been known for some time, but the wildest guesses were made as to the landing point. Efforts were made to defend most of the harbours along the Channel coast, with the inevitable result that the defence was scattered and weak everywhere. Harfleur was the favourite guess, and after that the Boulogne area.

But King Henry had his eyes fixed on the conquest of Lower Normandy first, i.e., the country to the south of the river Seine, and he had had enough of operating on the wrong side of a river: the landing must thus be to the south of the Seine, not the north of it. Consequently his choice fell upon the mouth of the little river Touques, the site of the modern Trouville.

On July 30 the fleet set sail with great ceremony. The wind being fair, the great expedition made the crossing in two days, and the landing was made on August 1, 1417. Feeble opposition was put up by 500 horsemen, and they were speedily dispersed. The disembarkation was then carried out without incident, and a camp was pitched on the west bank of the river.

The first act of the king, after returning thanks to God, was to appoint his brother the duke of Clarence to be commander-in-chief of the army, and to make no less than 48 new knights. A few miles to the south lay the powerful castle of Bonneville, and the earl of Huntingdon (who seems to have been the king's "maid of all work") was despatched at once to capture it. This proved a simple matter, the garrison offered to surrender unless relieved by August 9. No relief coming, it duly surrendered on that day. So far so good. Two days later the earl of Salisbury began what was to be his long line of conquests by capturing the castle of Auvillers (the modern Deauville). The road was now open to advance east against Honfleur (10 miles), or south against Lisieux (20 miles) or west against Caen (30 miles). The strategical situation of the English army was not dissimilar to that confronting Field-Marshal Montgomery after making his successful landing in 1944. Landings had been made in each case (some 30 miles apart), and against opposition, and modest beach-heads secured. The enemy had in each case expected the landing to be further east, and he was not for the moment capable of holding his ground, still less of driving the invader into the sea. The problem was, should a rapid advance be attempted, or should the ground gained be first consolidated? The decision come to in each case was roughly the same—an attempt to capture Caen before the main weight of the enemy's counter-attack could be mounted.

But here the similarity ends; for whereas the Germans responded rapidly and with vigour to the threatened attack, the French reaction was slow and supine.

The English king, having decided upon making Caen his immediate objective, had to guard against possible interference with his plan. This might come from two quarters—from Honfleur or from Rouen. He had no wish to spend precious time—as he had at Harfleur—besieging Honfleur, which had strong defence. On the other hand the menace from it could not be ignored. He consequently despatched a holding force to prevent any sortie from that town till he should be established at Caen.[1]

But the main danger was to be expected from the direction of Rouen and Paris. A strong force, under the commander-in-chief himself was accordingly thrown out in that direction. Marching swiftly, Clarence captured Lisieux town (but not castle) on August 4, and pushed on to Bernay 10 miles east of it. There being no sign of hostile approach here, Clarence turned west, evidently by pre-arrangement, and, marching rapidly, appeared before the gates of Caen on August 14, just in time to prevent the suburbs being burnt in order to provide the defenders with a good "field of fire". He also managed to take

[1] The only authority for this is a French one, but it seems in accordance with inherent military probability, and I accept it.

the Abbaye aux Dames by surprise. This was a smart piece of work by Clarence and gave the invasion a propitious start.

On the previous day the king had set out with the main army from Touques. Marching *via* Dives and Trearn, he on August 18 joined forces with the duke of Clarence before Caen. The army was reunited and Henry set up his headquarters in the Abbaye aux Hommes which Clarence had also captured. (See Sketch Map 4.)

* * *

It may be wondered what the French armed forces were doing, and what steps their government was taking to repel the invader. The short answer is that poor France was still distracted by civil strife, due to the insensate rivalry and hostility between the two leading factions—the followers of Armagnac and of Burgundy. The shifty Burgundy, whom no man could trust, had taken advantage of the impending invasion by the English to conduct a campaign of his own against Paris. Two days before the English expedition sailed, a Burgundian force took Troyes, and directly the duke heard that the English had effected their landing he took the field himself in the north, and advanced towards Paris as far as Corbie.

Faced by this threat, the French government, so far from sending help to Caen which they believed impregnable, recalled the Dauphin to Paris from Rouen where he was in command of a small force. Thus the English had a clear field for their attempt on Caen. In this matter one is constrained to sympathize with the distracted French government in Paris, facing attack from three quarters at once.

* * *

The medieval town of Caen cannot be adequately pictured from a verbal description; recourse should be had to the map which appears on p. 123. Soldiers who fought in the town in 1944 might be surprised to hear that the lower town was then an island; this was formed by two branches of the river Orne, for the northern branch has long since dived underground. The castle and hill to the north comprised the old town and the new town is still called the Isle de St. Jean, from the church of that name in the centre of the town. The castle had, and has, a very strong site, two of its sides being precipitous. The castle was the child of William I, strengthened later by his son Henry I. The old town which abutted on to the castle was surrounded by a strong and lofty wall, with numerous towers. A single bridge spanned the river and connected it to the new town, which was also surrounded by a wall. The western wall did not take the course of the river, but cut the island in two, the portion outside the wall being known as La Prairie (as it still is).[1]

The two famous Abbeys, aux Hommes and aux Dames (both built by William I), are a few hundred yards outside the old town, to the west and east of it respectively. They were each easily converted into powerful forts, and from their lofty towers splendid observation of the interior of the town was possible. Great care had been lavished on the defences, and Caen was generally believed to be impregnable–at least until the English had shown that Harfleur had belied that reputation.

The English had brought a large number of great cannons with them, and the slowness of the advance of the main body had probably been in order to keep their artillery with the army. (Some of these cannons were however sent there by boat up the river Orne.)

Arrangements were now made for a methodical siege, on the same lines as that of Harfleur. Gun positions were constructed, protective trenches dug, other and lighter guns were mounted on the roof and towers of the two abbeys, a collapsible bridge, constructed for the siege of Harfleur–stored there and brought on to Caen in sections–was thrown across the Orne in order to connect the besiegers on both sides of the river; mines were started, and all the paraphernalia of a medieval siege set up. The garrison, for their part, strengthened the walls, mounted light guns on them and prepared for desperate resistance.

---

[1] It is now a race-course, and unbuilt upon.

Henry decided to attack the new town first, and his plan was to make two breaches, one to the west for the main body, one to the east for the contingent of the duke of Clarence. For the main breach he sited a battery of heavy guns on the Prairie at a distance of 600 yards from the wall to be breached.[1] On the east the breaching guns were sited in the Abbaye aux Dames, at a shorter range. As soon as all the guns were in position the bombardment commenced. It was carried on without intermission until the morning of September 4, by which time practicable breaches had been made. A breach was also started in the south-west angle of the old town wall, but Henry desisted when he perceived that the church of St. Etienne just inside the angle was being damaged by the cannonade. He was ever a punctilious protector of churches.

On the morning of September 4, after hearing three masses, the king gave the signal by trumpet for a simultaneous assault at both breaches. The main assaulting party advanced in three lines, the leading men carrying fascines which they threw into the moat that encircled the wall, and then scrambled across over them. As they set foot on the breach, scaling ladders in hand, the defenders who by this time had manned the wall on each side of the breach, poured down upon the attackers crossbow-shafts, stones, darts, boiling water mixed with fat, lime to blind the eyes and some form of incendiary material, which proved very effective. Against this heroic and determined resistance the English could make no headway. But the king himself came up and with coolheadedness and spirit reorganized his troops and launched a fresh attack.

Meanwhile on the opposite side of the town the assault of Clarence's men was proceeding more favourably; the moat was filled and surmounted, the leading troops climbed the destroyed masonry and rubble of the wall, and one Harry Ingles–his name deserves perpetuation–reached the summit and jumped down into the town. His example was followed and a cheering

[1] Traces of the battery position can still be identified. See Appendix to this chapter.

mass of English soldiers forced their way forward, alongside the north wall, pushing on towards the sound of the fight
that their comrades were engaged in at the main breach. It
was the story of Badajos, enacted 400 years later. The French
defenders of the breach found themselves attacked from front
and rear. It was too much for them. They recoiled and scattered, and at last the main breach was won. The victorious
assailants, bursting through the breach met their comrades
inside, headed by the fiery duke of Clarence. King Henry was
soon across the breach himself, and the two royal brothers met
face to face. It was the greatest moment in the life of Clarence.

The attackers now swept through the whole of the new town,
driving the enemy back street by street, and causing heavy
casualties. In after years some French chroniclers accused the
English of a vile massacre, and a modern English historian has
deplored that Henry did not "forbid all massacre and pillage
as soon as resistance had ceased".[1] But did Dr. Wyllie pause for
a moment, before he wrote those words, to picture the scene,
and consider how the king should set about restraining indi-
vidual soldiers in the middle of the tumult and confusion that
inevitably follows the storming of a town that has refused to
surrender? By the custom of war in those days–and for a long
time afterwards–when a town refused the call to surrender and
it had to be breached no quarter was to be expected once the
attackers had got inside it. All adult males were potential
soldiers, civilians being indistinguishable from soldiers. The
only distinctions that could be made were those of sex and age
and the priesthood. Now Henry had strictly charged his troops
to respect women, children and priests, also churches and their
contents, and it is believed that his orders were very generally
complied with. On the evidence, and in view of the circumstances of the case, I can find nothing for which to condemn the
English king. Indeed, when all resistance had clearly ceased
he acted with marked leniency, doing all in his power to
reconcile the inhabitants to the English rule. One of the first

[1] *Wyllie*, III, 61.

extant documents after the siege records the marriage of an English soldier to a French girl.

The town was now in English hands, but the castle remained to be taken. Henry went about it in an unexpected way. He neither assaulted it nor bombarded it but quietly sat down and

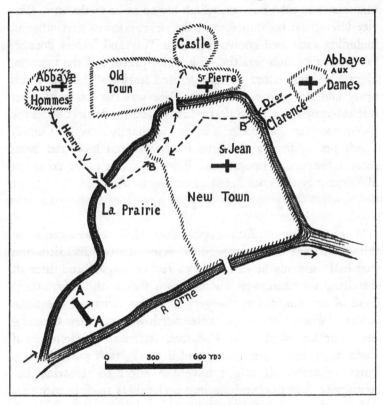

Sketch Map 4; THE SIEGE OF CAEN
A-A Main battery
B, B The breaches

suggested it should surrender. Five days later it agreed to do so, unless relieved by the 19th. No relief coming, it surrendered on the 20th on the most astonishingly easy terms. This surely shows that the English king was anxious to deal as leniently as possible with his opponents whom he hoped shortly to make his loyal subjects. Indeed he here, as always in the Duchy, acted in the most enlightened fashion.

*   *   *

Directly Caen had fallen the king despatched the duke of Gloucester to take Bayeux, which lay 20 miles to the west. The city offered no resistance, and the nearby towns and villages, including such well-known names as Tilly and Villers Bocage, followed suit, such was the power and prestige of the name of Henry V – augmented by exaggerated stories of the size of his army and the terror of his guns. Nor was the lesson of what might happen to a town that refused to surrender lost upon the Normans. The capital of Lower Normandy was in English hands and a firm and conveniently situated base had been secured for further operations. The first phase of the conquest of Normandy was completed according to plan.

*   *   *

What form should future operations take? Before examining this question it will be as well to review the political situation that had suddenly arisen. It was a rather tangled and difficult situation, for there was an unknown factor – the enigmatical duke of Burgundy. On the very day that Caen fell the duke captured Pontoise, only 20 miles north-west of Paris. Crossing the Seine he swept on to Chartres. It looked to Henry as if Paris might fall at any time, and if the English pushed on to Paris themselves it might have the effect of throwing the Armagnacs and Burgundians into each others arms, in common defence of the national capital.

Whether or not Henry had harbourd such an intention, he could not pursue it at the moment; moreover the conquest of Normandy was not yet accomplished. Should he then push east, south or west? Chartres was less than 20 miles from the border of Normandy; if Burgundy were to move in that direction and cross the border it might be awkward and difficult to remove him without open warfare, for he was theoretically an ally. An advance by the English army towards Chartres therefore seemed indicated.

Before putting this plan into effect the king sent out a force to the west of Bayeux to act as a sort of flank-guard in case of any danger developing from the direction of Brittany. This force he placed under the command of Gilbert Talbot, and he placed the trusty Umfraville in command at Caen during his own absence.

By October 1 all was ready for the resumption of the offensive and the army set out. It did not take the road from Caen to Falaise-so much trodden by English troops 500 years later— for Falaise was strongly fortified and would probably delay his army if attacked. Henry therefore by-passed it to the east and marched *via* Trun–the centre of the bottleneck of the "Falaise Pocket" of 1944.

There was no opposition all along the road, and Argentan[1] fell to him after a 40-mile march at the leisurely pace of 12 miles per day. Here the king halted and set up his headquarters, and from it he sent out detachments to make good the country to the east and south practically as far as the frontier of the Duchy. His object was to establish a line of fortified towns guarding this frontier against Burgundy or Armagnac, whichever should feel inclined to attack. Thus a line stretching from Verneuil in the north, southwards to Bellême and thence running west to Alençon was established. Alençon itself offered some slight resistance, but was in English hands well before the end of October.

All had gone well, and only Falaise remained to be taken for the king to be able to claim that he had the whole of southern Normandy in his hands. But Falaise would be a hard nut to crack, and the normal campaigning season was nearly at an end. Political problems had also loomed up in Brittany, Anjou and Maine. All three had become alarmed at the approach of the English army, and had called, though in vain, to Paris for

[1] The scene of Henry II's famous question, "Who will rid me of this turbulent priest?"

help. Receiving no response they took the prudent course of trying to come to terms with the invaders. To this Henry was not averse, and in a short space of time he had made a truce with them all. It was signed on November 16, and the coast was thus clear for the attack on Falaise. The season was, as I have said, late, but Edward III had shown his great-grandson that winter operations were quite feasible, and Henry V was ready to follow the example set him.

The castle and old town of Falaise – the birth-place of William the Conqueror – stands in a picturesque situation on a narrow outcrop of rock. Sharply below it on a little stream lies the lower town with the town washing-place immediately opposite the Castle. The town was surrounded by a wall and, with the castle, formed a strong military fortification. The English army encamped before it on December 1. There was now no need for haste, for the duke of Burgundy had fallen back to Troyes, and the Armagnacs remained quiescent. To storm the town would obviously be a costly operation. Time was no longer a consideration, but English lives were. The king therefore decided merely to blockade and bombard the town, trusting to hunger and cannon-balls to bring about its submission. He went further. Profiting by the experience before the walls of Harfleur, he took active steps to safeguard the health of his troops, and had huts constructed for them as winter quarters.

This plan proved completely successful: the town surrendered on January 2, 1418, and the castle a month later, after the attackers had managed by desperate efforts to make a breach 40 yards wide. This was due partly to the miners and partly to the very powerful artillery that the king brought against it. One cannon at least had the enormous calibre of 20 inches, as is proved by the fact that three cannon-balls of that dimension still lie inside the castle.

*   *   *

It was still winter, but there was to be no let-up in the operations. Three columns at least were sent out to conquer Western

Normandy. The duke of Gloucester commanded the biggest force, 3,000 strong. Its task was to reduce the Cotentin. In rapid succession the duke captured St. Lo, Carentan, Valognes, and the famous castle of St. Sauveur le Vicomte; but Cherbourg itself held him up for some months, being immensely strong.

In the centre, the earl of Huntingdon captured Coutances, Avranche and all the intervening country. Still further south Warwick accounted for the imposing castle of Domfront, but only after a lengthy siege.

In the spring of 1419 the duke of Clarence was sent in the opposite direction to clear up all the country as far as the line of the Seine below Rouen, a task that he accomplished with speed, and without much trouble.

By April practically the whole of Lower Normandy was in English hands and the second stage of the conquest was practically complete. There remained Upper Normandy, north of the Seine, and the capital itself, Rouen.

But before tackling this final task of conquest King Henry applied himself with his usual drive and thoroughness to the formidable task of reconciling his new subjects to English rule. The problem was an intricate one, and is not strictly relevant to this book. Suffice it to say that, pursuing an enlightened policy of appeasement, the king did all in his power by lenient and sympathetic treatment of the inhabitants to win them over, and he met with considerable, even surprising, success.

King Henry decided to lead the great campaign against Rouen in person. All through the month of May preparations went ahead, but when all was in train at the end of the month news came from Paris that altered the whole political situation. On the 29th an uprising against the hated Armagnac placed the city in the hands of the Burgundians. Here they took Armagnac prisoner and a few days later he was murdered by the mob. John the Fearless assumed the supreme power in the state, in close alliance with Queen Isabelle. What followed had been foreseen—and feared in the English camp: he immediately threw off the mask, allied himself with the men of Rouen and

sent troops to assist them against the English on the line of the
Seine, up to and including Rouen.

Thus when the English army approached Pont de L'Arche,
their intended crossing place in the advance on Rouen, they
found it strongly held, and the far bank lined with Burgundian
troops.

The crossing of the broad and deep river Seine in the presence
of the enemy in the month of June 1418 must be regarded as a
major military operation. The difficulties were great. The
bridge was defended by a walled town on the south side – the
side of approach – and the northern end was defended by a square
fort. The first endeavour of the English was to capture the town.
A fortnight was spent in vain attempts to take it by assault, and
a fresh plan had therefore to be devised. At Pont de L'Arche the
river contains a string of narrow islands. These, though nearer
to the south bank, have the effect of narrowing the 400-yard
wide stream to under 200 yards. The army was well provided
with boats and pontoons, thanks to the king's foresight. They
would now serve a useful purpose. It was a simple task to throw
a pontoon bridge from the south bank to the island 400 yards
down-stream of the bridge. A large number of small rowing boats
were then carried over this bridge by night. The north bank
of the island was lined with archers and a forlorn hope of
about 60 men under Sir John Cornwall, who had laid a bet
with a French knight that he would cross the river that night,
crept silently across the bridge on to the island in the early
morning. Embarking in the boats and covered by the fire of
archers on the island, his little party made the perilous crossing
with complete success. The French defenders of the bank
were taken by surprise, a landing was effected, the French
were routed and a bridgehead was established.[1]

The next step was to capture the square fort guarding the

[1] Wyllie finds the statement "hard to believe" that the archers were able to
cover the crossing, but I have satisfied myself from personal inspection that it was
perfectly possible. Covering fire by longbowmen at a landing had been practised
ever since the Battle of Cadsand in 1338. Though the average width of the river
is hereabouts nearly 400 yards, the island is 230 yards wide and the main stream
at this point only 170 yards.

northern end of the bridge. Some small guns, mounted on horses, a new development in artillery methods, assisted in the reduction of the fort. Meanwhile two pontoon bridges were thrown across the river one above and one below the town, and a strong force crossed by them to the northern side. Seeing that they were now effectually cut off, and overawed by Henry's vigorous measures, the town surrendered on July 20, 1418.

THE SIEGE OF ROUEN

Rouen, that still enchanting city of towers and spires, was in the fifteenth century one of the largest towns in France, with a population of perhaps 70,000. I measure its defensive wall as almost 6,000 yards.[1] The city had been strengthened and rein-forced since the 1415 campaign, and it was easily the most formidably defended place the invaders had yet encountered. The English king had been wise to delay attempting its reduc-tion till the ground was thoroughly prepared by the conquest of Lower Normandy, the amassing of siege stores and bridging material, the concentration of powerful forces and the blocking of the river above and below the city. The capture of Pont de L'Arche was the immediate "curtain raiser'. to the siege. Nine days after the fall of that town the English army approached the capital of Normandy, after it had been reconnoitred by the duke of Exeter who had brought out reinforcements from home.

The plan on p. 131 shows the lay-out of the city. The walls, which had recently been strengthened and provided with more than 60 towers, were pierced by six main gates; one was to the south on the bridge spanning the river, the remainder were sited at equal distances along the perimeter.[2] The walls were well manned with guns and the garrison had been worked up to a high state of morale by its intrepid commander Guy de Bouteille, ably seconded by the commander of the crossbowmen, Alain Blanchard.

[1] Wyllie gives the perimeter as 5 miles.
[2] The line of the walls is now marked by boulevards, with open circular spaces to mark the gateways.

The English army invested the town on all sides at the end of July and the king made his headquarters at the Chartreuse de Notre Dame de la Rose, opposite the Porte St. Hilaire and some 1,200 yards from it. (See Appendix.)

The tasks in front of the besiegers were multiple and difficult. Apart from the immense extent of the defensive line to be blockaded, the waterways above and below the town had to be effectively·blocked, and also the way barred to a possible relieving army from Paris.

This brings the duke of Burgundy once more on to the stage. After the murder of Armagnac, duke John and the Queen Isabelle had been in uneasy control of Paris. At the same time they made an uncertain and vague rapprochement with the Armagnacs and they announced that they would go to the help of Rouen. This possibility had to be guarded against.

The final complication was that at the beginning of the siege the army was deficient of a large number of troops, and–still more serious–of siege ordnance. Cherbourg, Domfront and Avranches, though on their last legs, had not actually surrendered at the outset, and most of the siege ordnance was tied up at those places and Gloucester's 3,000 troops were absent. Thus it was out of the question to attempt a breach and a storm, at any rate for some time to come, and Henry decided not to attempt one, but to sit down and starve out the town.

To this end most elaborate measures were adopted, full of interest to the military engineer. Here they can only be summarized. First a line of circumvallation had to be constructed. To judge from a contemporary drawing, it consisted of a wooden palisade and a ditch, which ultimately extended all round the perimeter. Then there was the blocking of the waterways. At the mouth of the Seine an Anglo-Portuguese fleet was in control, but it could not approach the city as Caudebec– midway between the capital and Harfleur–was held by the French. As a first step therefore the earl of Warwick was despatched to deal with this town and to secure the passage for the English fleet. This he did and the Fleet sailed upstream to within sight of Rouen, but could get no further. Nothing daunted, the sailors beached a portion of their ships and dragged them with sails set over-land across the three miles of the great loop in the Seine to the south of the city. Launching them again they drove the French craft back into the city. The waterway was then effectually blocked just out of gun-shot of the town by stretching three great chains across the river, one at water level, one 18 inches below and the other 18 inches above it.

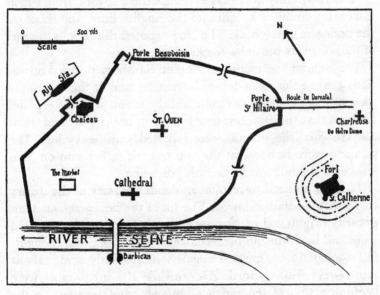

Sketch Map 5; THE SIEGE OF ROUEN

The next necessity was to ensure good communication between the troops situated to the north and to the south of the river. To ensure this an immense wooden bridge was constructed three miles above the town, great piles being driven into the river-bed and the roadway made wide enough to take all traffic.

The chief engineer, who must have been a man of no mean ability, deserves to be named. He was Sir Robert Babthorp, known as the king's controller.

A third preliminary step had to be taken before the city could
be considered well and truly besieged. Immediately to the
east of the city, and separated from it by some 300 yards of
marsh,[1] rose the mountainous-looking hill of St. Catherine,
some 400 feet high. On its summit was the fortified monastery
of St. Catherine, and nearby the small fort of St. Michel. This
hill was held as an outpost by the garrison, and was connected
with the town by a subterranean passage.[2]

It was obviously necessary to reduce this outwork, from which
the enemy could look right into the English lines, and shoot up
the besiegers in the back. The king deputed this task to the earl
of Salisbury. It proved a tough one.

Throughout the month of August, Salisbury pursued operations against this formidable obstruction, and at the end of the
month he launched an assault. But the ascent was so steep and
arduous that the attackers could progress but slowly, and when
they reached the summit were repulsed with heavy loss. The
garrison were however at the end of their tether and on September 2 the hill was in English possession.

There is no need to recount in detail the story of the dreary
three months that followed. The lot of the besiegers was temporarily brightened in November by the receipt of a cargo of
wine and beer, the gift of the citizens of London, who thought-
fully included 2,500 mugs. The garrison constantly made gallant
but always fruitless sorties. Meanwhile the inhabitants were
beginning to feel the pinch of hunger, and resorted to the
drastic step of thrusting out of the gates 12,000 unwanted
civilians—"bouches inutiles" they had been called when the
English did the same thing 200 years before at the famous siege
of Château Gaillard. Henry followed the example of the French
king on that occasion, and refused to let them pass. He however
tempered this severity by allowing his troops to pass to them a
portion of their own bread, and at Christmas he provided them
with a free meal.

[1] Wyllie states that it was 1 mile wide.
[2] The entrance to this tunnel can still be seen. No-one knows where its exit was,
but there seems little reason to doubt that it did reach right into the town.

The inhabitants also made frequent attempts to get messages through to the duke of Burgundy. One such message was carried by an old priest who bluntly told the duke that unless he relieved the city the inhabitants would surrender it and go over to the English side. The duke replied that he would do what he could. What he actually did was to take the sacred Oriflamme from the abbey at St. Denys and march with it as far as Pontoise, under 20 miles, and there he halted. Rouen was not relieved.

On the last day of the year the heroic garrison, urged on by the inhabitants, sent a message that they desired to surrender and, after lengthy negotiations, this was carried out on January 20, 1419. On that morning, perhaps the most auspicious day in the life of the English king, Henry rode out through the convent gateway (it still exists) and entered the city by the Beauvoisin Gate. His mien was modest, and he would have no military triumph. He was entering, not as a conqueror, but as a king "returning to his own", for he and the whole army devoutly believed that it was his by right and that the Valois kings were usurpers. His first steps therefore took him to the cathedral, where he returned thanks to God for his blessings. He was well received by the populace, and immediately set about trying to bring food and amelioration to his new subjects, who were in an appalling state of misery.

*　　　*　　　*

The military effect of the fall of the great city was prodigious. The other towns and castles of northern Normandy almost tumbled over one another in their haste to surrender, even before being summoned. A mere list, with the date of the submission of each is impressive. Lillebourne (January 31); Vernon (February 3); Mantes (February 5); Dieppe (February 8); Gournay (February 9); Eu (February 15); Honfleur (February 25). By the end of the month practically the whole of Normandy was in English hands except five great castles, Mont St. Michel (which was never captured), Château Gaillard, La Roche-Guyon, Gisors and Ivry. These fell after sieges of varying length. Normandy had, after a lapse of 200 years once again become a dependency of the English crown.

APPENDIX

A NOTE ON THE SOURCES

In general the sources remain much as before. Strecche may be said to increase in importance, and Monstrelet to decline. On the French side a new source must from now on be noticed, *Reductio Normanniae*, by Robert Blondel, which may be found in Stevenson's *Expulsion of the English from Normandy*, though it must be treated with caution for Blondel was a virulent Anglophobe. Rymer's *Foedera* remains, as always important and reliable for details on organization and supply and suchlike matters. Interesting items of information also are to be found increasingly in *Collection generale des Documents Français qui se trouve en Angleterre*, by J. Delpit. For the siege of Caen, Walsingham is particularly important and full details of authorities and local items are found in *Siège et Prise de Caen*, by L. Puiseux, a local historian writing in 1858. His story of the siege is the most detailed of any. For the siege of Rouen there are practically no French accounts from the aspect of the garrison, but there is a uniquely valuable account of the siege as a whole from the pen of an English soldier who fought in the retinue of Sir Gilbert Umfraville. His name was John Page, and that is about all we know of him, except that he was the author of a rhymed poem *The Siege of Rouen*, written in English (published in *Historical Collections of a London Citizen*, in the Camden Series (1876)). All modern historians base their account of the siege on this poem; indeed contemporary chroniclers did so too, including even Elmham. The fullest modern history of the siege comes again from the pen of Puiseux, *Siège et Prise de Rouen* (1867), whose map of the town and defences is invaluable. It was whilst writing this history that M. Puiseux discovered the forgotten site of the Chartreuse de Notre Dame de la Rose, which was occupied as the headquarters of Henry V during the siege, and which forms the subject of the appendix (p. 137).

JOHN STRECCHE'S ACCOUNT OF PONT DE L'ARCHE

The account of John Strecche, though no doubt picked up at first- or second-hand from some participant, is of little serious military significance, but it helps to place flesh on the dry bones of the chroniclers' history, besides being entertaining, in the manner of Froissart, for its lively conversations. As, moreover, it has never been done out of Latin into English, it seems worth while giving here my very free translation of the picturesque portions.

To start with, Strecche calls the town Pont Large (Ponte Largo), as no doubt did most English soldiers.[1] The first episode related by Strecche is out of place, but no matter. It concerns the action of Gilbert Umfraville, after effecting the crossing of the river. He surrounded the gateway tower on the northern bank (which we will call the barbican though Strecche calls it the "Bulwark") with an entrenchment, and on it he raised his own standard. When the garrison saw this they sent an English-speaking Scot up the barbican tower, to palaver with the English. (This in itself is of interest as showing the extent to which the French language was becoming extinct in the English army.) The following dialogue then ensued:

The Scot (in a loud voice): "Who is there? Who is the lord of that bulwark? Is he a gentleman?

Umfraville: "Who are you that asks the question?"

The Scot: "If you are a friend of the earl of Kyme (Umfraville) tell him that that standard of his will be in our hands before the hour of vespers."

Umfraville: "So be it, in the name of the Father. And I call God to witness that if my standard is attacked I shall defend it."

Then, as the Scot had foretold, about the hour of vespers 5,000 (!) armed men made a sortie from the barbican gate,

---

[1] In the same manner as Marlborough's soldiers called Bois le Duc "Boiled Duck".

but Umfraville with his handful of men drove them back into the barbican, pursued them and shot at them through the bars of the portcullis which they had lowered just in time, killing and capturing many men.

*   *   *

The other incident took place at the opening of the siege of Pont de L'Arche. A large band of armed rustics had taken up position on the northern bank of the river where they set up a din, shouting and clamouring the whole night long, to such an extent that the repose of the English king and his troops was disturbed. Henry in his wrath sent his favourite "maid of all work" Sir John Cornwall, to parley with the Lord Graville, the governor of the town. Cornwall entered upon his mission with evident relish, and there ensued at the castle gate the following remarkable conversation.

Graville: "Who are you, and what do you want?"

Cornwall: "I am the envoy of the English king, who has sent me to your camp to order you to restrain and punish those rustics yonder who set up a hideous din all night long, thereby disturbing the rest of the king and his army. Moreover you yourselves, if you care for honour, should maintain order and discipline in your camp."

Graville: "We cannot control these louts, so go away and do not vex us."

Cornwall: "Now it is clear that these rustics dominate you, since you dare not punish them. Let *us* into your camp for a short while and we will teach these rustics how to behave."

Graville (mildly): "This, I hope, it shall never be in your power to do."

Cornwall: "You are the lord in the town and you have there a pretty wife, for whom I undertake to give 2,000 crowns for the adornment of her head if I fail in my undertaking that within 15 days[1] our king's army shall cross the river and overpower you

---

[1] Wyllie, for some reason, follows Monstrelet in saying *one* day, which seems militarily improbable.

and those rustics; and you on your side, if I succeed, you shall give me your best charger with best appointments."

Graville: "This I promise, by the oath of a soldier."

The crossing was duly carried out, the French put to flight, while the rustics disappeared into the woods, never to reappear. Graville also fled, and hid himself. But Umfraville found him, and taxed him as follows (speaking in French):

"Graville, Graville, here rides John de Cornwall. You see now how our king has succeeded in crossing the river and in subduing both you and those rustics. Graville, I say, keep your word. Give me your charger, as you have promised."

Then the lord Graville gave Cornwall the charger as he had promised.

THE HEADQUARTERS OF HENRY V AT THE SIEGE OF ROUEN

The headquarters of Henry V were in the Chartreuse, or convent, of Notre Dame de la Rose. A century ago all record and recollection of its site had vanished. In 1867 M. Puiseux, when writing his *Siège et Prise de Rouen* made investigations (which he recorded in a long footnote), and he tracked it down to a site in the Rue de la Petite Chartreuse. This site is now accepted. It is 1,200 yards east of the town walls. Leaving the city by the Porte (now Place) St. Hilaire, proceed along the route de Darnatal (along which encamped the unfortunate *bouches inutiles* during the siege) for 1,200 yards. Then turn to the right down the Rue de la Petite Chartreuse, and on turning the corner to the right, there is a stone wall, on the left of the road, with a gateway through it. The wall is the old convent boundary, and the gateway is apparently the original gateway through which Henry V rode to receive the surrender of Rouen. You are now on historic ground.

Inside the wall is a kitchen garden. Looking half-left you see a detached two-storey building. The upper storey is latticed and modern (used as a granary drying-room); the lower storey is part of the original convent. Its external measurement I make to be 42 feet by 26 feet, and I believe it may be the actual lodgings occupied by the king (though Dr. Wyllie thinks differently). It is now used as a barn or lumber room.

The convent was only 26 years old, having been founded by Archbishop William de l'Estrange in 1392; his only proviso being that the best lodging in the building must always be at his disposal when he wished to stay. After the siege the convent fell on evil days. In 1565 the Huguenots burned the church, and the army of Henri IV did further damage. In 1703 the monks abandoned it altogether for another site. It speedily fell into decay and by 1867 little remained other than the abovementioned building.

No plaque or inscription marks the place, and it is neglected, ignored and, for all practical purposes, unknown. Yet the words of M. Puiseux are as true today as when they were written nearly 90 years ago: "Il porte l'empreinte des grands souvenirs, et l'archéologue s'arretera avec respect devant cette memorable relique du triomphe d'Angleterre et des dures epreuves que nos pères ont traversés."

CHAPTER VIII

THE TREATY OF TROYES AND THE BATTLE OF FRESNAY

EVEN while the siege of Rouen was in progress, King Henry was in tentative correspondence with count Bernard of Armagnac. This may occasion surprise, so a brief explanation is desirable.

The tangled and tortuous course of events in the diplomatic field at this period of the Hundred Years War is the despair of the historians. Fortunately it is not necessary for our purpose to enter into the matter in detail, but it may be summed up in the following way. Picture a triangular conference-table with one occupant on each side, each of whom is negotiating with his two neighbours simultaneously but separately, these negotiations being directed against the third party. There you have, with but slight exaggeration, the state of affairs at this time. Let us examine each party in turn.

King Henry of England disclosed his policy in a letter to one of his counsellors—a letter full of sound commonsense, for Henry, despite the fanatical side of his character, was a realist where military matters were concerned. The king of England was confident of being able to defeat any army ranged against him in the field, or to take any defended town that he chose. But such operations would entail time, money and casualties, all of which he could ill-afford. He had captured Normandy by force of arms, but if a similar process was to be necessary throughout France, the cost would prove too great. It was therefore essential to resort to diplomatic methods. Translated into plain terms, this meant that he must play off Burgundy against Armagnac, until the country, sighing for settled rule, would turn to him as the only one of the three capable of giving it.

The tergiversations of John, duke of Burgundy are more difficult to follow and explain. He undoubtedly hated the count of Armagnac like poison, and welcomed assistance from Henry in gaining the upper hand over his rival, but whenever he felt that Henry was becoming too powerful in France he drew back, blew cold over an English alliance, and even at times made some pretence of allying himself to Armagnac.

Count Bernard of Armagnac had a more straightforward policy: he hated Burgundy worse than poison, and would stick at nothing to thwart him – short of allowing the English to enter Paris.

Under these conditions, whenever the military situation fluctuated or seemed to, a fresh turn was given to the diplomatic exchanges. What we are here concerned with is, not the course of these fluctuations but their outcome. And the outcome came about in a totally unexpected way.

The chain of events that led up to this was as follows. Directly Rouen fell truces were made with Armagnac and Burgundy and this was followed up by a meeting at Meulan (on the Seine 25 miles below Paris), between the king of England and the queen of France (with Burgundy in attendance). Great precautions were taken against possible treachery, for Burgundy, as we have seen, was suspicious by nature – shifty men always are suspicious. The meeting place was fixed just to the west of the town (near the present railway station), and a ditch with palisaded bank was constructed all round it, to keep unwanted people outside, and to separate the English from the French troops.[1]

The conference lasted from May 29 to June 30, but was abortive. One important event, however, took place. Queen Isabelle brought with her the princess Catherine, to whom the king was to be affianced. Henry kissed her and immediately fell in love with her.

The duke of Burgundy, who had bent the knee to the king of England at Meulan, wasted no time in crossing to the other

---

[1] Part of this bank is still visible.

camp. Eleven days after the end of the conference he did obeissance to the Dauphin of France, in an endeavour to form an alliance against the English. For the moment this conference also was abortive.

The next step in the impending drama came from the English side. Henry, realizing full well the treacherous intent of duke John, broke off the truce the day after the conference was broken off, and struck swiftly and hard. The strongly defended town of Pontoise (which as its name indicates), bridges the river Oise, was distant only 11 miles from Meulan and 20 miles from Mantes, the nearest English garrison. A force was despatched by night to capture this town by a *coup de main*. The storming party, carrying scaling ladders, under the Captal de Buch, approached from the west, while a supporting party under the earl of Huntingdon made a wide circuit to south-east and approached it from the far side. The intention was that the arrival of the two columns should coincide, and that the stormers after effecting an entry should make a dash through the town to the other side and open the gate for Huntingdon's column. The first part worked well; the garrison were taken by surprise and the Captal's party entered, and according to programme made straight for the east gate. But the other column was nowhere to be seen. Meanwhile the whole garrison had been aroused, and it converged on the Captal's slender force. Things began to look serious, when suddenly Huntingdon's column (delayed by losing its way in the dark) arrived just in time to save the situation. Pontoise, for the first time in the Agincourt war (but by no means the last time) fell to an English attack and with it vast stores of every military kind. It was a shrewd, timely, and heavy blow, and it had all and more than all the effect that Henry had looked for. In the first place the duke of Burgundy panicked and hurriedly withdrew the king, Charles, to Troyes. This was just as well, for two days later the duke of Clarence appeared with a column at St. Denys, and on September 9 he was at the gates of Paris. In the second place it produced an effect quite unlooked for and undesired by the English king: it threw Burgundy and Armagnac into each others arms. They resolved to unite against the common enemy, and a meeting for this purpose was arranged to take place at Montereau, a town on the Seine, 20 miles above Paris. Burgundy, suspicious as ever, hesitated for three weeks and only consented to turn up after the most elaborate safeguards against treachery had been made. He had heard rumours of intended treachery, and this time they were not unfounded.

On September 10, 1419, the fateful meeting took place between the Dauphin and the duke of Burgundy. It was on the middle of the bridge over the river Yonne just above its con-fluence with the Seine. Precise details of what happened are at variance but what is perfectly clear is that Burgundy was brutally struck down and killed while engaged with the Dauphin (who however was not an accomplice). His followers were dispersed, and next day his body was taken to the town church and there buried.[1] The blow on the bridge of Montereau threw the Burgundians into the arms of Henry V: it did for Henry what he could never have done for himself unaided; it secured for his line the crown of France.

The immediate effect of the murder was that the Burgundians and Queen Isabelle both appealed to the English for help against the Armagnacs–the Burgundians in their desire for vengeance and the Queen because she desired to see on the throne of France her daughter Catherine whom she loved, rather than her son Charles, whom she did not love. (In the upshot, the reverse of her desires took place.)

King Henry could demand almost any terms he pleased, and his appellants had a pretty good idea what form they would take. The negotiations, however, were protracted, and it was not till the following spring that a settlement was reached. On April 9, 1420, the "Preliminary Articles" were signed. These

[1] The bridge was destroyed in the war of 1939–45. It spanned the Yonne, not (as Ramsay) the Seine. The church is only 100 yards from the bridge. The duke's body was removed to Dijon two years later, and no visible memorial of him is now in the church.

laid it down that on the death of King Charles VI the crown of England and France should be united in one person, that person being King Henry or his successor. But France was to retain its own laws and government under the king – a situation similar to that which obtained in the United Kingdom between 1603 and the Act of Union. Until the death of Charles VI, Henry Plantagenet should act as regent of France.

Though at the first glance it would appear that Henry had secured all his aims, there were two drawbacks. The first was that, according to the treaty, Normandy would come under the Paris Government (and the same applied to Aquitaine) instead of being under English control. This proviso however seems to have been ignored by both parties, as if by mutual consent. The second drawback was that Henry contracted to continue war against the territories still held by "the so-called Dauphin". But Henry yearned for peace, as we shall presently see.

On May 8, 1420, King Henry set out from Pontoise with a considerable army for Troyes, for the sealing of the treaty,[1] and to obtain a bride. He did not enter the French capital, but passed within sight of its walls, which were crowded with wondering inhabitants. Next day that still remarkable walled town of Provins was reached. On May 20 he entered the city of Troyes, escorted by the young duke of Burgundy, afterwards to be known as Philip the Good.

The meeting of the kings of England and France was ceremonious, but short.

Then, after kneeling dutifully before the Queen, Henry V kissed her daughter; after which they conversed amicably for some time. He then took his departure, recrossed the river to his hostel – and went to bed a happy man. But did he sleep that night? It seems at least doubtful, for the morrow, if all went well, was to see the crown put on his life's labours – in at least a figurative sense.

[1] Sometimes called, "the New Peace" to distinguish it from the Treaty of Bretigny which was "the Great Peace".

All *did* go well. The day May 21, 1420, opened with a joint meeting of the councils of the two potentates, at which the treaty was gone through and a few unimportant additions made.

The cathedral was selected as the place for the ceremony of sealing the treaty, in order to give it the greatest possible sanctity. Charles VI was not present, the Queen representing him. Both she and the king of England swore to the treaty, as also did a number of French notables.

Henry was of course delighted at the course events had taken, and he wrote that very day to his brother the regent in England declaring that it inaugurated "perpetual peace" between the two kingdoms.[1] When the news reached Paris "all hands were upraised to Heaven in transports of joy". And on June 14, there was a solemn procession to St. Paul's Cathedral in celebration of the happy event.[2]

But the signing and sealing of the treaty did not close the proceedings of that historic day. Later in the day the Cathedral witnessed the official betrothal of King Henry and the Princess Catherine. Twelve days later the wedding was duly solemnized in the church of St. Jean[3] with magnificent show. The bridal coach was drawn by eight snow-white English horses, the gift of the bridegroom, which must have been brought specially from England for the purpose. The marriage ceremony was performed in the French fashion by the Archbishop of Sens. "The day ended with the wine-cup and the blessing of the bed."

THE BATTLE OF FRESNAY

While the negotiations consummated at Troyes were proceeding, warfare of a rather sporadic nature was proceeding on the confines of Normandy. The last remaining castles in the Duchy were reduced one by one—Gisors, Dreux, Ivry. Last of all—appropriately—the famous Château Gaillard, the "Child of

---

[1] Edward III had expressed a like belief on the signing of the Treaty of Bretigny.
[2] As Professor Jacob points out, the association proposed by Mr. Winston Churchill in 1940 was a closer one than that enacted by the Treaty of Troyes.
[3] Only the nave of the original church survives.

one year" of Cœur de Lion.[1] Nearly all the fighting took the form of reduction or relief of castles and towns. Occasionally there would be a counter-effort by the French, which was in all cases brought to naught. The only real battle in the open field took place during the successful campaign of the earl of Salisbury (king's lieutenant in Lower Normandy) in the spring of 1420. The territory of Maine between Alençon and Le Mans had been temporarily overrun by the English in 1417, but not retained. The earl–"le redoubtable Comte de Salisbury" as a French historian calls him–now undertook the permanent conquest of this region. Advancing south from Alençon with an army of unknown strength he captured in succession, Ballon, Beaumont-le-Vicomte, and Montfort-le-Retrou.[2] He then laid siege to Fresnay-le-Vicomte.

Meanwhile, a large force was being assembled at Le Mans, a large proportion of it being a Scottish contingent that had recently landed in the country. This contingent was 6,000 strong, nearly half the total of English troops in the whole of Normandy at that time. On March 3, 1420, this army, under the command of Rieux, marshal of France, set out from Le Mans to relieve Fresnay, which lay 17 miles to the north. Salisbury evidently got wind of this intention and anticipated it. Without giving up the siege, he detached a force under the earl of Huntingdon and the earl marshal to deal with it. Huntingdon marched south, and the two armies met a short way to the south of Fresnay. Except for the fact that the English laid an ambush for the enemy on the road to Le Mans we have no details of the fight that ensued, nor reliable data as to numbers. The account in the most important source[3] gives the French 15,000, an obviously exaggerated figure, but even if we reduce it five-fold the numbers remaining will still give the contest that ensued the dignity of a battle–the battle of Fresnay. The same

---

[1] Its shell, mercifully preserved during the war of 1939–45, still stands grim and menacing over the river Seine.
[2] The ruined castles at these places still exist, all on naturally strong sites.
[3] *MS. Bodl. Digby No. 201*, as quoted by Francisque Michel in *Les Ecossais en France*, I. 118 N.

author puts the English at 3,500. Whatever we may make of this, it seems clear that the English were heavily outnumbered by the Franco-Scottish army. The latter seems to have been so confident of victory that the Scots adopted the extraordinary proceeding of taking with them their treasury containing the money for the payment of the troops during the campaign.

Whatever the respective numbers, and whatever the details of the fighting, all sources are in agreement that the result was a complete victory for the English.[1] According to the Bodleian writer, the French lost 3,000 in killed and the captures included their Marshal Rieux, six Scottish knights, the standard of Sir William Douglas (the Scottish commander,) 500 men-at-arms and 12,000 crowns in the Scottish treasury, and, indeed, everything in the allied camp. The Bodleian writer concludes: "And of the English only three were killed and no more, praised be God."

After the battle and the fall of Fresnay,[2] Salisbury rounded off his successful campaign by advancing up to Le Mans, and establishing the boundary there, though he does not appear to have occupied the actual town.

APPENDIX

THE SITE OF THE BATTLE OF FRESNAY

The *Vita* asserts vaguely that the battle took place "near Le Mans". There are difficulties about accepting this statement if we are also to accept the statement of the same authority, (which we may), that the English formed an ambush for the enemy. Le Mans is 20 miles from Fresnay. Salisbury could hardly have despatched Huntingdon's force to meet the enemy until he had certain information of their approach. However slowly they advanced, Huntingdon could therefore hardly have set out till the allies were within 10 miles of Fresnay. How then could he have laid an ambush for them "near Le Mans"?

---

[1] *Gloriosum triumphum* is how the *Vita* describes it.

[2] Situated on a rocky promontory overlooking the river Sarthe. If Salisbury stormed it, it must have been from the town side: the rock is unscalable.

Even if that were possible would an experienced commander such as Salisbury was, have detached a large portion of his small army to such a distance, and still maintained the siege of Fresnay? Moreover, the country near Le Mans does not lend itself to ambushes, which imply concealment on a pass or route by which the enemy is almost bound to come and from which he cannot easily diverge or deploy. Now the valley of the Sarthe to the immediate north of Le Mans is wide and flat, and the only feasible place for an ambush on the road to Fresnay is at the outskirts of Beaumont, 15 miles north of Le Mans. But Beaumont was already in English hands so the allies, whose objective was the relief of Fresnay would have avoided Beaumont. In short, the only place on the direct road from Le Mans to Fresnay at which I can envisage an ambush is at or near St. Christophe, four miles south of Fresnay. This is a likely distance from the main English army at which to make a stand against the enemy, moreover, the village stands upon a steep hill. The road between it and Fresnay runs through various cuttings all of which might form a possible site for an ambush, but I must admit that the present road has a modern appearance, as it winds down the hill. There is however, a direct track through the woods which I have not reconnoitred but which is likely to provide the required defiles for an ambush. These are my reasons for siting the battle about three miles from Fresnay, and naming the battle after that town. The battle deserves a name.

CHAPTER IX

BAUGÉ

FROM the moment the treaty of Troyes was signed, the long war between England and France which had continued intermittently since 1369 was technically over. Henceforth the armies of the two kingdoms were to fight under the banner of the regent of France against the French rebels of King Charles, (now called the Dauphinists). King Henry the regent, was bound by the Treaty to carry on war against these "rebels". That was the theory: in practice the warfare that ensued is treated by historians as a continuation of the Hundred Years War between England and France. As such we must consider it here, for though it was for some years to be waged nominally in the name of the king of France, all men knew that it was in reality a war of Englishmen, with some French allies, against other Frenchmen. Their nominal leader, the Dauphin, now came to be known contemptuously as "the king of Bourges", for it was at Bourges in central France that Charles the Dauphin set up his headquarters, and from Bourges he waged war against his own father. He was the dispossessed son.

King Henry allowed but one day for his honeymoon, and then set out for the siege of Sens, situated on the Seine, 40 miles to the west of Troyes. Thither Henry led his army, accompanied by the French king and the duke of Burgundy and both Courts. But the garrison had no heart for resistance and after a six-day siege it surrendered. The combined armies then turned their attention to Montereau, of notorious fame. The young duke of Burgundy was naturally spoiling for revenge, and he had not long to wait for it. The town was taken by storm on June 23, and the castle surrendered on July 1. Duke Philip entered the parish church, had the coffin containing the body of his murdered father opened, placed the remains in a fresh coffin, and had them sent for burial to the family vault at Dijon.

The next place for reduction was Melun, a powerfully defended town also on the Seine, 30 miles south-east of Paris. This
was a very different proposition. It was well defended, not only
by fortifications but by a resolute and enterprising commander,
the sire of Brabazan. The town was in three portions, the centre
being on an island with suburbs to the east and west. All three
portions were defended by walls and where necessary by a ditch.
The main English camp was on the west side, and the Burgundian camp on the east. Operations were started simultaneously
on both sides, but Henry soon perceived that it would be a
lengthy process and set about making systematic preparations,
such as his great-grandfather had done at the siege of Calais.
Lines of circumvallation were constructed on both sides of the
river, guns were placed in suitable sites and protected against
hostile fire.

The siege opened on July 9, and as it dragged on into the
autumn the zeal of some of the Burgundian leaders, (but not the
duke) began to weaken, and relations between the two camps
to deteriorate. But the king set his face resolutely against resort-
ing to a storm. Time was on his side; he could ill afford heavy
casualties, for the English army, (despite a large reinforcement
brought out by the duke of Bedford) was pitiably weak. Hunger
would do the work cheaper than missiles. As the weeks sped by
an unexpected reinforcement arrived in the allied camp. It
was a great cannon,[1] the gift of the citizens of London, who had
it constructed and sent out at their own expense. They named
it "The London", and it is claimed that it did great execution
and caused great consternation in the garrison.

But when November came round the garrison was in any
case at the end of its tether, and on the 17th of the month an
emissary came out to beg for terms. He approached Sir John
Cornwall, who refused to receive him till he had gone back and
trimmed his beard. This little contretemps did not unduly delay
the negotiations, and on the very next day capitulation terms

---

[1] *Maximum falaricam*, according to *Strecche* (op. cit., p. 183), but evidently a
cannon is indicated.

were agreed. A few days later the two kings with their retinues made a state entry into Paris amid the tumultuous greetings of its hard-tried inhabitants.

English garrisons had already been posted, in agreement with the Burgundians, at the Louvre, (where Henry took up his residence), the Bastille, and the Bois de Vincennes.

The king spent a strenuous month in Paris as regent of France, re-organizing the government. At the end of December Henry departed for Rouen, leaving his brother Clarence as his representative in Paris. On New Year's Eve he and his queen entered the capital of Normandy, and a month later they arrived in England, to receive from the London crowd as enthusiastic a welcome as on their return from the triumph of Agincourt.

When Henry V left France the military situation appeared satisfactory. The Dauphinists were quiescent, and the Anglo-Burgundian sway in northern France appeared to be unquestioned. But it was a deceptive calm. The duke of Burgundy had also left Paris for his duchy, and the simultaneous departure from the centre of the king and duke evidently encouraged the Dauphinists, who were by now recovering from the shock of the treaty of Troyes. They had bargained with the regent of Scotland for help, and ships were collected in France and Spain and sent north to transport the Scottish reinforcements promised by the regent. Moreover the Dauphinist leaders, sitting down and examining their map (if they had one) must have discovered that their strategical position offered great possibilities. This was due to the peculiar disposition of the Burgundian possessions. The old duchy of Burgundy, with the county of Burgundy to the east of it, covered between them all the territory from Savoy in the south-east to Auxerre in the north-west, with Dijon (160 miles south-east of Paris) as its capital. In addition to this, the duke had inherited the county of Artois (capital Arras) and Flanders to the north-east of it. Between these two blocks of Burgundian territory lay Champagne and Picardy. Champagne covered approximately the area between Troyes and the

river Marne, while north of it lay Picardy. Between them, these
two provinces embraced the lands of the Marne, Aisne and Oise,
nearly all of which were in Dauphinist hands. Indeed their influence extended to within 30 miles of Paris, the strongly fortified
town of Meaux being held by them. Finally, whilst holding
practically all the land south of the Loire, except Gascony, they
occupied stretches of the Seine and Yonne, to the south-east of
Paris. Thus, not only were the Burgundian territories cut off
from one another, but communication between Burgundy and
Paris was precarious, while that between Paris and Flanders
was in a similar situation.

Early in the New Year matters were worsened by the unexpected defection of Jacques d'Harcourt, sire of Tancarville, to
the side of the Dauphin. Harcourt, descendant of the Harcourt
who had proved so helpful to Edward III, was a bold and
enterprising soldier, and he quickly overran the valley of the
lower Somme from about Amiens to the sea. Thus, communications between the English and Flanders were virtually severed.

Meanwhile the duke of Clarence had not been idle. To begin
with, he swept south with an army almost to Orleans, a strongly
held Dauphinist city. In February, pursuant to instructions imparted to him by King Henry, he set out on a "punitive raid"
in Maine and Anjou. What the precise object of this was it is not
easy to say. Collecting an army of about 4,000 men at Bernay,
midway between Rouen and Caen, and taking the earl of Salisbury as his second-in-command, he advanced south-west to
Argentan, thence south to Alençon, and continued along the
route taken by Salisbury 12 months before, towards Le Mans.
Swerving to his left short of this town (a Dauphinist stronghold),
his army crossed the river Huisne 14 miles east of that town, and
thence marched 20 miles south-west to Luché, (seven miles east
of La Flêche). Here he crossed the river Loir, (not to be mistaken for the Loire, which is 25 miles further south). From
Luché he proceeded to Baugé, another 15 miles south-west,
whence after a few days halt he marched 22 miles due west to
the gates of Angers, the capital of Anjou. Up to this point the

English had encountered scarcely any opposition, but the gates of Angers were shut against them, and the grim and formidable-looking (as it still is) castle of King John did not invite attack. King Henry's orders did not apparently include the storming of defended towns, and to reduce Angers by starvation would have proved a lengthy operation. Clarence therefore fell back to the castle of Beaufort 15 miles east of Angers, and 10 miles south-west of Baugé.[1]

At Beaufort the duke halted his army and gave it a rest. What his next objective was is not clear to the historian and may not have been clear to Clarence. But in any case the matter was solved for him by the Dauphinists. When the news of the English incursion into Maine reached the Dauphin's head-quarters, he decided to employ against them the newly arrived Scottish army, strengthened by such local levies as were available. The army thus produced, slightly over 5,000 in number, assembled at Tours. The Scottish leaders were the Earls of Buchan and Wigtown, and the French were under the Constable de Lafayette. Exact dates of the movements of both sides in this campaign are missing, but it matters not for the understanding of the course of events.

The Allies evidently received information of the halt of the English in Baugé but instead of advancing direct to that place, they marched rather to the north of it, heading for La Flêche. This was presumably in order to place themselves in a position on the invader's line of retreat to Normandy. This shows that they envisaged a battle and considered themselves strong enough to challenge one.

On their arrival at the town of Lude, they may be presumed to have learnt of the new position of the English at Beaufort. Consequently they turned through a right angle to their left, and arrived at Baugé on the evening of Good Friday, March 21. They billeted most of their army in the village of Vieil Baugé, 2,000 yards south-west of the town.

---

[1] Four square towers of this ancient castle are visible on the left of the road thence to Baugé.

On the following day, Easter Eve, Buchan sent Lafayette to reconnoitre a position suitable for a battle between the two armies. The position was to be, not directly between the rival forces, but astride the road from Beaufort to Tours. This also was a sound move, for it would ensure that the position covered the line of retreat of the allies in case of defeat, whereas if they stood at Baugé they might be driven off this line into Maine and Normandy. Either Buchan or Lafayette was a good strategist.

Lafayette carried out his reconnaissance in the morning, and selected a position at La Lande Chasles, five miles south by east of Baugé.

Meanwhile the duke of Clarence was still halted in Beaufort, with foragers–mainly archers–dispersed over the country-side. One of these parties on approaching Baugé ran into a party of Scots and took some of them prisoners. It is likely that these foragers were under the command of Sir Gilbert Umfraville who sent back the prisoners to headquarters to be interrogated. Clarence was at dinner when they arrived and he carried out the questioning himself, still seated at table. Up till this moment, he had been totally unaware of the propinquity of the enemy. He expressed his annoyance at their appearance on this particular day, for his own troops were dispersed and the next day would be Easter Sunday when he was hardly prepared to fight. Yet he was anxious not to allow two days to elapse before offering battle in case the enemy should elude him. The duke of Clarence was a fiery soldier, imbued with the offensive spirit, a firm believer in its virtues and in his own ability to defeat the French. Moreover he was spoiling for a fight in the open, having missed Agincourt. Not a moment was to be lost; the enemy must not be allowed to give him the slip. Therefore in spite of the fact that his troops were dangerously dispersed and few if any archers (apart from his own body-guard) were immediately available he sprang up from the dinner table leaving his food unfinished, exclaiming, "Let us go against them. They are ours!"

The duke then sent off messengers to his captains to prepare their men-at-arms for battle, without waiting for the archers to come in. He would go on with his men-at-arms, leaving the earl of Salisbury to collect the remainder and bring them on as soon as possible. This course appeared unduly rash to the earl of Huntingdon, but he failed to dissuade Clarence from it.

The duke then set out with a force of men-at-arms numbering something between 1,000 and 1,500 to do battle with the allied army. The little cavalcade moved off at best speed, and in high heart. Sir Gilbert Umfraville and Sir John Grey were apparently out with the foragers when the force set out, and on hearing the news they "chipped in" to the column with only a few personal retainers, while it was on its way. When Umfraville heard what the duke's intentions were he also counselled prudence. But the duke would not hear of it. According to the rhymed chronicle of John Hardyng the following conversation took place. Umfraville reminded the duke that to-morrow was Easter Day, and that it would be better to keep church that day and fight on the Monday. Clarence, possibly misunderstanding Sir Gilbert's motives, replied hotly, "If thou art afraid go home and keep the church," and he reminded the knight that *he* had had the luck to fight at Agincourt, whereas Clarence had not. Umfraville expostulated that he had had no intention of deserting his master: "Nay, my Lord: my cousin Grey and myself have but ten men with us, yet you shall never say that we thus left you." And they rode on together conversing earnestly.[1]

The road approaches Baugé from the south and converges on that from La Lande Chasles. Now it so happened that just as the English were approaching the town, the sire of Layafette was also approaching it with his officers on the conclusion of his reconnaissance. The two parties thus were marching on approximately parallel roads. Presently they came in sight of one another, and Lafayette immediately galloped at full speed into the town shouting a warning to the troops as he entered. To reach it he had to cross the little river Couosnon (only nine feet

---

[1] Since both speakers were dead within an hour of the conversation it is hard to know how its purport could reach Hardyng. The only explanation must be that one of Umfraville's retinue riding close behind his master heard snatches of their converse.

wide at this point), and his warning cries just enabled the few nearby soldiers who were off-duty, to rush to the bridge and man it ere the pursuing English arrived. The English and Scots arrived simultaneously and there followed a hot fight for the possession of the bridge, of sufficiently long duration to enable the earl of Buchan to assemble his main force in or near Vieil Baugé. This village lies on a slight ridge running parallel to the river – and about 300 yards from it.

Though the river itself was but a poor obstacle to mounted men the valley was boggy, which made a crossing other than by the bridge difficult. It was however attempted by Clarence and some of his troops whilst the struggle for the bridge was proceeding. It seems that for the most part his men had to dismount and lead their horses across, and we may picture Clarence himself floundering across in full armour, closely followed by page leading his charger. On gaining the far bank the Scots on the bridge, finding their flank turned, retreated, and the mounted English burst across and pursued them in a northerly direction into the town. Some of the Scots shut themselves up in the parish church, where they were besieged by the exultant English, and confused fighting took place in the streets.

But this was not to the liking of Clarence. His tiny force was rapidly becoming disseminated and the main body of the enemy had yet to be encountered. He therefore halted the troops that still remained under his own hand, and tried to reorganize them on the gentle slope leading up to the Vieil Baugé ridge. He can by now have had with him only a few hundred men, and we can picture them halted, dismounted, resting their panting horses after the nine mile *chevauchée* followed by the exhausting passage across the marsh. Most of the leaders of the tiny band were with him – the earls of Huntingdon and Somerset, the Lord Roos, Sir Gilbert Umfraville, Sir John Grey and others.

Meanwhile events of moment were taking place "the other side the hill". Buchan, by great exertions had managed to collect a considerable proportion of his army, hidden by the village of Vieil Baugé, and he now led them forward over the ridge to join issue with the English. In number they were, to quote a French chronicler Fénin, "incomparably more numerous than the English,"[1] Dr. Waugh computes them as at least 5,000 strong. Moreover they had the advantage of the higher ground. Undeterred by these disadvantages the English duke instantly decided to take the offensive himself. Mounting his horse and ordering his men to follow, he charged straight up the hill into a sea of enemies. Resplendent with his banner flowing and wearing a helmet encircled with a ducal coronet of gold and jewels, he must have been a conspicuous figure, an obvious target for the hostile missiles. Indeed his onset was almost tantamount to suicide.

Be that as it may, the Franco-Scottish army also advanced and the clash must have taken place just below the ridge top, and along the road joining Baugé to Vieil Baugé.[2] The English were almost at once engulfed in the midst of the enemy and a confused and indescribable mêlée took place. One of the first to fall was the gallant Thomas, duke of Clarence. After quoting various circumstantial and detailed accounts by French and Scottish chroniclers, each claiming the honour of striking the mortal blow for their own countrymen, Dr. Waugh coldly concludes, "In short, Clarence died by an unknown hand".[3] It is not surprising that there should be competition in lying to substantiate the claim to have slain in battle the heir presumptive to the English Crown. Such a catastrophe had never previously been known, and it was only to occur once again in English history.

As the mêlée continued, fresh troops were continually being drawn into it as the tail of the strung-out English column came up, while fresh troops were also joining Buchan's forces.

Yet the issue was never in doubt; many of the English were borne down into the marsh by sheer weight of numbers, and either captured there or dispersed. Besides Clarence, Umfraville

[1] *Memoirs de Pierre de Fénin*, p. 154.
[2] A stone monument at this spot commemorates the battle.
[3] Wyllie and Waugh, III, p. 305, n.

and Lord Roos lost their lives, while the earls of Huntingdon and
Somerset were both captured. The engagement–it is hardly
correct to call it a battle[1]–cannot have lasted long. According
to the most reliable account, that of Buchan and Wigtown to
the Dauphin, written at midnight that night, it started at one
hour before sunset and it was over by dusk.

While these exciting events were being enacted what was the
earl of Salisbury doing? It will be remembered that he had
received orders to collect the scattered archers and bring them
on in the tracks of the duke as soon as he possibly could. This
the experienced and faithful Salisbury proceeded to do. But
there is an annoying absence of specific information about his
movements. It is true that all the English and Burgundian
sources are in substantial agreement, but there is not only complete absence of corroboration on the French and Scottish side
but certain difficulties about accepting the English account.
In fact, Waugh, who has delved more deeply into the whole
affair of Baugé than anyone, and to whom I am greatly indebted
for his thorough researches and marshalling of evidence, practically discards the accepted Anglo-Burgundian story. For the
reasons why I part company with him in this matter see the
Appendix to this chapter.

The English account states that the earl of Salisbury, bringing
up the remainder of the army, reached the battlefield at dusk,
attacked and drove back the allies who were in position on the
field and retrieved the bodies of Clarence and other leaders,
which were then being carried off in a cart. The body of Clarence was taken away and sent back to England for burial. The
last part at least of this story is certainly correct; Clarence's
body *was* sent to England.

I will now give my own reconstruction of the story, but it is
necessarily conjectural. As soon as he had collected sufficient
archers, the earl of Salisbury set out along the road taken by the
duke. Whether he left orders for the dismounted archers, the
varlets and the baggage train to follow on must remain an open

---

[1] Dr. Waugh calls it "a disorderly scuffle". Op. cit., III, p. 309.

question; fortunately it is immaterial. Marching at top speed the relieving force reached the scene of the fight before it was completely dark. All was quiet, but figures could be seen groping about on the battlefield. They were quickly ridden down and a cart that was hurrying from the field was overtaken and captured. Its grim contents were the dead bodies of the duke and some of his leading captains. In this dramatic form was the dismal intelligence conveyed to Salisbury that the little English force that had set out so joyously only a few hours before had been practically wiped out. It was clear that the allied army must have been of considerable size to effect this, and equally clear that nothing was to be gained now by seeking another encounter with it. It must have been with unspeakably heavy hearts that Salisbury and his archers retraced their steps to Beaufort, bearing with them the body of their beloved leader; for we are told that even many Dauphinists mourned his death. He was (according to St. Remy) esteemed for "his goodness and humility". His military reputation was high and the king seems to have placed more confidence in him than in any of his brothers.

Early next morning, being Easter Day, what remained of the English army begun its sad and hazardous retreat. The prospects of its ever seeing Normandy again cannot have appeared bright, for a superior and victorious army stood in the way. But Salisbury showed his metal, and skilfully evaded the enemy, taking the road to La Flêche instead of the one they had advanced by through Luché. The army managed to reach and to cross the Loir by an improvised bridge of carts and timber which the far-sighted earl had had collected during the march. They entered Le Mans by a *ruse de guerre*, broke down the bridge over the Sarthe behind them, and regained Normandy without ever seeing their opponents.

Indeed, the battle had ended rather tamely for the Franco-Scots. In the last few minutes of daylight the bulk of their army had set off in pursuit of the few fugitives towards the north, leaving the battlefield almost abandoned. Returning from the

pursuit late that night the Scottish leaders took up their residence
in Baugé town whence at midnight they indited a letter to the
Dauphin reporting their victory and appealing to him to advance with them into Normandy. Some troops were next day
posted at Ludé in the expectation that the English might try
to cross the Loir at that point, but no other steps appear to have
been taken to cut off the retreat of the enemy. If any steps were
taken they were ineffectual. Dr. Waugh sums up this final
phrase of the affair:

"In the sequel English generalship and morale appeared at their
best, and the French saw many of the fruits of victory slip from
their grasp."[1]

COMMENTS ON BAUGÉ

Baugé holds a place of its own in the military history of the
Hundred Years War. It is a mistake to call it–as some English
historians have–a skirmish. It was the direct opposite of a
skirmish; rather it was a mêlée. The main clash can scarcely
have lasted more than twenty minutes at most, and only a few
hundred Englishmen were engaged. It was a formless, almost
chaotic scrimmage, hardly worthy of the name of battle and
there is nothing to be learnt from it either for that or for any
other generation. But its results were out of all proportion to its
size and nature. And this for two reasons. Easily first was the
fact that the heir presumptive to the thrones of England and
France had been killed. Such a disaster had never happened
previously in recorded English history. Thomas, duke of
Clarence, though he had missed Agincourt, had a high military
reputation.[2] Forceful, ardent and quite fearless, he was an
attractive and appealing character, a knight *sans peur et sans re-
proche*. Indeed his ardour and fearlessness had been his undoing.

The second reason for the importance of the battle was that
it was the first time in the Hundred Years War that an English
army had suffered such a defeat–and the fact that its victors
were mainly Scots did not diminish the sensation, for French

[1] Op. cit., III, p. 298.   [2] Gained originally in Gascony.

propaganda successfully belittled the part played by their allies.

As for the English side, no truer or more exact verdict could be passed than "defeated but not disgraced". When King Henry heard the dire news of the disaster at Baugé and the death of his favourite brother his countenance remained unmoved – and he set about preparing a new army. In the meantime the Dauphin had been stirred into action. The appeal from Buchan found him in Poitiers, and he announced his intention of invading Normandy. But his movements were dilatory, if not hesitant. Arrived in Tours, he remained there several days. During his visit he gave a dinner to the Scottish lords, and to it he invited the captured earls of Huntingdon and Somerset – a pleasing touch of chivalry on the part of a prince about whom little that is flattering has been written. He then made Buchan Constable of France – a tactful, but astonishing honour to a foreigner – and in his company advanced to Le Mans, which was recaptured without difficulty. Here for some unknown reason he halted and made it his headquarters.

Meanwhile the earl of Salisbury had been "scraping the barrel" (of the garrisons in Normandy), to reinforce his depleted army, adding to it a number of Norman knights and their retainers. Early in May, when the French laid siege to Alençon, he marched to its relief. The two armies drew up just outside the town facing one another, but neither would attack. The English were inferior in numbers, but the Dauphin did not relish the idea of a battle with the English in the open. He shortly afterwards raised the siege and marched off in an easterly direction, to besiege Chartres, which was garrisoned in the main by Burgundians.

As a riposte to this, Salisbury undertook the bold project of a raid into Anjou. There was a touch of studied defiance and challenge about this raid, for it set out to do exactly the same thing, and in the same way, as the ill-fated raid of Clarence less than two months before. Moreover it succeeded in its aim: the walls of Angers were again reached without much let or hindrance, and on the return journey large quantities of booty were captured. The earl wrote a jubilant letter about it to the king, and claimed that the English troops were never in better heart. Dr. Waugh rounds off this spring campaign in the following terms:

"In the whole Hundred Years War there was nothing more resolute, prudent and skilful than Salisbury's conduct of the affairs under his direction."[1]

It may be so, but there seems to me to be an absence of firm facts to warrant so unqualified a claim—especially as on the very next page he writes that, had the Dauphin invaded Normandy boldly, Salibury might have been destroyed and the war ended. On this showing, some at least of Salisbury's success was due to the mistakes of his opponent.

Whatever be the truth of this estimate, we can at least agree that, by putting a bold face upon it, Salisbury was able to "keep his end up" in Normandy till the arrival of his king with a fresh army, and to retrieve in a remarkable fashion a situation that looked almost desperate on the morrow of Baugé.

APPENDIX

THE SOURCES

There seems to be more discrepancies and more sheer hard lying on the part of the chroniclers regarding Baugé, than about almost any medieval battle that I know. There may be two reasons for this. In the first place, the chroniclers of four different nationalities or parties are concerned—English, French and Scottish, and Burgundian. Each of the first three would be biased in favour of his own country, and the Burgundians might be fairly neutral, thus making a fourth point of view.

In the second place, there was a natural emulation on the part of the Scots and French to claim the credit for the death of Clarence, and both parties compiled most circumstantial and positive, but mutually incompatible stories of this episode. As

[1] Op. cit., III, p. 315.

for the English, they were equally naturally at pains to em-
phasize the part played in the final stage of the battle by the
arrival of Salisbury's troops. Dr. Waugh cites a long list of
sources, but there are only three principal ones, the remainder
contributing comparatively little of value. These three are
Vita et Gesta Henrici Quinti, (cited as *Vita*) by the "Pseudo"
Elmham, for the English side, *Liber Pluscardine* for the Scottish
side and *Histoire Chronologique du Roy Charles VI*, by Gilles le
Bouvier, (sometimes known as le Heraut Berry), on the French
side. This valuable work is inaccessible to most people for it is
hidden away in Godefroy's *Histoire de Charles VI*, a ghastly folio
volume lacking a table of contents and with an almost useless
index, published in 1658. To make matters still more confusing,
it would appear from Dr. Waugh's method of citation that the
references are to *L'Histoire de Charles VII* not *L'Histoire de
Charles VI*. To these may be added *Chroniques d'Anjou et de
Maine*, though it is not strictly a contemporary source, being
written 100 years later, contains much useful material.

THE PART PLAYED BY THE EARL OF SALISBURY

In the body of this chapter I indicated that I could not accept
the reconstruction of Dr. Waugh in this matter. In brief, the
only statement that he utilizes in the English accounts is that the
body of Clarence was recovered on the battlefield. This fact can
hardly be disputed, for the army did bring the body back to
Normandy with them, whence it was sent to England. But this
explanation of the matter is that the episode of the recovery
took place next morning. This thesis seems to me to raise more
difficulties than are provided by the English account. In order
to make it possible for an English force to perambulate the
battlefield next day, he suggests that most of the Dauphinist
troops were on the east side of Baugé looking for the English
there. But could there be a more unlikely quarter for the English
to be in? In the first moments of confusion and semi-darkness
immediately after the battle was over—a period of relaxation
after all battles—the episode described above was quite con-

ceivable, but on the grounds of inherent military probability I cannot conceive it happening in broad daylight next day. Nor on the same grounds can I believe that Salisbury would have sent a flank-guard right up to Baugé, whilst trying to slip away unobserved. Such a flank-guard would necessarily approach the battlefield from the west, and thus would have to pass through Vieil Baugé, a place that would then be occupied by some of the enemy. The only possible direction from which they could have approached the field would be the south. Moreover, assuming that they did succeed in recovering the bodies, they would have to make a detour to the south in order to avoid being intercepted by the enemy. This would give the main army a long start, and how could they be expected to catch up a quickly marching army, encumbered as they would be with dead bodies? In short, this thesis sounds to me wildly improbable.

CHAPTER X

HENRY V'S LAST CAMPAIGN

D URING the months of April and May, 1421, King Henry was busy raising a new army to take to France. It was not a large army—900 men-at-arms, 3,300 archers, but it was unusually well found in ancillary troops, sappers, miners, pioneers, siege train, etc. The troops were indentured for six months. The above facts show that the king did not anticipate a winter campaign, but was ready to undertake sieges.

By the beginning of June all was ready; leaving his pregnant queen in England, Henry, at the stern call of duty, set sail for France on 10th of the month. He and his army made a speedy passage from Dover, arriving at Calais the same day. Since his ultimate destination was Paris, some people have speculated as to why he did not select the Southampton-Harfleur route, evidently overlooking the slow and uncertain nature of sea voyages before the days of fore-and-aft rigging. By the Southampton route more than half the journey would be by water; moreover the distance from Southampton to Paris is 70 miles more than by Dover. Furthermore, by clever use of the tides the sea crossing to Calais could usually be assured, while the chance of interception by a hostile fleet was almost negligible. A landing in France at the firmly established well-found base of Calais would provide a firmer start for the campaign than would the newly acquired base of Harfleur.

There was also a strategical reason for the Calais route, as well as the logistical one set out above. It is unusual for medieval commanders to give to posterity the reasons for their courses of action, and we are usually reduced to deducing them from their actions. In this case however the king himself gave the main strategical reason for his selection of the Calais route. The situation in Picardy was bad: duke Philip had done little to suppress the Dauphinist leader Harcourt, and he probably appealed to the English king for help. At any rate he was very pleased at the prospect of receiving it. Henry had confidence in the power and ability of the earl of Salisbury to hold the enemy for the time being on the borders of Normandy, and he considered it the soundest strategy to start by making good the disturbed and disputed country that separated Paris from Calais. This he could best do by landing at Calais and joining forces with what ever army the Burgundians might provide.

*   *   *

At Calais, then, the English army landed. An advanced guard was sent forward to Paris at once, and the remainder marched straight to Montreuil, 25 miles south. In this pleasant town of historic memories the English king and Burgundian duke met and conferred together. There was ample need for a conference, for on the road Henry had learnt of the advance of the Dauphin to Chartres, which city was then being besieged by him. The earl of Salisbury was by that time far away on his Anjou raid. Should Chartres fall and the Dauphin advance on Paris in the absence of a field army ready to oppose him, there might well be a rising in Paris which the earl of Exeter might find impossible to quell. Anything might then happen. Clearly the presence of the English king with his steadying influence was required in the Isle de France, if only to raise the morale of the defenders. Henry and Philip rode south together from Montreuil discussing the new situation that had arisen. The Burgundian was amenable to the arguments of the Englishman, and agreed to take the field single-handed against Harcourt, thus allowing the English army to push on to the relief of Chartres. The two princes passed over or by the field of Crecy in the course of their ride, and Henry spent a pleasant day's boar-hunting in Crecy forest. At Abbeville the duke turned back to take command of his own army assembled at Arras, while the English army pushed on for the valley of the Seine. Between Vernon and

Pontoise they were quartered, whilst the king rode straight to
Paris, to confer with Exeter and the French government and
court.

Henry did not stay long in Paris, for the military situation had
been transformed, almost overnight. The very sound of the
name of the redoubtable English captain had achieved this. On
the news of his landing and approach, the Dauphin, who had
boasted loudly of his intention to do battle with the English
king if he should get the chance, incontinently broke up the
siege of Chartres and retreated in a southerly direction. The
moment for an English counter-offensive had clearly come.
Confidence in the army and the Paris government was restored,
while the Dauphinists were correspondingly depressed. The
question was, what form should this offensive take? On the
eastern border of Normandy, 25 miles north of Chartres and
50 miles west of Paris, lay the town of Dreux, very strongly
defended. It was the only considerable Dauphinist stronghold
remaining west of the capital. Should the Dauphin be immediately pursued or should this stronghold first be reduced? Without more information as to relative strengths and dispositions it
is hard to say, though on general strategical principles one
would favour an immediate pursuit and engagement of the
chief enemy in the field. The fact is, details of this last campaign
of Henry V are distressingly and distractingly meagre, and
without them, criticism is, or should be, stifled.[1]

Whether sound or not, Henry decided that his first objective
should be the reduction of Dreux. This town, in any case, lay on
the route to Chartres and the Loire, and if the siege was not prolonged the delay in the pursuit of the Dauphin might not be
material. On July 8, Henry rejoined his army at Mantes, and
next day, somewhat surprisingly, he was joined by the duke of
Burgundy, with a considerable number of reinforcements at his
back. He had come, very faithfully, to the help of his ally in the
relief of Chartres. This being no longer necessary, Henry sent

[1] Wyllie, Ramsay, Kingsford and Newall have between them pretty well
"scraped the barrel", thereby showing up the more the scantiness of its contents.

him back to deal with Harcourt, but he was much touched at the fidelity of young Philip.

On July 18 he laid siege to Dreux. This was a strongly situated town, but the strength of all defence lies ultimately in the will and spirit of the defenders. The garrison of Dreux, though nearly a thousand strong, were weak in spirit, and after three weeks of siege they asked for terms. On the 20th the English entered the town, and the advance was at once resumed.

Chartres was entered amid great rejoicings. The garrison, both English and Burgundians, had behaved admirably and received Henry's thanks.

On the approach of the English army, the Dauphin, who had temporarily set his headquarters at Vendôme, 12 miles north of Blois, fell back south of the river Loire and was now reported to be concentrating in the Beaugency area, ten miles upstream from Blois. Thither King Henry marched, his army having been reinforced by some Norman levies as well as by detachments from the English garrisons. We can but guess however, at its size, though it seems pretty safe to assume that it was well inferior to the Dauphinist army.

The little town of Beaugency does not belie its name. It is picturesquely poised on an eminence on the north bank of the Loire, with its rather grim castle donjon looking down on the many-arched bridge, which remains today much as it was five centuries ago. The English army arrived opposite the town on September 8, and immediately attacked it. The actual town was taken by assault, but the castle held out. The bridge, which was commanded by the castle, could with difficulty be used while the castle remained intact and as the Dauphinist army was not in sight on the far bank it was necessary to send a reconnoitring force by some other passage.

The river Loire, though wide, is shallow, and a ford was found downstream at St. Dye. By this ford, a force under the command of the earl of Suffolk crossed, and scoured the countryside for the enemy. Working their way downstream they reached the outskirts of Blois without obtaining news of the enemy. No one in the English camp knew where they had gone to–and no one knows today. They disappeared for the time being from the Loire, and from the pages of history.

And now an event that always haunted a medieval army occurred–the outbreak of an epidemic. What its exact nature was we do not know, but it is certain that it carried off a large number of the troops, and at the same time food began to run out. A move to a more salubrious and more fertile area was imperative. Should the army move upstream towards Orleans or downstream towards Tours? Whichever direction they took, it was unlikely that they would now bring the Dauphin to battle; he had shown his colours: evidently he had no intention of crossing swords with his formidable opponent. The probability is that he was well on the way to Chinon, 35 miles south-west of Tours. Henry decided that he must change his objective. He was now confronted with the same problem that had confronted Edward III 60 years before–how to bring to heel an opponent who declined to fight–for it takes two to make a battle. Here, for almost the first time, Henry parted company from his great-grandfather, who had broken the enemy's will by widespread devastation of his country. Henry was regent, and hoped shortly to be king of the land in which he was fighting; he had pledged himself to reduce the places held by the Dauphin, and he now returned to that objective. The obvious area in which to operate was that debatable region to the east and south-east of Paris in Brie and Champagne which, if held by the enemy, threatened to cut off the province of Burgundy from Paris and from Flanders. He therefore turned his face towards the north-east, seeking the lands watered by the rivers Yonne, Seine and Marne. On the way the army passed Orleans. Though some of the suburbs of this great city were captured, there could be no question of sitting down and besieging it with his small army, now racked with disease. The march was resumed, he himself marching north-east to Nemours, near Montereau, and no doubt he lodged in the still-existing castle there. Other troops marched east via Montargis to Villeneuve, an important town on the Yonne, which was immediately attacked. The Burgundians had tried in vain to take it in the previous February, but this time there was but little spirit in the garrison. Perhaps they recollected that the English king had never yet attacked a town that he had not captured, and they decided to anticipate the inevitable and come to terms at once. In a few days the whole valley of the Yonne as far south as Auxerre was cleared of the enemy, and all eyes were now turned upon the one remaining Dauphinist stronghold in those parts, the city of Meaux. Thither the army by diverse routes now directed its steps, the pestilence having apparently abated to a large extent. Descending the valley of the Yonne as far as Sens, the army split up into three divisions, moving on a broad front. One continued to hug the Yonne, treading in the footsteps of that other English army that had followed Edward III in his last campaign. The second struck further to the east, and crossed the Seine at Nogent. The third, still further east, crossed at Pont-sur-Seine, where Edward III's army had crossed in the opposite direction on its way to Burgundy. Thus both these English monarchs traversed much the same ground in their last campaigns. The three columns concentrated on Meaux, which was reached on October 6.

THE SIEGE OF MEAUX

The city of Meaux lies on the river Marne, 25 miles east of Paris. Ten miles on the Paris side, also situated on the Marne, is the town of Lagny. The importance of Meaux lay in the fact that it was the strongest defended post held by the Dauphinists in the region of Paris; from it the communications between the capital and both Burgundy and Flanders could be cut, and from its propinquity, it was a potential menace to the capital itself. It was also the centre for a pillaging band which terrorized the countryside, and led to urgent appeals being made to the English army for its destruction. Until it had fallen, Henry could not claim that he had in any sense carried out his contract to rid the land of Dauphinist dominance in the towns of northern France. There are indeed indications that after the capture of this last stronghold in the north Henry would regard his task as morally accomplished, and that he might then make peace with the Dauphin faction in the south. For in the course of the siege when matters were not going well he complained that he found himself short of men "in the point and conclusion of his labours".

The king had no misconceptions as to the immensity of the task that faced him. No quick and easy reduction of Meaux was to be looked for. In it as we have said, had collected the "scally-wags" of divers nations, English deserters, Scots, wild Irishmen, and the riff-raff of the French population that had ranged themselves under the banner of the Bastard of Vaurus, " a byeword for ferocious cruelty" as Ramsay calls him.[1] All these men had, metaphorically speaking, halters round their necks and they would sell their lives dearly.

Henry therefore made careful and methodical preparations before approaching the town. He made the rendezvous for his army at Lagny, where he had constructed "many wooden engines" according to Monstrelet. This is interesting as showing that nearly a century after the introduction of gunpowder artillery the old mechanical "engines of war" were still employed to supplement the cannons. These "wooden engines" were no doubt ballista, trebuchets and mangonels, throwing great stones, or even carcases of horses into the besieged town, together with "sows" or movable overhead cover for the attackers and possibly rams working at the foot of the walls of the town.

When all was ready, and not till then, he sent the earl of Exeter to make a sudden dash and thus capture the suburbs before the enemy could get wind of it and burn down their buildings. This was successful; Exeter having established himself in the suburbs on October 6, the remainder of the army followed in a few days.

The city of Meaux lay upon the northern apex of a hairpin bend of the river Marne, here about 70 yards wide, a deep, and

[1] Ramsay, op. cit., I, p. 297.

normally slow-flowing stream. A wall and moat surrounded the town, and it was well supplied with artillery. To the south of the river, and inside the bend, which thus protected it on three sides, lay the market, which also was surrounded with a wall while its southern side was protected by a canal, which converted it into an island. Thus, with the river as additional protection, the market was more strongly defended than the town itself.

The king divided his army (which was about 2,500 strong) into four divisions. His own was stationed to the north, his headquarters being St. Faro Abbey. To the east was the earl of March, and to the west the earl of Exeter. South of the river, facing the market, was the earl of Warwick.

It is interesting to note that the Bretons were at this time very divided in their loyalties, and that Arthur of Brittany and his troops assisted in the siege of Meaux, whilst his brother Richard supported the Dauphin.

As a preliminary to the siege, lines of circumvallation and contravallation (that is, facing inwards and outwards) were constructed. King Henry then turned his attention to the reduction of the town. When all his engines and cannons had been placed in position he commenced the systematic bombardment of the gates and walls. The amount of damage done was at first not considerable, or the garrison must have been particularly vigorous in their repair work, because when the month of December came round little impression appears to have been made on the defences. In that month there was prolonged rain and the Marne overflowed its banks, sweeping away the bridge of boats that Henry had constructed to maintain communication with Warwick's division on the south side of the river and forcing the English to evacuate their front trenches. Nearly all the boats were in the possession of the garrison, and Warwick's division was for some days dangerously isolated. The garrison took advantage of this to make sorties by boat. The meadows also were flooded and the king was obliged to send his horses away in order to obtain forage. For food he was largely dependent on a supply line to Paris (much of it being brought from

England), and this was constantly cut or threatened by raiding parties. He was thus forced to picquet the road with troops all the way between his camp and the capital. Thus the see-saw contest proceeded; for every step on the one side a counter was devised on the other.

To add to the difficulties and hardships of the attackers, a sickness epidemic–a feature of most medieval sieges–made its appearance, and the fighting strength was thus reduced at a time when appeals for help were received from Normandy.[1] But whatever the disappointments and difficulties might have been, the king pursued his purpose relentlessly. He had never yet abandoned a siege once he had undertaken it and the very possibility of such a course probably never occurred to him, and he showed his contempt for the faint hearts that began to appear around him. Even the gallant Sir John Cornwall departed for England on sick leave.

Christmas came and went, and still the king remained with his army before the walls of Meaux–like Edward III before Calais. But all was not well with the garrison. The nominal commander was something of a nonentity, and messages were smuggled out of the town to the famous Guy de Nesle, the sire of Offémont, to come and assume command. Offémont responded to this somewhat unattractive offer early in March, (1422). On the 9th of the month, he, with 40 companions, managed to steal through the English lines under cover of darkness and reach a point where the garrison, by pre-arrangement, had let down some scaling ladders (wrapped in cloth to muffle the noise). His leading men had successfully passed over the moat by a plank and were climbing the ladders when they heard a splash behind them. The sire was in the act of following them over the moat when the plank–an old one–broke with his weight and deposited him in the water. Now Offémont was wearing his full armour and its weight bore him down and he was in danger of drowning. Frantic efforts were made to rescue

---

[1] Salisbury had twice to ask for help, first in the recapture of Avranches, and later in that of Meulan.

him in the darkness. Two lances were handed to him, which he
grasped; but, we are told, they were "left in his hands". One
can picture the scene, the excitement, the confusion and the
resulting clamour. The noise roused the soporific English
sentries; the guard was called out and it rushed to the spot.
Presumably they were confronted with the rather comic spectacle of a knight in armour up to his neck in the water of the
moat, and brandishing two lances–an aquatic Don Quixote.
At any rate Guy and all his men were captured.[1]

This failure so disheartened the garrison that the very next
day they abandoned the town and took refuge in the market.
Before doing this they transferred as much food and stores as
possible into the market. These were seen crossing the bridge
that connected the town with the market and a vigorous attack
was launched in the effort to prevent the move. It came too late
to be really effective, but it prevented the desperadoes in control
in the city from setting the whole place on fire and slaying all
the inhabitants who preferred surrender. The inhabitants as a
matter of fact were only too glad to admit the English and to aid
them in driving out the Dauphinists.

The bulk of the garrison made good their escape across the
river to the market, and King Henry entered the town and
transferred his headquarters thither.

The first phase of this great siege was over, but the second–
the reduction of the market–was to prove even more arduous.
The leaders of the garrison were desperate, knowing that little
mercy was to be expected if the place fell, while the patience of
the English was becoming strained, and their tempers steeled by
the fierce, implacable spirit of their king. Thus the siege of
Meaux became an epic, famous throughout the century.

Henry's first attack was directed against the northern face of
the market. The garrison had broken down the bridge behind
them, and the king set about restoring it. This he did by means
of a *beffroi* or movable tower which was manhandled through

---

[1] This episode has been described by some writers as an attempt to relieve the
town. It was not. It was an attempt to smuggle in a new Commander.

the streets and on to the English end of the bridge. Halting short of the gap in the bridge, a kind of drawbridge was let down from the *beffroi* and the gap thus bridged. This operation was covered by a "barrage" of missiles from a large number of "engines" stationed at the end of the bridge.

The next step was to obtain possession of the flour mills which lined the southern bank of the river by the bridge (as they still do). To accomplish this the king occupied a small island in midstream not far from the bridge. Here he posted a strong force of cannons which directed a heavy bombardment on to the mills, thus enabling the infantry to cross the bridge and capture them in a gallant attack in which the earl of Worcester lost his life. This success not only gave a covered line of approach to the north face of the market but also a foothold on the bank under its walls.

The next step was taken by the earl of Warwick against the southern face of the market. Here he managed to establish his troops across the canal and, covered by a "sow" or movable pent-house, his troops got close up to the wall of an outwork which they took by assault. From here it was possible to direct a very damaging fire on to the interior of the market.

It was now the turn of the western division. The earl of Exeter had handed over the actual command to Sir Walter Hungerford, who was a more experienced commander in siege work. The new commander soon made his presence felt. On this side there was an appreciable space between the river bank and the curtain wall. He was able to throw small wooden foot-bridges across, and thus to establish a lodging at the foot of a wall. Protected by a "sow", his miners now sunk a mine, despite a number of desperate and well-led sorties by the garrison.

Last of all, it was the turn of the eastern face. Here the earl of March had a problem all his own, for the river on this side was unusually wide and swift—so swift that boats and bridging could with difficulty be employed. King Henry proved equal to the occasion. He had two large barges lashed together, and on them he constructed a species of *beffroi*, topped with a drawbridge which could be pushed out and lowered on to the top of the wall on that side.[1] It would be impossible to conceal this lofty erection from the eyes of the garrison, who must have watched its progress with trepidation. Appeals to the Dauphin had met with no better response than the appeals of the garrison of Harfleur to his brother Louis had been. Charles was at that moment living a life of luxury in far-off Bourges. Easter had come and gone (Henry granted the enemy a few days truce for the sacred feast), the siege had now lasted over six months; time after time the garrison had countered every attempt of their enemy to effect an entry, but time after time that inexorable foe, like a ferret that has its teeth into a rabbit, returned with some fresh attack. And now yet another attack was plainly brewing. Though food was still plentiful this was the last straw: King Henry had broken their spirit, the voice of their leaders was silenced and the garrison sued for terms.

Henry V was now in one of his grimmest and most unpleasant moods. He and his army had been kept under arms right through the winter, suffering loss and privations, and even insults from the Bastard of Vaurus and his ruffians. He consented to grant terms but they should be "just" terms, which meant that they would not be tempered with mercy. Most of the garrison were to get away with their lives, but there was a long list of exceptions—persons whose lives would be at the disposal of the king, Charles, and his regent, King Henry. The capitulation was written in English only, although it was ostensibly in the names of both kings. This was probably intended as a purposed form of humiliation. Among the names exempted from mercy we find the mysterious phrase, "One that blewe and sounded an Horne during the siege".[2] Thereby must hang some tale but it is lost to history. Some people have connected it with another story,

---

[1] Some writers have regarded this and the other *beffrois* as unique of their kind, the invention of the king's fertile brain. But *beffrois* were a recognized weapon of siege warfare, and the floating one was a counterpart of that constructed by that "leveller of castles" Philip Augustus in his famous siege of Château Gaillard. A huge *beffroi* known as Pompey's Bridge was used as late as A.D. 1601 at the Siege of Ostend.

[2] Rymer's *Foedera*, X, p. 212.

namely that an ass was dragged up to the top of the wall and belaboured till it brayed, when the garrison shouted to the English outside to come to the help of their king who was calling for them. Henry V seems to have had no sense of humour, this being the least attractive side to his complex character and he was much offended by this puerile prank. The condition in the terms of surrender that gave most satisfaction to friend and even foe was the fate accorded to the villainous Bastard of Vaurus. He was ordered to be hanged on the very elm tree outside the town which he had used as a gallows for his many victims in the past.

It was on May 2, 1422, that the capitulation was signed, the siege having lasted longer than any other of King Henry's sieges. Dr. Waugh describes this siege as, "Perhaps Henry's master-piece",[1] a well-deserved tribute. At the first blush, it might be regarded as rather disappointing that such a place should hold out against the might of England at her strongest for over six months, but such events must be judged in the context of their time. The physical strengths of medieval armies was compara-tively small; what swayed the course of history was the moral effect of the operations of those armies, and even more, of their leaders. Here was seen a prince who had never known defeat; disappointments he had had, but he had always managed to overcome them and to come out on top. His iron will had invariably triumphed, and a superstitious generation was pre-pared to regard it as in some way the verdict of God. Much the same had been the case with a previous soldier-king of England, Edward III. In his last campaign he fought no battle; he cap-tured no great town, yet by his persistence in the maintenance of his aim he eventually broke the spirit of his enemies. In like manner his great-grandson in this protracted siege broke the spirit of his enemies; and not only those within the walls of Meaux. The siege had been closely watched from the outside by the neighbouring towns and castles held by the Dauphinists. On its fall they fell too, with scarcely a blow struck. As a result, by

[1] Op. cit., III, p. 338.

the end of June, all Northern France except Guise, St. Valery and Le Crotoy, were in the hands of the Anglo-Burgundians.

* * *

After the capture of Meaux, King Henry returned to Paris, where he met his queen, who had borne him a son, Henry by name, during the siege. In Paris he devoted himself for a time to diplomacy, striving to build up a great alliance against the Dauphin's party. His next campaign, he decided, should be waged in conjunction with the young duke of Burgundy against the elusive Jacques d'Harcourt. The latter had made his base of operations Le Crotoy on the estuary of the Somme. The earl of Warwick was already operating in that direction, and was laying siege to St. Valery, on the opposite side of the estuary. But before plans for this campaign had been fully concerted, the strategical situation was suddenly and unexpectedly altered by a fomidable-looking offensive on the part of the Dauphin, directed at the Burgundian province of Nevers, which lay between the Orleanais and Burgundy. La Charité on the Loire was taken and Cosne on the same river, 50 miles south-east of Orleans, was besieged. The garrison agreed to surrender if not relieved by August 12. Instantly the duke of Burgundy abandoned all thought of proceeding against Harcourt and turned to the south. He had a curious correspondence with the Dauphin in which the two princes agreed to meet in battle on a field to be selected outside the town of Cosne. Thither duke Philip marched with his main army. Being short of archers, he begged Henry to lend him some. The king jumped at this opportunity to show his staunchness to his ally. Not only would he lend archers, but his whole available army, and more still, he would lead it in person.

Late in July the English army, with some adherents from Picardy, concentrated for the campaign near Paris, and began its long march to the south. The route lay through Corbeil, 15 miles south of Paris. Up to this point the king accompanied his army, but found himself unable to ride as he was suffering from some malady, probably dysentry. He was therefore constrained to ride in a horse litter, suffering great pain all the time. Beyond

Corbeil he found it impossible to go, reluctantly handing over the command to the duke of Bedford (who had escorted Queen Catherine from England, bringing some much-needed reinforcements with him). Marching south-east the English army joined forces with that of Burgundy at Vezelay on the Yonne on August 4. The Burgundian army was at full strength and the combined force must have been a formidable one. Continuing on their way (English and Burgundians being mixed in the same formations in order to prevent jealousy) they reached the outskirts of Cosne on the 11th. On the next day the town was due to surrender, the day fixed for the battle.

Of the Dauphin or his army there was no sign. Evidently he had fought shy of the contest. Possibly he had heard a report that the regent was present in person. Whatever the reason, the Dauphinist army had retreated towards Bourges, leaving a mere fringe of patrols on the opposite (west) side of the river.

Duke Philip now took an extraordinary decision. Instead of pursuing the retreating enemy, seizing the opportunity presented by the English troops or at least of retaking La Charité, he immediately fell back to Troyes and disbanded his army. Was his heart in the struggle? It seems doubtful. The English army perforce fell back too, sick at heart. Had their king been still with them, they must have reflected, things might have gone otherwise. But there was worse to come. The king was dying. Bedford was summoned in haste to his bedside at Vincennes, whither the stricken king had been removed.

Bedford, Warwick and other leaders assembled round his bed, while Henry, with two hours of life left him, gave his instructions and advice for the future regulation of affairs. His body might be wracked with pain, but his brain worked as coolly and lucidly as ever. To his eldest brother John of Bedford he bequeathed the regency, with the earnest injunction that he should never give up the contest till all France recognized the treaty of Troyes. Shortly afterwards he died peacefully. The sun of England had set.

*   *   *

This book is not a biography of a great king, but we must pause for a while to assess the military talents of Henry of Monmouth.[1] We cannot be sure that he was a great strategist like Edward III, for there is not enough to go upon. Apart from the Agincourt campaign, his warfare consisted for the most part of a series of sieges. Whereas Edward III thought in terms of the movements of armies, Henry's thoughts seemed more concerned with steps of diplomacy. Nor in the field of tactics is there much to be learnt from his actions. How then, it may be asked, did he make such a tremendous impression as a soldier not only upon his own people but upon allies and enemies alike! I think the explanation is that his military greatness lay in the moral sphere. He built up his army on the double foundation of discipline and fervour. The discipline he imparted was astonishingly strict for the age in which he lived, and it stood him in good stead. When things were going badly the fervour, or belief in a cause, was also most marked. He imbued his army with the same firm faith in the righteousness of his cause as he himself held. And all this was stoked up by the fires of religion. In these matters he was perhaps the prototype of Oliver Cromwell, who achieved nothing spectacular as a strategist or tactician, but yet produced an army ready, at long last, to "go anywhere and do anything". Another quality contributing to his military success was his resolution – his refusal to be downcast or to "let up" on anything to which he had put his hand. This, in conjunction with careful forethought and preparation, resulted in success invariably crowning his efforts. His careful forethought was shown strikingly when preparing for his last (and unfought) campaign in the north. Before undertaking it he made arrangements with the people of Amiens to provide food for his army, and even fixed with them the prices that should be paid.

[1] Various French writers of later days have had savage things to say of Henry V. A recent writer delights to call him "The Cut-throat King". But it was not always so. Contemporary French writers, Dauphinist as well as Burgundian, wrote little that was bad and they were practically unanimous in praising his strict sense of justice and his implacable – moderns would say harsh – execution of it. The story goes that on one occasion when one of his brothers was pleading for a malefactor the king answered him, "If it had been even you, my brother, I would have hanged you for it".

None of the above qualities is spectacular, but when combined in one person they represent a formidable combination. But that is not all. Overriding and informing them all was the innate greatness of the man, a greatness that is born witness to by friend and foe alike, a greatness of spirit and character that made all his brothers his dutiful slaves, even after his death. We hear of no petty quarrels among his captains. This was the true greatness that had shone in the character of his great-grandfather, and, in a lesser degree, in his great-uncle the Black Prince, as also in his grandfather, John of Gaunt, whose resoluteness and remorseless determination carried him through difficulties that would have submerged a lesser man. Truly those Plantagenet princes were a "mighty breed of men".

CHAPTER XI

CRAVANT

HENRY V was dead. The linch-pin had fallen out of the coach. John, duke of Bedford, did his best to replace it. It was no easy task, as he must have realized when reviewing the situation that confronted him. We have seen how English fortunes ebbed during the absence in England of the king–not so much from any failings on the part of his subordinates as in the encouragement and improved morale that was thereby engendered in the Dauphinist camp. This swing in military fortune was again to be expected. Bedford was quite a good general, as was shortly to be demonstrated, but he lacked the position and prestige of the late king, and also the military reputation of his dead brother, Thomas of Clarence.

Let us give this military situation a brief glance. The English troops were spread out over an enormous area, nearly as large as England south of a line from the Wash to the Severn estuary. They were pitifully few in numbers for this purpose, probably less than 15,000 combatant troops in all. Bedford saw, as clearly as his brother (who indeed had impressed the point upon him), that his task could only be accomplished if the Burgundian connection was maintained. Ominous cracks were already appearing in it. Duke Philip's conduct during the illness of Henry had been peculiar, not to say suspicious. It would require all the tact and patience at the command of the new regent to cement the uneasy alliance. Fortunately, he was not lacking in experienced and in trusty generals–the chief among them being Salisbury and Warwick–and the morale of the English troops was, so far as we can estimate, still unimpaired; the capture of Meaux and the hasty retreat of the Dauphin from Cosne had evidently raised it. Even so, the prospects of success were not bright, for only a month after the death of the English king, that

of the French king followed. This added to the difficulties confronting Bedford, for no longer could orders be issued to the
French in the name of their own king, Charles VI, but in that
of an absentee infant king, whom Bedford had had proclaimed
in Paris as Henry VI of England and France.

Two factors, however, improved the prospects. One was the
inertness of the Dauphin who, apart from proclaiming himself
king of France as Charles VII, took no active steps to make good
his claim. He was reported to be living in luxury in Bourges.
The other factor was the sterling character of the duke of Bedford. Now that Henry V was dead there was no better or
fitter person in the land to carry on his work than his brother
John. Lacking Henry's harshness, he possessed to the full his
flair for diplomacy and his strong sense of justice. To these
qualities he added a sincere desire to establish enlightened
government in France, and strict fidelity to the terms of the
Treaty of Troyes. The details of his civil government lie outside
the scope of this book, but it may be recorded here that he was
outstandingly successful in winning over the leading Burgundians in Paris, to whom he entrusted practically all the reins of
government, even appointing his old opponent at the siege of
Rouen, Guy de Bouteille, as captain of Paris. The populace
tended to follow their leaders, with the result that in future
military operations there was usually a strong contingent of
French (Burgundian) volunteers, who formed a useful reinforcement to the depleted ranks of the army.

To describe the course of the war during the first year or two
of the reign of Henry VI must be the despair of the historian. It
is as difficult to discern any clear-cut pattern in it as in much of
the Great Civil War.

Military operations were sporadic, spasmodic and of varying
fortunes. They consisted, for the most part, of sudden raids by
one side or the other, followed by sieges of castles, their capture
and recapture almost *ad nauseam*. It is, however, possible to
generalize, and to sum up the strategy of the duke of Bedford as
an attempt to "tidy up" the military situation before proceeding

to further advances. In this he was only following the recent strategy of Henry V. For twelve months, then, after the accession of Henry VI the situation in France may be said to be static.

By a bold stroke the French gained possession of Meulan; the ever-victorious earl of Salisbury, who had become "the handmaid" of the government just as Henry of Lancaster had been in the Crecy War, was sent to retake it, which he very speedily did. A more serious affair occurred in Anjou. Sir John de la Pole had been ordered to take a force to reduce the formidable fortress of Mont St. Michel. Disregarding his orders, de la Pole carried out a raid into Anjou, up to the gates of Angers, with a small force about 1,600 strong. History continued to repeat itself, for the sire Aumâle with a superior Dauphinist army based on Tours cut in behind him, and waylaid him near Laval on the homeward way. The English force was cut up and its commander deservedly made a prisoner.

As a counter to this setback in the west the English were enjoying marked successes in the north-east, where "the thorn in the flesh" of the Burgundians, Jacques d'Harcourt, was at last being seriously tackled by the earl of Warwick. First of all, Noyelles on the estuary of the Somme was captured. As a result, Harcourt fell back, withdrawing his forces into Le Crotoy. This town was then besieged vigorously and methodically by Sir Ralph Boutellier, and after some months it fell. The detested depredations of Harcourt in Picardy were thus brought to an end, to the great relief of the populace.

On the diplomatic plane, John of Bedford was proving himself a worthy brother to Henry V. His efforts culminated in April 1423 in the tri-partite Treaty of Amiens, a defensive alliance between England, Burgundy and Brittany. It was a great achievement to bring in Brittany, for her duke had been acting in as shifty a manner as the late duke of Burgundy, first leaning towards one side and then to the other. King Henry had laid the foundations of this *rapprochement*, but full credit must be accorded to his brother for bringing it to fruition. This he accomplished largely by means of two notable marriages. He himself espoused Duke Philip's fifth sister, Anne, while Arthur of Brittany, brother of the duke (who fought in the English ranks), married Philip's eldest sister. The duke of Brittany signed this treaty despite the treaty contracted in the previous year at Sablé with the Dauphin. But both Burgundy and Brittany had their tongues in their cheeks when they signed the Amiens treaty.

To revert to the military aspect. The "tidying up" process was not yet complete. The duke of Bedford himself did something towards it in an indirect way. In May he journeyed to Troyes to receive the hand of his fiancée, Anne of Burgundy, and on the way back to Paris he fell upon the garrison of Pont-sur-Seine, which had recently fallen into Dauphinist hands, and captured the place. He followed this up by clearing up other bad spots. But Champagne was not yet clear of the enemy, and Bedford deputed to his most efficient general, the earl of Salisbury, the task of completing the operation. Salisbury commenced by laying siege to Montaiguillon, a small stronghold near Provins, 50 miles south-east of Paris. Though small, Montaiguillon proved unexpectedly strong and tough, and the siege was a long one. Whilst thus engaged Salisbury received yet another task. After the fiasco of Cosne in the summer of 1422 the Dauphin had remained quiescent. But the death of Henry V, and the resistance of such places as Le Crotoy and Montaiguillon, seem to have spurred him into action. In the summer of 1423 he formed a new army at Bourges. It must have been of considerable size, for he collected it from over a wide area. A large proportion of it was the Scottish contingent under their marshal, Sir John Stewart of Darnley. There were also contingents from Aragon and even from Lombardy. Stewart was given the chief command, with the count of Vendôme as his second. This army the Dauphin despatched into Burgundy, with orders to take the town of Cravant as a first step. Various motives have been suggested for this step. For one thing, it was the region most remote from any English garrisons, and the Dauphin had already clearly shown that he preferred being ranged against Burgundians than against English troops. Further, a blow directed against the duchy of Burgundy, while it might relieve the pressure on Montaiguillon, would prepare the way to re-establishing a channel of communications with the remnants of his forces in Picardy and Champagne. To strike at the hostile strategic flank whilst at the same time covering his own communications and threatening the enemy's sensitive spot–his capital–was sound strategy. The degree of success that might be expected from it would depend largely on the reactions of the duke of Bedford.

Bedford's reaction was prompt and vigorous. Reinforcing Salisbury's army with the troops recently brought from England by the earl marshal and Lord Willoughby–about 1,000 in number–he ordered Salisbury to march at once to the relief of Cravant. At the same time the dowager duchess of Burgundy also collected and sent a contingent, which was to form part of Salisbury's army. Auxerre, situated nine miles north-west of Cravant, both towns being on the Yonne, was selected as the rendezvous for the two corps. Thither Salisbury set out in the latter part of July, leaving a small force to continue the siege. The distance was 40 miles and his route would take him through Sens, where he would strike the route of Bedford's army in its march to Cosne the previous year. Thence the two armies marched by the same road, passing through Joigny and Villeneuve, ascending the wide and rather dull valley of the Yonne.

The size of the English army is given by Waurin as 4,000, a likely enough figure under the circumstances; and as Waurin was himself present and is a reliable chronicler we may safely accept it. Of the Burgundian army we have no information, but it was collected hastily and it is likely to have been neither large nor of good quality. As for the Franco-Scottish army, Waurin is silent, and St. Remy merely states that it was large. Considering the wide area from which it was recruited, and the very large number of casualties incurred in the battle, it must have outnumbered the Anglo-Burgundians by two or three times.

The Burgundians were the first to arrive at Auxerre and, on

July 29, they were joined by the English. It was high time, for the garrison of Cravant were so short of food that they were reduced to eating horses, cats, and even mice. The leaders of the Burgundians, delighted that the English should help, and that their leader should be the great earl of Salisbury, came out of the town on the English approach and escorted them with ceremony into the cathedral city where they received a hearty welcome. Though the two parties had been allies for four years no pitched battle had yet taken place in which both were present. Relations were most cordial and the Burgundians gladly placed themselves under the orders of Salisbury.

The first act was to summon a council of war for that evening, to be held in the nave of the cathedral, which then bore much the same appearance as it does today (though the chancel is newer. On the spot one can easily picture this war council in session. While the council is debating, we will pass on to a description of the beleaguered town of Cravant.

The valley of the Yonne between Auxerre and Cravant is bordered on its eastern side by a line of hills, rising at their highest point, two miles short of Cravant, to some 500 feet above the valley. The town is situated on the southern end of this line, where it descends into the valley. Thus, its northern portion is 100 feet higher than the southern, which is at river level. Three of the medieval gates still stand, and at the highest point of the wall there is a watch-tower, of which more anon. The peculiar thing to note about the situation is that the town does not embrace or even touch the river, which flows past it at a distance at the nearest point of only 160 yards. (It may be conjectured that the river has changed its bed since the original walls of the town were laid out.) The bridge opposite the middle of the town was intact. The river is 40 to 60 yards wide, shallow but not swift, as it flows through the broad valley to Auxerre.

We will return to Auxerre cathedral, where the war council was being held. Whether Waurin was actually present is not known, but it seems likely, for he reported its decisions in great detail. The master-hand of Salisbury is clearly visible throughout, his main object being to weld into one fighting machine two different nationalities. This would not be easy, for the English of those days had a sublime contempt for all foreigners, and were hasty of temper. A quite trivial incident might wreck the whole partnership.

The decisions reported by Waurin may be re-arranged and tabulated as follows:

1. The two national contingents were to form one indivisible army.

2. To ensure this, every man in each contingent was to live in harmony with the others.

3. Two marshals were appointed to control the movements and discipline of the troops, one English and one Burgundian.

4. Each soldier was to carry on his person two days food.

5. Supplementary food for future days was to be provided by the townsmen of Auxerre and sent forward to the army.

6. Each archer was to provide himself with a wooden stake pointed at each end, to plant in the ground to his front.

7. Each soldier was to keep his exact station in the ranks; penalty for falling out being corporal punishment.

8. One hundred and twenty men-at-arms, 60 English and 60 Burgundian, were next morning to go forward as scouts in front of the army.

9. On getting near the enemy, everyone was to dismount, and the horses were to be led a good half-mile to the rear.

10. No prisoners were to be taken until the issue of the battle had been decided. (A wise provision, for the procedure of taking prisoners, including the arrangement of ransom terms, might be a lengthy matter.)

The allied army retired to rest in a happy and confident frame of mind, feeling that its leaders knew their business. Early next morning, July 30, divine service was held, and at 10 a.m. the whole army marched out, "with much brotherly affection" declares Waurin.

Following the right or eastern bank of the river the army marched slowly, the heat being extreme. At about four miles short of Cravant the enemy was sighted "a short league" away, at a place that I will discuss presently. There the army halted for the day. It was a short march, but no doubt Salisbury desired another 24 hours in which his newly-formed army might shake down together.

On Saturday the 31st the march was continued; but not in the same direction. For the French were seen to be drawn up in an extremely strong position.[1] This is given vaguely as "one mile from Cravant", and no one seems to have tried to identify the exact position. But I think it can be easily done. When passing up the valley by road or train on the other bank, the line of hills appears to be continuous, unbroken by any gap in the line of heights. But if one takes the valley road from Cravant along the right bank, at about one-and-a-half miles downstream from Cravant, a sudden cleft in the heights appears at a point where the ridge is at its highest and steepest. This cleft cuts right through it at right angles. If the French held the crest of the gorge with their left resting on the marshy river valley, which there can be little doubt they did, the position would be well-nigh impregnable to a medieval army, and Salisbury was well advised not to attempt it. Instead, he fell back slightly and then crossed to the west of the river at Vincelles, some four miles short of Cravant.[2] Having crossed the river the army advanced south until it came opposite Cravant. But the river separated it from the town to be relieved and the enemy was found to be lining the right bank. What had happened was that the French army, drawn up on its lofty position, had had a good view of the allied army during its turning movement and had consequently moved parallel to it, "descending the hill" as we are explicitly told, prepared to contest the river crossing.

Stated in this way, the manoeuvre of the English commander

[1] They had been waiting in that position for three days, so they evidently had early information of the Allies' approach.

[2] Ramsay, who seems to have misread Waurin, makes them cross at Champs, nearly three miles further downstream.

does not look impressive, especially if one works on a small-scale map. For such a map does not show the cleft through the ridge, nor the relationship of the river to the town. In actual fact Salisbury's experienced eye told him that the hill position was not to be tackled, while his scouts had no doubt by this time reported to him that the river ran only 160 yards from the western wall of the town. Thus, if the French tried to oppose the crossing there they would be within missile range of the garrison on the town wall: they would find themselves between two fires.

Nevertheless, the fact remains that when the allies reached the river opposite Cravant they found the French lining the far bank, in spite of any hostile action from the garrison of the town. I fancy they must have provided themselves with some form of parados to their position on the river bank, foreseeing such an eventuality.

THE BATTLE OF CRAVANT (See Sketch Map 6, p. 191)

Salisbury ranged his army along the western bank; the English, who must have formed the major portion of the army, being in the front line. Lord Willoughby had the command of the right, and Salisbury the left.

A long pause–a common feature of medieval battles–now ensued. But after some three hours of waiting for the French to move, Salisbury decided to attack. According to Waurin, no doubt an eye-witness, the earl suddenly shouted, "St. George! Banner advance!" and himself dashed into the water, closely followed by his men-at-arms, while the archers, according to their wont, provided "covering fire". Waurin's account is most circumstantial and rings true. The men crossed "each as best he could", the water reaching in some cases to the knees and in others to the waist.[1] The English men-at-arms must have divested themselves of a great part of their armour (though it is curious that Waurin omits all reference to this) and most of

---

[1] From local intelligence (for I could not obtain a boat to make my own soundings when visiting the scene) I learnt that it is about 3 ft. deep, at the present time, with some deep pockets. At this point it is 60 yards wide.

them managed to reach the far bank. Seeing this, the Burgundians followed them into the water. A bitter fight then ensued in the narrow strip of ground between river and town.

Meanwhile, on the right, Lord Willoughby had attacked the bridge. It was held by a Scottish contingent who resisted stoutly, and the contest was fierce.[1]

Eventually the day went in favour of the English on the bridge, and the French began to give way. Perceiving this, the garrison commander, who could see every movement from his watch-tower less than 500 yards away, gave the signal to the troops manning the wall, and a sortie was made from the western gate right into the backs of the French engaged in the bridge struggle. The gallant garrison were so weak with hunger that they could scarcely stagger out, but it was the last straw, and the French army took to flight. But escape was difficult: flight direct to the rear was, of course, intercepted by the town; while to the north the ridge had an almost cliff-like steepness, and for men in armour it would be unscalable. Only to the south was there a practicable line of retreat, and to reach it the fugitives had to pass through the gauntlet constituted by the line of English troops on the one side and the garrison on the other. It seems probable that very few men-at-arms can have made good their escape. Certainly that must have been the case with the Scottish Corps, for they were in the front line, and we are told that the Lombards and Spaniards were the first to fly. The Scots, on the other hand, suffered very heavy casualties – one account gives 4,000 killed, another 3,000. For the French contingent Waurin gives 1,200 killed, including no less than 300 to 400 of noble birth. Even French chroniclers admit to a loss of 2,000 to 3,000 Frenchmen. Many prisoners were taken, one account making the number as high as 2,000. Most important of them all were the two commanders of the army, the Constable of Scotland and the count of Ventadour. The unfortunate Sir John Stewart of Darnley was not only captured but lost an

---

[1] When at a later date the bridge was widened, many skeletons were dredged out of the river under the bridge, a silent testimony to the fight that had waged above it.

eye. (Next time he crossed swords with the English he was again taken prisoner.) The Dauphinist army scattered like sheep with-

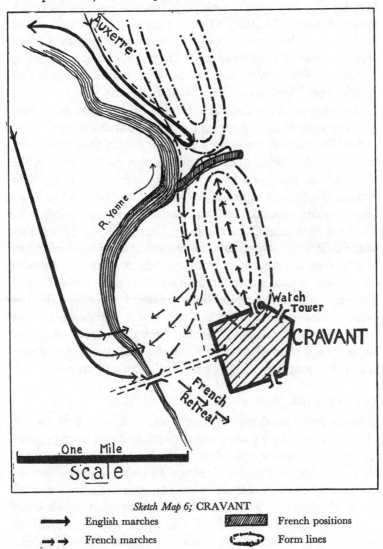

Sketch Map 6; CRAVANT

➡ English marches		French positions	
➡ French marches		Form lines	

out a shepherd. A contingent was sent in pursuit of them, while the remainder of the allied army entered the gates of Cravant to receive a tumultuous welcome. The following day, Sunday, was spent in the town, the pursuers had returned. On the following Monday the two armies took their leave of one another and marched away, the Burgundians to Dijon and the bulk of the English army back to the siege of Montaiguillon. The French army had literally ceased to exist. The victory was 100 per cent. complete. Thus, by a sudden blow of unlimited dash and daring, the Dauphinist offensive plan for the year 1423 was broken beyond repair. When news of the victory reached Paris, bonfires were lit in the streets by the delighted citizens.

But the results of the battle went even further than this. Salisbury was able to send a corps under the earl marshal to assist the Burgundian, John of Luxemburg, in Eastern Champagne, in driving the French right across the river Meuse into Lorraine. More striking still, another corps under the earl of Suffolk, who had been present at Cravant, plunged into the heart of Burgundy as far as Macon, 100 miles south of Cravant and on the borders of Bourbon, a Dauphinist territory. Thereabouts he captured several strong places, the details of which Waurin unfortunately does not provide. Suffolk then detached Captain Glasdale (afterwards to be prominent at Orleans) still further south to the strong castle of La Roche which he "brought to the obedience of King Henry of England and France". With this series of successes the campaign of 1423 practically came to an end.

COMMENTS ON THE BATTLE

No two medieval battles were alike, and none that I know of even approached Cravant in similarity. It was a crisp, clear-cut affair without vicissitudes; and it bore the clear impress of that great soldier Thomas Montagu, earl of Salisbury. From the bare record of his almost unbroken successes and from the confidence that Henry V placed in him, we knew that this could hardly fail to be so, but the details of his work and methods were lacking. One cannot, therefore, be too grateful to John Waurin for his very full and convincing account of the battle, and particularly of the events leading up to it. Waurin tells us just what we wished to know, the things about which most medieval chroniclers are so aggravatingly silent, either because they were clerics and did not know, or because they were soldiers and assumed everyone knew.

Thus we learn six things at least to explain Salisbury's military success. Notice first his successful efforts to weld together the heterogeneous elements in his army on the very eve of battle; the tact with which he employed exactly the same number of Burgundians as English; the sharing of the duties of marshal; the strict injuctions as to mutual behaviour.[1] Notice next his careful foresight and planning–he thought out eventualities and was ready for them. Next, his care for strict discipline, doubtless inherited from his late master. Next, his experienced eye, which told him that the French position was impregnable but that it could be successfully circumvented. Next, his dash and drive in hazarding a wide river crossing under the eyes and missiles of the enemy; and, finally, the fighting spirit that he must have communicated to his troops that induced them to undertake what seemed such a hazardous operation.

I have referred to the sort of details that Waurin, almost alone among ancient chroniclers, provides. These details throw valuable light on what we call logistics and the fighting methods of his age.[2] When Professor Newall in his *The English Conquest of Normandy* wishes to treat of such matters he goes to Cravant for his authority (though quoting Monstrelet instead of the source which the latter copied). As regards weapons and armour, Waurin tells us how the weight of the armour on that hot July day–the very height of the summer–bore down on and wearied the men-at-arms, and he mentions specifically that these men-at-arms were provided with lances, hatchets and swords. Shields had by this time practically disappeared from the battlefield, owing to the increased protection given by plate armour.

[1] The British army has for centuries had to fight with allies, and it is tempting to trace the success of Marlborough and Wellington in their relations with their allies to the example set them by such men as the earl of Salisbury.

[2] The injunction against taking prisoners is an interesting one, doubtless a hark-back to Agincourt.

APPENDIX

Considering the importance of the battle of Cravant the chroniclers paid remarkably little attention to it, with one noteable exception. This is, perhaps, not to be wondered at on the part of the French writers, but the Scots had nothing to be ashamed about, still less the English; yet both nations have dealt with it perfunctorily. Walsingham had finished writing and Edward Hall, nearly a century later, only provides a list of names. Nor have the Scots much to say about their defeat. It is left to a single Burgundian writer, serving in the English ranks, to provide us with over nine-tenths of the details of the battle. John de Waurin had, it will be recalled, also fought on the English side eight years before on the field of Agincourt, of which battle he provided the most valuable account. It is the same for Cravant. Indeed, it is a case of, "Eclipse first; the rest nowhere". Of the Burgundians, Le Fèvre (sire of St. Remy) condensed his compatriot's account, merely adding a few facts concerning numbers. Monstrelet also condensed, but added nothing whatever. Chastellaine ignored the battle.

The chief French chronicler to notice the battle was Gilles le Bouvier, or Berry the Herald, whose chronicle for the battle is in Godefroy's *Histoire de Charles VII* (1661) (just as his account of Baugé was hidden in the same author's *Charles VI*). His account, though short, adds some particulars as regards personnel on the Dauphinist side, and does not attempt to conceal the extent of the disaster; indeed, he says that the French lost 2,000 to 3,000 in killed and captured. The chronicle of Guillaume Cousinot is also difficult to track down, for it is embodied in a volume edited by Vallet de Viriville in 1850 entitled *Chronique de la Pucelle*, and is generally cited as *Gestes des Nobles Français*, though there is nothing on the title page to indicate its presence in the volume. Cousinot seems to have drawn his account mainly from le Bouvier, but he is even more emphatic about the catastrophic nature of the French defeat. More than once he uses the phrase that it was "grand dommage au roy Charles".

No modern English writer has attempted an adequate description of the battle.

VISITING THE BATTLEFIELD

Cravant is one of the easiest battlefields to find and to follow, although it is one of the least known. Motorists rush past it, within a few yards of its western gate, without so much as seeing it; for the modern road, instead of entering the walled town, bends sharply to the right,[1] and the motorist's eyes are glued to the road. Yet they have just passed over the very bridge on which Lord Willoughby had such a tussle with the Scottish defenders–the same bridge that had echoed to the feet of English soldiers only 12 months before, en route to the relief of Cosne. The town wall is almost intact and the three gateways plainly visible, whilst the watch-tower is in an excellent state of repair. This remarkable tower contains a girdle of circular apertures high up in its wall, too small for the discharge of any missile and quite obviously intended solely as look-outs. I know of no similar tower in England, though some may exist on the Continent. The tower obviously played an important part, not only in the actual battle but in the defence of the town during the siege. Approach to the town from every direction is clearly visible from it.

There is no good hotel in Cravant, but accommodation is easy in the interesting old town of Auxerre, only nine miles to the north, and there is a good train service between the two towns.

Thanks to Waurin's careful description it is easy to follow the course of the battle and to picture the scene, standing on the river bank within sight of the bridge. The watch-tower can also be ascended and from it every detail of the ground can be seen. There can, indeed, be comparatively few other medieval battles where one is so sure of the topographical features as Cravant.

---

[1] On the bend of the road there is a conveniently situated cafe, also ignored by the motorists.

CHAPTER XII

VERNEUIL:
"A SECOND AGINCOURT"

AFTER the victory of Cravant, affairs, both military and political, continued to go well for the English. On the political side this was almost entirely due to the regent, John, duke of Bedford, who is assessed by Oman as "almost the equal of Henry V as soldier, administrator and diplomatist".[1] By his good sense, fair dealing and tact he managed to endear himself to the Burgundian party, whom he placed in charge of the government in all regions except Normandy. The *Bourgeois de Paris*, a reliable witness, writes of him:

"This Duke was a strenuous man, humane and just, who loved greatly those of the French *noblesse* who adhered to him, virtuously striving to raise them to honour. Wherefore as long as he lived he was greatly admired and cherished by Normans and French of his party."

The details of his administration do not concern us here, but they had a direct bearing upon the military operations, inasmuch as a close and cordial cooperation in the field was maintained between the English and Burgundian armies.

This was well illustrated during the autumn and winter of 1423 in the eastern region where the Burgundian leader, John of Luxemburg, worked hand-in-hand with the earl of Salisbury and his lieutenant, Sir Thomas Rempston. The "tidying up" process continued steadily in the Laon-St. Quentin area, against the garrisons that were still holding out under the Dauphinist leaders La Hire and Poton de Xantrailles, whom we now meet for the first time. Occasional setbacks there were; notably the loss of Compiègne by the Burgundians and their failure to retake it. Bedford had to do the work for them himself early in the following year.

The year 1423 had been a good one for the allies. That of

[1] *Political History of England*, IV, p. 289.

1424 was to bring even more striking successes, and this despite the fact that the English, with their allies, were contending against not only the Dauphinists but also the Scots. A constant trickle of Scottish troops had been landing in the country for some years, and in April 1424 a complete army of 6,500 troops under the "war-battered" earl of Douglas landed and joined forces with the Dauphinists in the south. Alexander Douglas, in superseding his son-in-law the earl of Buchan, broke the promise he had made that he would join Henry V if King James were restored to Scotland. James was released and he re-entered Scotland in March, but, despite this, a month later Douglas landed in France, where the Dauphin created him duke of Touraine.

Meanwhile, the English successes were continuing. The ubiquitous and indefatigable earl of Salisbury, with Burgundian aid, subdued nearly all the towns and castles that still held out in the eastern theatre while in the north Le Crotoy fell in March.

Hitherto, the duke of Bedford had confined himself strictly to the instructions bequeathed to him by his brother; and he had carried them out with considerable success. He had established sound and settled government in Paris; he had safeguarded the English conquests in Normandy; he had "tidied up" nearly the whole of the region of northern France; and, above all, he had maintained friendly relations and close co-operation with Burgundy. The time had now come when he felt he could strike out on a line of policy of his own, of a more ambitious nature. In other words, he decided to carry the war into the enemy's country, starting with the conquest of Anjou and Maine. He was encouraged thereto by the numerous contingents of reinforcements that had of recent months joined him from England (notably among them being that of John, Lord Talbot) and amounting in all to about 5,000 men.

The first step was to collect a field army, for at the moment most of the troops were swallowed up in the ever-increasing number of garrisons, and in the scattered columns laying siege to towns and castles, or repelling local raids.

The basis of this army of invasion was the English reinforcement. Next came the contingents from garrison towns. The Normandy garrisons were squeezed dry: out of 4,000 troops so employed Bedford laid hands on 2,000. Finally, he called off the mobile columns, including one now operating far to the south, in Burgundy, under the earl of Salisbury. (Its progress had been so marked that towns as far distant as Lyons began to tremble for their safety.)

By these means the regent managed to assemble at Rouen by mid-July an army at least 10,000 strong. Thither he himself went on the 20th of the month, for he had determined to mark the importance of the operation by taking the command himself. It is probable that it was while at Rouen that the news reached him that the Dauphinists were also collecting a large army, with evident aggressive intentions.

The French command had indeed thrown off the semi-stupor which had afflicted them ever since the day of Agincourt. A resolute attempt was to be made to drive the invader out of Normandy. To this end a levy was declared throughout southern France. Fresh Scottish contingents were enticed over, and mercenaries were raised in Lombardy and elswhere. By these means an army something over 15,000 strong was raised. It assembled along the lower Loire, with advanced headquarters at Le Mans, 40 miles north of that river. By a coincidence both armies were ready to set out practically simultaneously. Furthermore, they both directed their steps towards the same objective.

Some months previously the town of Ivry, 30 miles west of Paris, had been captured by a sudden raid. Bedford despatched the earl of Suffolk to retake it in June. The town fell to him at once, but the garrison shut themselves up in the castle. Mining operations were then resorted to. On July 5, however, the garrison agreed to surrender on August 14, unless previously relieved.[1] It was natural, therefore, that both armies should set their faces in that direction, the one to relieve it, the other to

[1] Most authorities give the date as August 15, the Feast of the Assumption, but Martin Simpson has shown in the *English Historical Review* that the eve of the Feast, not the Feast-day itself is correct. (E.H.R., January 1934.)

effect its speedy fall and, if possible, to cross swords with its opponents. Since the French also announced this intention, a battle appeared imminent.

On August 11, the duke of Bedford marched south from Rouen, arriving the same day at Evreux, 20 miles north-west of Ivry. A contingent of Burgundians under L'Isle Adam had joined the army and, at the last moment, the earl of Salisbury. Meanwhile, the French army was approaching Ivry from Le Mans, 75 miles to the south-west, and had reached Noancourt, 15 miles short of the town. On the 13th, Bedford resumed his march, and that evening joined forces with the earl of Suffolk before the castle of Ivry.

The rival hosts were now within a day's march of each other, and the English fully expected a battle on the morrow – the day fixed for the surrender. The regent drew up his army, ready for attack; but nothing happened; or rather, all that happened was that the garrison marched out and surrendered. It turned out that the advanced scouts of the relieving army had come into contact with the English patrols; it had then been reported to the Franco-Scottish leaders that the main English army had anticipated them. A council of war was thereupon held to decide what action to take. It was of a stormy nature. On the one hand were the Scots and the younger French leaders; on the other, the senior French commanders. The Scots had been "kicking up their heels" at Tours for four months, and were spoiling for a fight with their detested opponents; but the French leaders, the duke of Alençon and the viscounts of Narbonne and Aumâle, had not forgotten the lesson of Agincourt, and were anxious to avoid battle and fall back. Eventually a compromise was reached. The army was to avoid a battle in the open with the English, but was to try and capture as many English towns on the Norman border as could be done without drawing on a battle. A start would be made with the little walled town of Verneuil, which they had passed on their left hand during the previous advance (see Sketch Map 5). Thither they directed their march, and next day effected an entry by the simple expedient of declaring that the English army had been defeated and was in full retreat.[1] Meanwhile the duke of Bedford, after receiving the keys of Ivry castle and leaving a substantial garrison, had taken what appears on the face of it an astonishing step. Sending off Suffolk with 1,600 men to shadow the French army, he himself returned with his main army that day, August 14, to Evreux. This step has baffled most students, and, indeed, the whole campaign has been baffling owing to the mistake in the date of the surrender. Bedford regained Evreux that night and spent the next day, the Feast of the Assumption, in pious devotions in the cathedral. The only possible explanation is that he had taken the measure of the French generals, realized that there was no danger of immediate attack, and depended on Suffolk to keep him informed of their movements. Meanwhile, being of an intensely religious nature, he was desirous of celebrating the feast in Evreux cathedral. However we look upon it, we cannot palliate such a transgression of an elementary principle of strategy, one which makes it impossible to rate John of Bedford in the very highest rank of military commanders.

Thus, August 15 was spent by the two armies quietly in the respective towns of Evreux and Verneuil, while Suffolk camped in the open between the two, near Breteuil and Damville, some 12 miles north-east of Verneuil (Sketch Map 1). That evening Suffolk sent word to the regent that the French were in possession of Verneuil and Bedford resolved to march next day to meet them in the field. But before doing so he took another step that requires some explanation. He sent away L'Isle Adam with his Burgundian contingent (stated by *The Brut, Continuation* as 3,000 men) to resume their siege operations in Picardy, stating that he had no need of so large an army. One can but suppose that he had in mind his brother's famous remark on the eve of Agincourt, and reckoned to stimulate the pride and confidence of his troops thereby. If this be so, it was

---

[1] As corroboration of this story, they marched some unfortunate Scots troops in sight of the garrison, tied to their horses tails, to represent English prisoners.

certainly a magnificent gesture, and one is loath to condemn it.

On August 16, then, the English army set out to meet its opponents once more, and halted that night at Damville, a 12-mile march.[1] Here, again, a query arises. Why halt so far from the enemy? His troops had had a whole day's rest, and it should have been possible at least to join forces with Suffolk, and to marshall the whole army for battle within reach of Verneuil. Of course it is possible that Bedford possessed more precise and accurate information as to the situation and intentions of the enemy than we are aware of; but it is not likely, for that enemy was himself at the time in two minds as to what to do. Controversy was again raging: to fight or not to fight! And again Douglas and his men were emphatically for fighting. The northerners were not proving very congenial comrades to their allies, one of whom commented on the fanatical hatred displayed by them for their English opponents. However, the Scots got their way this time, and next morning, August 17, the whole allied army was deployed for battle on the open plain one mile to the north of the walls of Verneuil. From its ramparts, and especially from the grim and gaunt Tour Gris of Henry I, spectators of the oncoming battle were to have an excellent view.

*   *   *

A description of the *terrain* will not take long. The ground has changed but little since the battle, in spite of its contiguity to the town. The old town-ditch and traces of the ramparts still remain. To the north the ground is almost flat for one mile. Just to the left of the Damville road lies the farm of St. Denis, the site of a chapel built on the battlefield over the graves of the French dead. It thus pin-points the battlefield as precisely as the abbey at Hastings or the church on Shrewsbury battlefield. The Damville road then slopes very gently downwards for 600 yards into a slight dip at the edge of the forest, through a gap

---

[1] Some Norman contingents, seeing that a battle appeared inevitable next day, deserted and went home. This must have caused the Regent to regret his action in parting with his Burgundians.

in which the road passes. The ground then rises gently through the forest. The country is cultivated, open and hedgeless, as it probably was at the time of the battle.

THE BATTLE (Sketch Map 7, see p. 205)

On the morning of August 17, 1424, the Franco-Scottish army was early astir, for even if messages had not passed on the previous evening between Bedford and Douglas, as some aver, they were fully aware of the approach of the English army. There are not lacking symptoms of confusion and muddle in the marshalling of this heterogenous array, with at least three tongues–French, English and Italian–and contingents drawn from a wide area, including Brittany. Things were not made easier by the acrimonious conduct of the Scottish leaders who quarrelled among themselves for precedence. There was, doubtless, some intermixture of nationalities, but in the main it may be said that the French occupied the left and the Scots the right of the position. Each division was nominally in three lines, but the three soon became merged in one. On the two flanks were posted smallish bodies of mounted men, as at Agincourt, the remainder of the army being dismounted. The crossbowmen, of whom we hear but little, were interspersed among the men-at-arms. Of artillery in either army we hear nothing. One may picture each division as occupying a frontage of about 500 yards, i.e. 1,000 yards in all; the Damville road dividing the two divisions, and the front line passing through the modern 2-kilometre stone (measured from Verneuil).

The supreme commander was the count d'Aumâle, but it is safe to say that during the battle he exercised no practical influence on its course and particularly on the Scottish division.

While the allied army was debouching on to the plain of Verneuil the English were marching through the forest of Piseux, collecting the scattered forces of the earl of Suffolk *en route*. The combined strength of the army was now reduced to between 8,000 and 9,000, or rather more than half their opponents. The regent's chief lieutenant was the earl of Salisbury.

Nearly all the leaders who afterwards distinguished themselves in the war were present, including the earl of Suffolk, Lord Scales, Sir John Fastolf and Captain Gladstone, the only notable absentee being Lord John Talbot.

*   *   *

As the English descended the hill through the opening in the forest, the allied host could be seen drawn up for battle about one mile away. A glance was sufficient to show Bedford that their flanks were "in the air" but that they were supported by mounted troops. The march continued, down into the dip and up the very gentle slope towards the allied position. At a convenient distance outside missile range Bedford halted and deployed his army, drawing it up parallel to and on the same frontage as his opponents. For Bedford was a conventional soldier of the age of chivalry. Not for him was the surprise action, or the flank attack. He conformed to the practice of his great-grandfather, his grandfather and his brother. After all, he had good precedents. Moreover, he followed his brother's formation at Agincourt pretty closely: everyone was dismounted, the front was in two divisions (of which he himself commanded the right, and Salisbury the left), the men-at-arms occupying the centre of each division, and the archers both flanks (see appendix), and the front consisted of a single line. The sole departure from Agincourt practice was that the regent provided a mobile reserve (described by Waurin as a baggage-guard) of 2,000 archers, whom he stationed to the west of the road, whilst the baggage was slightly further in rear and to the east of the road. Mindful of the fate of the English baggage at Agincourt, Bedford took novel steps to safeguard it: the vehicles were drawn up in close order along the perimeter, while the horses, tethered head to tail in pairs, were placed immediately outside it, in order to supply additional protection to the camp or leaguer other than that supplied by the pages and varlets. Moreover the latter, having no horses to hold, would be free to ply their weapons in active defence.

*   *   *

When both the armies had completed their deployment a pause ensued, a normal precursor of a medieval battle as we have seen. This was to be no chance clash such as the affair of Baugé, but a rare and ordered ordeal by battle on the part of the main armies of England and France–the first for nearly nine years–the only abnormality being the absence of the head of the French state, the 22-year-old Dauphin. It was even more than that: it was, in a sense, an ordeal by battle of three nations, for the Scots regarded themselves as fighting for Scotland and against England rather than for France. And they had Cravant to revenge.

During this pre-battle pause, the duke of Bedford sent forward a herald to Alexander, earl of Douglas, enquiring blandly as to what rules he proposed to observe in the coming fight. If the record is correct he received the grim reply that the Scots would neither give nor receive any quarter.

At about four o'clock, according to Bedford, the two hosts, as if by mutual compact, advanced simultaneously–again as at Agincourt; indeed, that name must have been in the forefront of every man's mind on the field. The duke of Bedford gave the traditional signal, "Avaunt, banners!" and the troops, after kneeling down and reverently kissing the ground, responded with, "St. George, Bedford". The allies countered with "St. Denis, Monjoie!" The English line then stepped forward, slowly and deliberately, uttering what Fortescue describes as

"a mighty cry, the forerunner of that stern and appalling shout which, four centuries later was to strike hesitation into so fine a soldier as Soult."

The allies, on the other hand, advanced impetuously and raggedly–for which the youthful Scottish troops were afterwards blamed.

Each archer carried a double-pointed stake, and when within missile range, say 250 yards, they halted and the stakes were planted in front of the front line. Up to this moment the

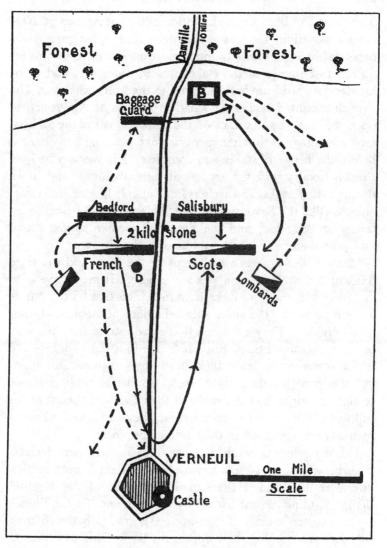

Sketch Map 7; VERNEUIL

D Ferme St. Denis

B English baggage

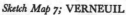 } English

 } French

procedure had been a close imitation of that at Agincourt. Now came a variation. The season was high summer, the ground was presumably at its hardest, and some trouble and time was required to hammer in the stakes which, moreover, had to be handed forward from hand to hand to the front-rank men. The French mounted bodies who had orders, as at Agincourt, to open the battle by an attack on the flanks or rear of the archers, took advantage of the time spent in stake-planting and charged before the hedge of stakes was complete. The western body of French cavalry took the archers at a disadvantage and broke through their ranks. The archers instinctively herded into closer clumps (like the Saxons at Mount Badon, and the English infantry at Waterloo) and the French horsemen surged round and past them, and pushed on against the reserve.

Many of the archers were swept to the rear, and the right flank of Bedford's division was left exposed. It must have been an anxious moment for duke John in this his first battle. But he was supported by the admirable behaviour of the men-at-arms of his division. They exhibited that steadfastness that had now become characteristic of English troops in a tight corner—and which was never to desert them in the ages to come. Disregarding the peril on their right, these wonderful soldiers strode straight on right into the ranks of their foes and, bereft of the support of their bowmen on the right, they laid into the French men-at-arms stationed in their immediate front.

The struggle was tough, tougher than at Agincourt declares Waurin, who should know having been present in both battles. But after 45 minutes the superior prowess of the English, though fighting against odds of over two to one (for the French army consisted mainly of men-at-arms), gradually forced their way forward pushing their opponents back. Bedford is said to have wielded a two-handed axe (reminiscent of Harold at Hastings). He had dismounted from the bay charger that had carried him into the battle; he was "large of body, strong of limbs, wise and bold in arms" writes Waurin, and John Hardyng declares that "the regent was there that day as a lion".

Aumâle's own division which was engaged with Bedford's division gradually crumbled up under the intolerable pressure; and then arrived the moment of breaking-strain when a complete formation turns and flees to a man. The French men-at-arms scattered and made for the sheltering walls of Verneuil. Indeed, it is likely that the knowledge of the friendly shelter so close in the rear increased the temptation to retreat. But, alas for them, the pursuit was so close and hotly carried out that many of the fugitives could not reach the gates but plunged into the town ditch, where large numbers of them were drowned,[1] and Aumâle himself was killed.

The presence of this town ditch proved an additional god-send to Bedford for it enabled him to call off the pursuit, collect his scattered troops and return to the battlefield, where fighting was still going on.

This brings us to the earl of Salisbury's division on the English left, where his troops were ranged against the Scots. An even stiffer resistance was put up by these young and untried but doughty troops, who were, of course, picked men of splendid fighting material. They gave as good as they received, or nearly so, for some time, and the sight of their allies on their left quitting the field did not dismay them. Here for the moment we must leave them, fighting lustily in a foreign land for a foreign king.

The mounted body on the allied right flank consisted of 600 Lombard mercenaries. Fine horsemen they were, and under good leadership. Their commander could see that the hostile waggon-leaguer was in their immediate front, apparently unguarded by the English archers in the rear, who were by now engaged with the oncoming French cavalry. The Lombards seized their opportunity, and swinging round the English left flank attacked the baggage. It is, of course, impossible to say how far this encircling movement was influenced by the fire of the archers on Salisbury's left flank. Horses in a mounted action have a way of "taking charge" and swerving away from the missiles, carrying their riders with them willy-nilly. Be this as

[1] One report states that the inhabitants closed the gates in their faces.

it may, the result was a complete success for the bold Italian horsemen. They cut down the pages and varlets who offered resistance, broke into and pillaged the baggage-leaguer and loosed and made away with a number of the tethered horses. This was pretty smart work, especially as it was carried out almost under the eyes of the English reserve. The attention of the latter, however, was taken up by the tussle with the cavalry on the other flank, though their commander is open to criticism for not detaching some of his numerous formation to the help of the hard-pressed pages.

The triumph of the Lombards, however, was short lived. As soon as the French cavalry had been disposed of, the reserve turned on the Italians and drove them pell-mell in utter flight right off the field. The success of the French cavalry had been considerable, if only temporary. There is good evidence of fugitives fleeing far to the rear, declaring, in the manner of such people, that all was lost. One of them, a captain Young, was afterwards charged with taking no less than 500 men off the field for which he was afterwards hanged, drawn and quartered – a fate which, complacently observes *The Brut*, was quite right.

Meanwhile, the fight between Salisbury's division and the Scots was proceeding. The reserve, having now successfully disposed of both parties of enemy cavalry was available for further action. But Bedford, far away in pursuit of Aumâle's division, was in no position to give them orders. It mattered not. English archers had shown at Agincourt and elsewhere that they possessed in a high degree, in addition to their other virtues, that of initiative. Looking round for a fresh foe, they could see, and hear, the battle still waging on the left front. This presented a grand opportunity to repeat the example of the captal de Buch in a similar situation at Poitiers. Forming up again and wheeling round to their right they charged into the exposed right flank of the Scottish division, uttering what the good Waurin calls "un merveilleu cry" (sic).[1] The unfortunate Scots, assailed from

---

[1] Ferdinand Lot goes perhaps too far when he calls this action "une initiative inattendue, inouie à l'époque." (Op. cit., II, p. 23.)

two sides at once, were now almost at their last gasp. But yet worse was to come.

We left Bedford with his division on the bank of the town ditch, reassembling his victorious troops. Breathless and fatigued as they must have been after nearly an hour's violent physical exertion followed by a pursuit, or, more likely, a painful waddle in full armour in the heat of a summer day, fain would they rest, and scout for drinking-water to relieve their parched lips. But there was more work to be done. Salisbury, outnumbered as he was by his opponents, must be supported. Back into the fight the weary men-at-arms therefore plodded. They arrived in time to strike into the rear of the Scots. This action sealed the fate of the northerners. Now completely surrounded there was nothing left to them but to sell their lives dearly. Escape was impossible, surrender was out of the question, for had not they declared that there was to be no quarter on either side? And it is pretty evident that they were slaughtered where they stood, almost to a man. The exultant English hacked them down with triumphant cries of, "A Clarence! A Clarence!" an obvious allusion to the Battle of Baugé (though it had already been avenged at Cravant).

When the last Scot lay prone the battle came to an end. A great part of the French rank and file had escaped but their leaders had stayed to fight it out, and they were one and all accounted for: Aumâle, the commander, Narbonne, Ventadour, Tonnerre, all were dead, and the duke of Alençon and the marshal Lafayette were prisoners.[1] The Scottish losses were catastrophic, as was only to be expected under the circumstances. Douglas, his son James, and his son-in-law the earl of Buchan, his second-in-command, were also dead. No less than fifty Scottish Gentlemen of rank died that day. Thereafter till the end of the war no considerable Scottish force took the field.

Two days later Bedford wrote a letter to Sir Thomas Rempston, at Guise, stating by count of the heralds no less than 7,262

[1] *Harl*, MS. 788, gives the names of 35 French Lords and Knights taken prisoner. Only about 200 prisoners in all were made.

enemies were killed. In a victory bulletin to London the regent might have purposely exaggerated the number of dead, but it seems unlikely that he should do so to one of his junior officers in France. Moreover, the number seems inherently probable; of 6,000 Scots only a handful can have escaped, and this would leave about 1,500 Frenchmen killed out of perhaps 10,000–ten per cent. No wonder this battle has been likened to that of Agincourt and dubbed by French writers "Un autre Azincourt".

The English losses were about 1,000, a by no means negligible figure. But it was worth the sacrifice. The French army was leaderless, dispirited and dispersed. The Scottish army had ceased to exist. That evening English troops entered Verneuil, and next day a solemn service of thanksgiving was held in the great church. They had much to be thankful for. It was, indeed, a second Agincourt.

*   *   *

I have only one comment on the battle. Search my memory how I will, I cannot call to mind any medieval battle that involved so happy a co-operation of different formations at a critical juncture as that of Salisbury's division, Bedford's men-at-arms and the English reserve at the battle of Verneuil.

APPENDIX

SOURCES

Owing to the scarcity of modern literature on the battle I will devote more space than usual to the subject of sources. They are fairly numerous, at least 19 contemporary or near-contemporary writers dealing with it, though most of them very briefly. They can be grouped under four headings, English, Burgundian, Dauphinist and Scottish, and they differ but little from the chroniclers of Baugé. The main differences are as follows. On the English side we get an invaluable contribution in *Harleian* MS. 53, included in Brie's edition of *The Brut* as *Continuation H.*

This was first printed by Brie in 1906, and it had not been used by any historian previous to that date nor, so far as I can ascertain, by any historian since. But it is essential to the understanding of the battle, the author being the sole authority for the pursuit of Aumâle by Bedford's division to the town walls, and the subsequent return of the English to the field. We have reached an arid period in our English chroniclers (which possibly accounts for the neglect of the reign of Henry VI by historians). But it is, perhaps, legitimate to include the sixteenth-century chronicler Edward Hall, who adds some useful details about the battle, including the statement that the English had archers in the centre as well as on the wings. Of the Burgundians, though Monstrelet's account is the best known, that of Waurin is *facile princeps*, which is not surprising seeing that he fought in the English ranks, though in what capacity and in what part of the field we unfortunately do not know.

Both Monstrelet and Le Fèvre copy Waurin slavishly. A newcomer among the Burgundians, however, deserves mention, the Bourgeois de Paris, whose *Journal*, though more concerned with the political and social events in Paris, is the work of a contemporary, and fairly reliable one. Of the Dauphinists, perhaps the most original is Raoulet (whom we have cited earlier), and the most copious Thomas Basin, in his *Histoire de Charles VII* (translated from the original Latin into French by E. Samarin). The only really useful Scottish source is again the *Liber Pluscardine*.

No modern writer shows evidence of having visited the battlefield except H. R. Clinton, in his *From Crécy to Assaye* (1881) but he was, of course, handicapped by not having the use of *The Brut*, so his account is incomplete. Other modern writers seem to treat the battle perfunctorily and uncritically: for example, the most recent, Professor Ferdinand Lot, solemnly repeats without comment the (inevitable) story that Bedford struck down Douglas with his own hand. Lot seems, as ever, more interested in the numbers engaged than in the actual fighting. Though usually a careful student of English sources, he does not seem to have been aware of *The Brut Continuation*. And, of course, the English historians Fortescue, Ramsay and Oman laboured under the same disadvantage. (It is a pity Dr. Waugh did not turn his attention to this period.)

It is, perhaps, not surprising that Scottish and French historians have paid little attention to the battle. For example, Michelet in his *History of France* devotes exactly two lines to it. Of the most recent French writer, Ferdinand Lot I have already spoken, and there is really no one else worthy of mention but Vallet de Viriville, who incorporates the most detailed account in his *Histoire de Charles VII* (1861). Du Fresnes de Beaucourt is almost valueless for our purpose.

Finally, for the most documented and best informed, though brief, account of the battle we are indebted to an American, Professor R. A. Newall, whose *The English Conquest of Normandy* was published in 1924. Since that date the only reference to the battle or campaign I can find in the English tongue is an article in the *English Historical Review* for January 1934 by Martin A. Simpson, who, however, stops short of the actual battle.

*   *   *

THE NUMBERS

English. The most careful and most reliable computation of the English numbers has been made by Professor Newall in his *The English Conquest of Normandy*. He computes that Bedford set out from Rouen with 10,000 troops. To these must be added the contingent under Suffolk at Ivry; but we must deduct the garrison left at Ivry, the Burgundian contingent sent away, and the deserters from the Norman contingent on the eve of the battle. We shall probably not be far wrong in assessing the number that actually took part in the battle at between 8,000 and 9,000. This practically tallies with the figure of 9,000 given in *The Brut Continuation*.

French. Here we are confronted by an unusual phenomenon. Almost invariably we find in medieval times that the protagonists on each side exaggerate the numbers of their enemies and diminish that of their own side, but here we get the exact opposite. The average figure given by the Dauphinists (and Burgundians) is 18,000 to 20,000 Franco-Scots; whilst the duke of Bedford puts it as low as 14,000 in his letter to Sir Thomas Rempston. It is true that, writing only two days after the battle, he could make no more than a guess from the evidence of his own eyes, and his knowledge of the numbers slain and taken. Apart from these assessments, the only firm figures we have to work on is the number of Scots. We may asume that every available man was put into the field, and, allowing for four months' wastage, the total must have been at least 6,000. Now all the accounts seem to imply that the main constituent of the allied army was French, to whom must be added the Lombards. If we put this figure at about 9,000 we get a total of about 15,000. Splitting the difference between the assessments of Bedford and the French we get 17,000. If we split the difference between 15,000 and 17,000 we get a total of about 16,000, and that is as far as we can go. The fact that the allied casualities in killed and captured, and excluding wounded, amounted to nearly 8,000, shows that the grand total cannot have been far short of 16,000.

Few modern writers attempt an assessment of the numbers. Ramsay states briefly that the English "may have been 2,000 to 3,000 men" and leaves it at that. One would be glad to know the reasoning that led to this conclusion. Oman gives no figures at all, and Lot, after citing fairly fully the medieval figures, which are unanimous in giving a clear superiority to the French, refers inconsequentially to this superiority as "réelle ou prétendue" (p. 24). But this lame conclusion–or inconclusion– does not surprise us.

* * *

THE RECONSTRUCTION OF THE BATTLE

Until *The Brut Continuation H* was published the heavy losses of the French compared with the Scots was something of a puzzle. But this invaluable document ties up the battle into a comprehensive whole. It also establishes an unusual action in medieval warfare – the concentration on to the vital point of two widely separated units at the critical moment.

This document also enables us to locate the French division on the left of the line. Previous chroniclers were hopelessly at variance on the point, French sources placing Frenchmen in the front line and Scots in the third; whereas the Scottish source, the *Liber Pluscardine*, reverses this position. The fact is, both nations were anxious to appear to have borne the brunt of the fighting. In reality both accounts can be reconciled if we predicate, as I have done, that the Scots, as a formation, were on the right, and the French on the left. On this assumption, and on this alone, the battle seems to make sense, though I am not aware that anyone has suggested this formation before.

I have also disregarded the statement of Waurin (followed by nearly all writers) that the formation in rear was a baggage-guard. Doubtless the guarding of the baggage formed part of its duties, but there must have been more to it than that. Otherwise how are we to explain the original situation of this body, not with nor directly in front of the baggage-leaguer, but on the other flank? The commander of the reserve cannot have believed that his primary duty was to guard the baggage. Moreover, Bedford would hardly have allotted upwards of 20 per cent. of his force for this sole duty.

The last point concerns the formation of the archers. Practically all writers have taken Waurin's statement that the archers were "on the wings" to mean that they were formed in two bodies only, on the two flanks of the army. But this would constitute a striking departure from the formation of Agincourt and Crecy, and we have seen that in all other respects except the reserve (for which there was an obvious explanation) Bedford copied the Agincourt formation almost slavishly. It seemed evident to me that Waurin carelessly omitted the words "of divisions" after "on the flanks", and that his intention was to say that they took up the normal formation, that is, on both flanks of each division (though there may in addition have been, as at Agincourt, bodies of "army archers", as we might call them, on the extreme flanks of the line). Partial confirmation of this view is given by *Hall's Chronicle* which avers that archers were posted both in the front of the battle and on the wings.

CHAPTER XIII

FROM VERNEUIL TO ORLEANS

ON the morrow of the battle of Verneuil the prospects for the English cause were bright. A French field army no longer existed and the Dauphin would find it impossible to create a new one at short notice, for he had spent all available money in raising the one that had just foundered. Humanly speaking, there was nothing to prevent Bedford from advancing straight on Bourges and capturing it. Such action might have resulted in the ending of the war, for the Dauphinists, seeing the utter impotence of the French government, might have lost heart and given up the contest—even as did the inhabitants of Paris in 1360. Of course the Dauphin might have fallen back and set up another capital still further south, such as Toulouse,[1] and the war might have dragged on. Even so, an advance on Bourges would seem to have held out the best chances of a decision and the end of hostilities.

But the duke of Bedford did not take it. Instead he clung to his original plan, the conquest of Maine and Anjou, though he extended his objective to include the reduction of all the territory to the north of the Loire, and an attempt in the west to capture that almost impregnable fortress, Mont St. Michel.

To effect this he divided and scattered his army, entrusting the campaign in Maine to Sir John Fastolf and Lord Scales, the advance to the Loire to the earls of Salisbury and Suffolk, while Sir Nicholas Burdet was directed against Mont St. Michel. He himself departed to Rouen, ostensibly to punish the Norman deserters from Verneuil.

This conduct may appear supine to modern students of war, but before condemning Bedford too severely we should remember two things. First, in those days a war of sieges, such as was now being resumed, was the normal method of fighting;

[1] And his domains might then have become the prototype of "Vichy France".

second, both Edward III after Crecy and Henry V after Agincourt had not seized somewhat similar opportunities. There
may therefore have been some adverse factors against such a
course of which we, at this distance of time, are not aware. But,
not knowing of any such, it is difficult for us to place John of
Bedford in the highest rank of generals.

But whatever criticism may be passed on the regent, the
military situation remained favourable and indeed continued to
improve. In all but one theatre progress was registered. It was
perhaps slow, but it was sure, and in the months immediately
following the battle of Verneuil, the greater part of Maine and
Anjou was over-run, the campaign towards the Loire was put in
motion, and the few strongholds still holding out in Picardy and
Champagne surrendered, and with them the formidable captain La Hire. Best of all perhaps was the loyal and successful
co-operation of the duke of Burgundy. He conducted a campaign
far to the south and almost reached the town of Macon. Only
opposite Mont St. Michel was the general advance stayed.

*   *   *

It seemed to be a case of "all over but the shouting", when
suddenly one of those totally unexpected turns of fortune
occurred which are at once so upsetting to calculations yet so
intriguing to the military historian. To explain what was about
to happen we must hark back to the previous year, and dabble
in purely political history.

It all started in a simple and apparently harmless way. The
young Jacqueline, countess of Hainault and Holland in her
own right, had married the boorish duke of Brabant. In 1421
she quarrelled with her husband and fled to the court of England,
where she fell in love with the very presentable duke of Gloucester. After some difficulty, she obtained a dubious divorce and
married Duke Humphrey. Now the duke of Brabant had
assumed the government of Hainault and Holland, and Jacqueline was naturally eager to regain her own dominions. Equally
naturally, as it seems to me, her new husband was eager to help

her regain her just rights. To this end, he started raising contingents in England to help in the work of ejecting the Brabanters. For this he has been unmercifully condemned by practically all historians, for complications were bound to arise. The trouble was that the duke of Brabant came of the younger branch of the family of Burgundy, and duke Philip hotly espoused the cause of his cousin.

Matters came to a head in October, 1424, when Duke Humphrey and countess Jacqueline landed in Flanders with a contingent of mercenaries. Very soon the countess was in possession of her old domains, and Humphrey sent a force into Brabant which ravaged the country up to the gates of Brussels. The fat was in the fire. Duke Philip threatened even to go to war with England, and a heated correspondence passed between him and Gloucester. Humphrey wrote that Philip ought to espouse the cause of Jacqueline rather than that of duke John of Brabant, and technically there is much to be said for this view. But the sentence that really roused Burgundy was to the effect that he had stated something "contrary to the truth". Philip declared this to be a reflection on his honour and he challenged the Englishman to a duel, the Emperor to be the judge. Humphrey accepted the challenge, and as the Emperor was not forthcoming, Burgundy agreed to accept Philip's suggestion of Bedford as judge–a nice compliment to Duke John. It required all Bedford's tact, diplomacy and patience extending over several months to soothe the feelings of the irate Burgundian.[1]

The threatened breach between the two countries was eventually healed in an unexpected way. The tide of war turned against the Hainault cause, Humphrey went back to England in a somewhat equivocal manner, and never returned to the Continent.

Though Humphrey no doubt deserved the opprobrius epithets cast at him, one cannot overlook the romantic side that was bound to appeal to a high-metalled youth at the side of a

[1] His efforts even extended to taking part himself in a joust, a thing he had never done before; he probably lacked something of the martial ardour of his three brothers.

beautiful countess in distress. His conduct was human and understandable; but the consequences were almost disastrous, and with anyone but Bedford in the saddle they would have ended in an open breach with Burgundy, and the end of all English rule in France. And although the breach had been patched up it had unfortunate after-effects: it slowed up the tempo of the war in France at a time when it was looking so promising, and it was the beginning of the "rift in the lute" between England and Burgundy.

For the above reasons, we can pass rapidly over such military operations as there were during this period. The advance in Maine and Beauce (between Chartres and the Loire) came to a standstill, and it was not resumed till the arrival on the scene in the summer of 1425 of the earl of Salisbury with reinforcements.[1] He then carried out yet another of his successful campaigns. After a final "tidying up" of Champagne, he pushed westwards into Beauce, captured Etampes and Rambouillet, and drove forward into Maine. The town of Le Mans, its capital, fell to him on August 10, and Mayenne soon afterwards, and this completed the conquest of Maine. Owing to the absence of any English chroniclers of the period, details are lacking, as they are for most of Salisbury's operations in the war. After this the war languished, the duke of Gloucester again being the indirect cause. This time it was owing to his disturbing influence in home politics—in particular his quarrel with his uncle, Cardinal Beaufort—which entailed the presence of Bedford in England from December, 1425, to April, 1427. Gloucester was the protector in England, but Beaufort was the practical head of the government. Consequently there was a struggle for power between the two men which lasted for nearly 20 years.

While Bedford was in England the only operations that need be noticed were in Brittany, where that arrant turncoat, Jean V, duke of Brittany had now thrown in his lot with the Dauphin. In January, 1426, therefore, a small English force under Sir

[1] Salisbury paid frequent visits to England, and no doubt these visits had the double object—not only of raising reinforcements, but of providing some "Notes from the Front" for their training.

Thomas Rempston invaded the Duchy, and at one time penetrated as far as the capital. Rempston then established his base in the little town of St. James-de-Beuvron, on the border of Normandy, midway between Avranches (held by Suffolk) and Fougères.

The brother of the duke of Brittany, Arthur of Richemont, who had recently been made Constable of France, raised an army to take to the help of his brother and in February, 1426, he advanced to besiege St. James. His army was about 16,000 strong, while that of Rempston's garrison was a mere 600.[1]

The constable had brought with him a powerful force of artillery, and with it he soon made two breaches in the walls. On March 6 he assaulted, and a long fierce struggle took place, lasting till the evening. The hard-pressed garrison then held a council of war and decided on a desperate expedient. Leaving a portion of his tiny force to hold the enemy in the breaches, Rempston with the remainder crept out through a sally port, got right round the enemy and attacked them in the rear uttering the war cry: "Salisbury! St. George!". Thus assailed on two sides at once the French gave way, despite the huge disparity in numbers; many of them were driven into a nearby lake and drowned, the remainder fell back to their camp suffering heavily. But that was not the end. During the night a panic set in, and burning their tents and abandoning artillery and stores, the whole army dribbled away and did not stop till they had reached their original point of departure near Fougères. Their casualties are given as 600 killed, 50 captured and 18 standards.[2] De Beaucourt's summing up is:

"Thus fled his army–routed by an enemy 20 times its inferior in numbers. Thus terminated in a most lamentable reverse an expedition in which he had placed all his hopes."

This extraordinary "Rout of St. James"–one of the most

---

[1] These figures come from French sources and are accepted by both Dr. Cosneau, in his admirable *Le Connétable de Richemont* and by Du Fresne de Beaucourt in his *Histoire de Charles VI*.

[2] Edward Hall claims that the English captured 14 "great guns", 14 barrels of powder, 300 pipes of wine, 200 pipes of biscuit and flour, 200 "frailes" [*sic*] of figs and raisins, and 500 barrels of herrings—no doubt in preparation for Lent.

astonishing episodes in the Hundred Years War–puzzled the French chroniclers at the time and French historians since (it has escaped comment by English historians). A contemporary English source for the battle might throw light on it, but there is not one. Various excuses were put forward, but they sound mere palliatives. Whatever the true explanation, the consequences were clear: Arthur de Richemont retreated into Anjou and remained there inactive throughout the ensuing summer. The English remained unmolested at St. James. Two days after the battle the earl of Suffolk, who had evidently learnt of the victory, arrived at St. James with 1,500 troops, rightly resolved to take advantage of this unexpected success. He is, however, open to criticism for not having arrived even earlier. Possibly he had "written off" the town in view of the immense superiority of the French.

The earl of Suffolk now united his force to the garrison and advanced towards Rennes. This town lies 45 miles to the west of St. James; midway between the two is the walled town of Dol (where Harold Godwinson had so distinguished himself when fighting under the banner of Duke William of Normandy). Suffolk occupied Dol without any let or hindrance from the constable de Richemont or Jean V. Further advance proved unnecessary, for the vacillating duke of Brittany now decided that it was time to change his coat again. He sent to apply for a three months' truce, which Suffolk granted. After a little more fighting in the following year this truce ripened into a treaty which was signed in the summer of 1427. By it Jean V recognized Henry VI as king of France. His *volte face* had been complete.

Meanwhile the regent had returned to France, and the arrival of reinforcements enabled him to put fresh vigour into the war. He sent an army 2,000 strong under Warwick and Suffolk into the eastern theatre of the war. On July 1 they laid siege to Montargis, 60 miles south-east of Paris and 40 miles east of Orleans. The siege lasted two months, and was of interest for two reasons. It brought into prominence, in an effort to relieve it, not only La Hire (now released) but a new figure in the

person of a bastard son of the late duke of Orleans, known as the
Count de Dunois. These two enterprising leaders fell upon a
portion of the besieging force, cut it to pieces, captured Suffolk's
brother and relieved the town. The English retreated, leaving
most of their guns. This was the first "ray of sunshine" (as de
Beaucourt called it) that the French had enjoyed; Charles VII
described it, at a time when Joan of Arc was still alive, as "le
commencement et cause de nostre bonheur". This was an un-
doubted set-back for the English cause, but exactly how far it
set back their progress in the campaign of conquest it is hard to
say. The "ray of sunshine" warmed the hearts of the Dauphinists and there were some slight reactions in the west; but the
English were apparently not discouraged, nor put off from their
resolution to pursue the war vigorously. The trouble was a shortage of troops. It should be noted that for over two years the
English had been operating single-handed, for the duke of Burgundy, though he had not openly broken with his allies, had
withdrawn his field troops into the Low Countries for the war
against Jacqueline. The only Burgundian leader who still kept
the field was John de Luxembourg, who—ever faithful to the
House of Lancaster—was operating in the Argonne in eastern
France. The earl of Salisbury was sent home once more to raise
fresh troops, and spent the latter part of 1427 and the spring of
1428 engaged in that duty. His task was not rendered easier by
the persistent efforts of Humphrey of Gloucester to revive the
war in the Low Countries on behalf of the Countess Jacqueline.
Any troops that he could collect for this purpose necessarily
reduced the number available for France. Eventually Bedford
succeeded in putting a stop to the whole project and Salisbury
was able to produce a small army 2,700 strong. With this force
he sailed from Sandwich on July 19 and landed at Calais on
July 24, 1428, whence he pushed straight on via Amiens to Paris.

While Salisbury was collecting reinforcements in England
two isolated actions took place in Maine that deserve notice, for
they introduce a new figure to the war with whom we shall
have a good deal to do before we finish—John, Lord Talbot.

When Bedford returned from England in the spring of 1427 he had brought in his train Lord Talbot. His first engagement was at the capture of Pontorson by the earl of Warwick. Later he took part in the siege of Montargis, and when the spring of 1428 came round he collected a force at Alençon for some project of which our French informant does not tell us the nature. Whilst thus employed, a message reached him from the garrison of Le Mans, some 30 miles to the south, that the French under the ubiquitous La Hire had seized the town and that they were cooped up in the Tour Ribendèle. Talbot's response was immediate. Marching with only 300 men, "this valiant English chevalier" as the Frenchman Cousinot called him,[1] arrived outside the walls between dawn and sunrise, in other words at the most favourable moment for attack. His troops over-ran the somnolent guards, and rushed into the town shouting "St. George!" The surprise and success was complete; aided by the friendly inhabitants, the French were ejected and the imprisoned garrison rescued.

The second action occurred shortly afterwards when, by another swoop, Talbot captured the town of Laval (midway between Angers and Avranches) which had till then always held out against the English.

These two actions, which were to become typical of Talbot's methods, made a great impression on contemporary French opinion, though they seem to have been allowed to go unrecorded in England.

APPENDIX

THE SOURCES

The four years that intervene between the battle of Verneuil and the siege of Orleans is a bad period for sources. There is an almost complete blank in English chronicle history, while for military operations France is only slightly better provided for. Waurin is almost silent and we must rely more than one would wish on Monstrelet for the Burgundian side. It is true the *Bour-*

---

[1] *Chronique de la Pucelle* by G. Cousinot, p. 252.

geois de Paris is becoming important, but more for the political than for the military aspect, for he was a civilian resident in Paris. Thus, for the battle of St. James the nearest English chronicler that we can make use of is Edward Hall who wrote a good 100 years later, albeit that his military information is often quite good. Monstrelet's account of St. James is also useful (though ignored by Ramsay for some reason), but, though Ramsay cites *le Bourgeois* for the battle, this author gives no account of it. On the Dauphinist side there are only two real accounts. Easily the best is that of G. Gruel in his *Chronique d'Arthur de Richemont.* The other is *Chronique de la Pucelle,* by G. Cousinot. Of modern histories for the battle we have none in England. In France we have Dr. E. Cosneau's *Le Connétable de Richemont*—the best account—and the *Histories of Charles VII,* by M. Vallet de Viriville (1863) and du Fresne de Beaucourt (1881). In the rather disjointed account of the period by the former I can find no description of the battle, but the latter contains a fair account.

But it is a bleak period for sources on both sides.

CHAPTER XIV

THE SIEGE OF ORLEANS

LATE in July, 1428, Thomas Montague, earl of Salisbury, entered Paris at the head of his army of 2,700 men. The question now arose: how should this army be employed? By collecting contingents from all over occupied France, it was found possible to raise the numbers to about 5,000. Long and careful war councils were held in order to decide on the plan, for it was agreed that a vigorous effort must now be made to bring the war to a conclusion.

Two schools of thought soon arose; the first school advocated the completion of the conquest of Anjou, which meant in practice the capture of Angers its capital; the other school favoured the capture of Orleans. There can be little doubt as to which of these plans represented the soundest strategy. Orleans lies midway between Paris and Bourges, the Dauphin's capital, about 60 miles from each; whilst Angers was more than twice as far from it. Anjou was an old domain of the Plantagenet kings, and its complete domination would not have any direct effect on the Dauphin's cause. It was a very indirect approach to the main objective – the Dauphin's capital. Orleans, as we have seen, constituted the direct approach which is generally the soundest form of strategy. Moreover, its capture would breach the river Loire, which had become the *de facto* boundary of the Dauphinist domains. To rupture this line had long been the aim of the English leaders, but nothing permanent had been accomplished. Orleans was not only midway between the two capitals, but the nearest point to Paris on the vital river Loire. An English army operating in that sector would thus be more easily supplied and reinforced than any other point on the river. But the duke of Bedford favoured the Anjou plan. It is surprising that he should do so, for his previous attempt to conquer Maine and Anjou, though it had made some progress, had not weakened the will of the Dauphinists to fight on, and four more years of warfare had not brought the end appreciably nearer.

For all these reasons the earl of Salisbury, now the most experienced and uniformly successful general on the English side, favoured the direct approach–the maintenance of the objective–which was to hit the enemy where it would hurt him most.

After some weeks of argument the Orleans school prevailed. The regent regretfully acquiesced in it and in mid-August the invading army set out.[1]

THE ORLEANS CAMPAIGN

The earl of Salisbury, decided to make Chartres his first objective. Retaking on the way four towns that had fallen back into Dauphinist hands, he entered the city in the latter half of August and then turned sharply south-east towards Janville 26 miles distant. On the way he captured a number of places with the minimum of resistance except at Puiset, ten miles north of Janville, which had to be stormed.

Janville was a walled town (much of its moat still exists) and had a resolute garrison. Something curious happened here. According to Hall, Bedford intended to reduce the garrison by siege, but his troops, angered by some action on the part of the garrison, "took the bit in their teeth" after only a few days siege, and assaulted the town and took it by storm, "after the most formidable assault that we have ever seen" as Salisbury himself wrote to the mayor and aldermen of the city of London. Sismondi, however, avers that the garrison offered to surrender but that Salisbury, with implacable harshness, would not listen to them but preferred to take it by storm.[2] This seems improbable, to say the least. The English army was already over-small

---

[1] It is sometimes asserted that Bedford was not aware of Salisbury's intention, on the grounds that Salisbury set off in the direction of Anjou and that Bedford in a famous letter to Henry VI wrote, "Alle things prospered for you till the time of the seage of Orleans, taken God knows by what advice". But Salisbury set out towards Anjou, in order to deceive the enemy, not his own side. As for Bedford's letter, it lays the duke open to the suspicion of prevarication or at least of a *suggestio falsi*, for though he disliked the Orleans project there is no evidence that he did anything to prevent it or to reprimand Salisbury for undertaking it.

[2] *Histoire des Français*, XIII, p. 87.

for the task before it: why then should its commander go out of
his way to endanger the lives of his men in a preliminary operation if he could secure his end without striking a single blow?

Janville lies 15 miles north of Orleans, and Salisbury decided
(probably in advance) to make of it a sort of forward base, or
supply depot, for his army during what he foresaw might be a
long and arduous siege of Orleans. The town was well situated
for its purpose, being on the direct road from Paris to Orleans
and only a day's march from the latter.

The establishment of this base being completed, the next
stage of a carefully thought out strategical plan was taken in
hand. This was to isolate the city by water, by capturing the
Dauphinist defended towns immediately above and below it:
that is to say, Jargeau above and Beaugency and Meung below
the city. First he turned his attention to the downstream towns.
Meung and Beaugency lie 12 and 20 miles respectively below
Orleans, both on the northern bank of the Loire. Obviously
Meung was the first town to be secured. Now the road from
Janville to Meung passes within a few kilometres of Orleans, and
it was necessary to use this road for the artillery that might be
required in the siege. On September 8, therefore, Salisbury
posted a left flank-guard on the outskirts of the city to safeguard
the passage of his artillery to the siege. As things happened, the
guns were not required, for Meung surrendered tamely,
and Salisbury was enabled to pass on to the siege of Beaugency.
This proved to be not quite so simple a task, for the château and
the abbey, which had been fortified, were just within range of
the near end of the many-arched bridge. The garrison confined their defence to the château and bridge. But the English,
being now in possession of the bridge at Meung, were able to
approach it from the southern bank. The siege opened on September 20, and on the 25th a simultaneous attack was made
upon the château from the north and on the bridge from the
south after an artillery bombardment. There seems to have been
a tussle on the bridge, and one can picture knights in armour
being hurled over its parapet into the river, for mail armour has

been dredged from the river bed beneath the bridge.[1] The attack was successful and on the 26th the garrison surrendered, and the inhabitants swore fidelity to King Henry VI.

The first stage in the great operation had thus been accomplished and Salisbury, in a letter to the mayor of London, showed justifiable pride in it. He stated that 40 towns, châteaux and fortified churches had fallen into his hands, and this was no empty claim for all 40 have been identified by M. Lognon, and repeated by A. de Villaret.[2]

Salisbury wasted no time, but switched his troops at once to the eastern side of Orleans, and on October 2, Sir William de la Pole laid siege to Jargeau, 12 miles up-stream. Though defended by formidable ramparts and ditch this town only held out for three days, and shortly afterwards Chateauneuf, ten miles further upstream, also fell. Orleans was thus doubly blocked by water on each side and the English army could now settle down to the siege of this redoubtable city. In the words of M. de Villaret:

"Salisbury, with the audacity that proclaims assurance of success, attacked the ancient city, the final hope of the poor King of Bourges and the last rampart of his power."[3]

Jargeau lies on the southern bank of the Loire, and thus enabled de la Pole to march thence to Orleans along this bank and approach the city from the south. This he did on October 7, and appeared in front of the bridge leading across the river into the city the same day. Five days later he was joined by the earl of Salisbury at the head of the main army, who presumably crossed the Loire by the Meung bridge. The whole army now encamped in Olivet, the southern suburb of the city. The earl's chief lieutenants were the earl of Suffolk, his brother de la Pole, Lords Ros and Scales, and Sir William Glasdale. Owing to the necessity of leaving detachments and garrisons on the road his

---

[1] It can now be seen in the town museum. The lower part of the Abbey is now a restaurant and from its terrace the bridge is in full view and the whole scene can be easily envisaged.

[2] *Campagnes des Anglais dans L'Orleanais, La Beauce, Chartraine, et le Gatinais* (Orleans 1893).

[3] Op. cit., p. 70.

army probably did not exceed 4,000 men at this juncture.[1] It was later to be joined by about 1,500 Burgundians, whom Duke John had allowed to take the pay of England. The English artillery was fewer in numbers and less powerful than that of the garrison, but some of the guns could reach the centre of the city at a range of over 1,000 yards.

As for the city of Orleans, an attack had been feared for some years past, and the defences had been greatly strengthened until it was probably the best-defended town in the whole of the Dauphin's dominions. It was also well provided with artillery and ammunition. In the city was at least one great ballista. Side by side with it were some surprisingly big guns. Some of the stone cannon-balls weighed as much as 192 lb., and one of them is recorded as engaging an English ferry – a moving target – at a range that I compute as about 1,400 yards. There were no fewer than 71 guns, many of them made of leather, mounted on the walls. The regular garrison was around 2,400[2] and another 3,000 milice were found from the civil population, which numbered over 30,000.

The river was nearly 400 yards broad, shallow, rapid, but navigable, with numerous sand-banks and islands. Over one of these a bridge, 350 metres long, joined the town to the south bank. (See Sketch Map 8, p. 231.) As this bridge comes prominently into the story it must be described. It consisted of nineteen arches, and was built A.D. 1100-1133. (It was demolished in 1760, but the old piles can still be seen when the water is low.) On the southernmost of these arches, and separated from the bank by a drawbridge, a fort with two towers, called Les Tourelles, had been built. An earthwork had also been thrown up on the southern bank as a sort of barbican or horn-work. The city wall was massive, with towers and bastions, and there were five powerfully defended gates.

---

[1] Boucher de Molandon, in *L'Armée Anglaise vaincue par Jeanne d'Arc*, in an exhaustive research makes the number 3,467 "plus 898 pages". Louis Jarry, in an equally careful account, makes it 3,189.

[2] This is de Molandon's figure. Ferdinand Lot reduces it to 1,570, and appears to ignore the *milice*.

Altogether, it was the most formidable obstacle that had confronted the English since the siege of Rouen. It is not surprising if the regent viewed with apprehension the attempt to reduce it with Salisbury's tiny army.

The earl of Salisbury opened operations in the normal style — that is, he directed a cannonade against the Tourelles and the town. After a few days he reckoned that the work was ripe for assault and launched his troops to the attack of the horn-work. The French resisted so strenuously that Salisbury promptly changed his plan. He had brought a large force of miners with him and, having presumably reduced the guns of the horn-work to silence, he set his miners to work against the foundations of the fort. After two days of this the garrison lost heart, abandoned the horn-work and, surprisingly as it seems to us, the Tourelles too, breaking down two arches of the bridge behind them. (The French assert, most improbably, that the English also broke an arch.)

Thus, the first step in the reduction of the town had been achieved, and Salisbury at once set about the second. Having hastily repaired the Tourelles, the next step was reconnaissance, on the result of which he would base his plan of attack. The earl therefore established what we should call his observation post high up in the tower of the Tourelles. At a quiet moment during the dinner hour, when the French gunners had gone to their meal, leaving their cannons loaded and laid, the English commander took a party of his chief officers with him and ascended to this observation post. From it they had a good look at the city and discussed plans for the assault. Now it happened that a lad, the son of one of the gunners, was playing about among the French cannon and, whether for a lark or because he spotted the English party looking out from the Tourelles, he touched off one of the cannons. The earl of Salisbury heard the shot coming and ducked. The cannon-ball hit the lintel of the window, dislodging an iron bar which struck the earl on the side of the face, removing half of it. Since the details of this story are almost the only items that come from English sources, it may be of interest to reproduce the passage in our earliest printed source, *The Brut*, which was almost contemporaneous with the event:

"And tho at the laste, as he was busi to seke and loke upon his ordynaunce, for to gete it [the town] if he might, a fals thef, a traitour withynne the towne, shotte a gonne, and the stone smot this good Earle of Salusbury, and he was dede through the stroke; wherefore was made grete doole and sorrowe for hys dethe, long tyme afterward, for the greate doughtynesse and manhood that was found in hym, and in hys governaunce at all tymes."

The stricken earl was removed to Meung where he died eight days later, after adjuring his officers gathered round his

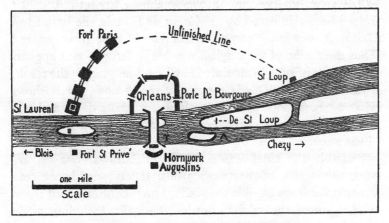

Sketch Map 8: THE SIEGE OF ORLEANS

| ▄▄ | Line of forts | A | Isle de St. Aignan |
| T | Tourelles | C | Isle de Charlemagne |

bed to persevere with the war till they had obtained complete victory. His death was a calamity indeed. The French were fully aware of the extent of it, and the poem *Le Mistère d'Orleans* puts into the mouth of William Glasdale this lamentation:

> Luy qui a fait et soustenu
> Du tout nostre ost par sa vaillance,
> Et qui très bien entretenu,
> Qu'il avoit conquis toute la France.

There can be no doubt that Salisbury, who had brought almost as many miners as artillerymen to the siege, had every intention of taking the town by assault; and had he been spared he would probably have succeeded, for the garrison was then thoroughly demoralized, as we shall see. He was succeeded in the command by the earl of Suffolk, who was opposed to any action of a hazardous nature, and instead of persevering with an operation so well begun, tamely withdrew the field army to winter quarters in the neighbouring towns. He left an isolated garrison under the captain, Sir William Glasdale, in the Tourelles and in a fortification which they threw up round the church of the Augustins immediately to the south of it. Yet though the French in the vicinity were now in overwhelming strength, and had indeed been reinforced by the Count de Dunois, the bastard of Orleans,[1] they left it completely unmolested for three weeks.[2] Thus the action of the English was not so fatuous as it appears to our eyes; it was a "calculated risk", and judging by the result, a justifiable one. This is a point of significance, for it shows what a tremendous power morale was in those days, and will explain much that is otherwise inexplicable in the further course of the siege.

Probably the chief reason for the withdrawal was to preserve the health of the troops whilst billets were being constructed for them outside the walls. The inhabitants had razed to the ground the suburbs outside the walls, including many churches, in order that the besieging army might not find ready-made billets. Again it may be that the breathing space was required in order to bring up heavy ordnance to breach the town walls.

Whatever be the truth of this, and we shall never know the full reasons, the army began to flow back to the siege in December. John Lord Talbot also arrived on December 1,[3] and he and Lord Scales were now associated in the chief command with the earl of Suffolk. This seems an odd and unsatisfactory arrange-

[1] Half-brother of the Duke of Orleans, who had been captured at Agincourt and was still a prisoner in England.

[2] Miss Sackville-West well writes: "The English held the French in a snake-like fascination."

[3] Most accounts assert that Talbot shared the command with Suffolk and Scales on the death of Salisbury–which is impossible.

ment. The explanation probably is that Bedford had lost confidence in Suffolk as an independent commander. It may, indeed, be significant that three years previously he had been replaced whilst in command at Pontorson for some reason unknown to us. John Talbot was a remarkable man. He spent no fewer than 50 years under arms, and was at this time about 46 years old. He soon became known to the French as "The English Achilles", and it is significant that at first his was the only English name known to Joan of Arc.

We can probably deduce the English plan of operations from what followed. The attempt to take the town by a *coup de main* had failed, so recourse was now had to a normal siege procedure of mining and bombardment. But there were abnormal difficulties. The perimeter of the town was 2,000 yards. To construct a besieging line 700 yards outside the wall would require nearly 4,000 yards of fortifications, excluding works on the south bank. These would require a long time to construct, nor were there sufficient troops adequately to man them when constructed. What was to be done? Common-sense would suggest that the work should be commenced on the critical side, *i.e.*, the western, whence reinforcements might arrive from the Dauphin's headquarters at Chinon, and that as time went on and the besieging army was increased, the line might, if necessary, be drawn right round the town, if it had not before then surrendered. This is precisely the procedure followed by the English army.

Here a reference should be made to the map. First of all, a great base camp, as it may be called, was constructed round the church of St. Laurent, on the northern bank, connected with the Tourelles by a fort on the Isle of Charlemagne. Thence in succession to the north a line of four forts (called bastilles), connected by communication trenches, were constructed. An isolated fort was also constructed at St. Loup, one-and-a-half miles east of the town. This work took until about the beginning of April to complete; and meanwhile the eastern side of the town was perforce left open; through this gap reinforcements and supplies could enter the town without much danger, being screened on their way by a forest belt, though occasionally they were cut off. To anticipate, work was put in hand on entrenching this gap, and constructing a bastille, when early in April the Burgundian mercenaries incontinently departed and there were insufficient troops left to complete the work.[1] The siege operations were mainly of an artillery nature though there were occasional sorties and sallies, and reinforcements in driblets got through. And thus things went on till the beginning of February. The Dauphin now at last bestirred himself and he assembled a relieving force. It was based on Blois, 40 miles downstream from Orleans, and was put under the command of Charles of Bourbon, count of Clermont.

*   *   *

THE BATTLE OF THE HERRINGS (February 12, 1429)

Meanwhile Lent was approaching, the season when fish must be the staple diet. A convoy was therefore fitted out at Paris and despatched to Orleans early in February. Its commander was Sir John Fastolf, and it consisted of 300 wagon-loads of herrings and other commodities. The escort, all mounted, consisted of about 1,000 archers and some Paris militia. On the 11th of the month it reached the little village of Rouvray, five miles north of Janville, where it spent the night. Next morning it was just setting out when mounted patrols, evidently forming the vanguard of a French army, appeared on the sky-line to the south-west. It was indeed the army of Count Clermont, which was approaching. News of the march of the convoy had reached Blois, and Clermont had instantly decided to march north-east in the endeavour to cut it off from its destination.

Fastolf was a general of great experience. Quick to realize the extent of the danger, he took a step most unusual, if not unprecedented, at that period: he halted his whole convoy and escort in an open space on the road to Janville one mile south of Rouvray.

[1] The ground is now a built-up area and all signs of any entrenchments or works have vanished.

He had recognized that his slow-moving convoy had but little chance of reaching the protection that Janville might provide; and that if caught on the march the line of wagons, which must have been about three miles long, could not be adequately protected by his small force against a mounted adversary who was in fact thrice as numerous as his own escort. He promptly halted and constructed with his wagons a leaguer. It had two openings: these openings he defended with archers; the remainder of the army taking cover inside. Thus when the French came up they found in their path what we might now call a "hedgehog".

This was something novel in medieval warfare, but the count of Clermont, the French commander, fitted his tactics to the novel situation. He was provided with a large number of cannons (of small calibre), whereas the English had none. Instead, therefore, of making a direct attack on them he ordered an artillery bombardment. To this, of course, the English had no reply and they had to "sit and suffer" while casualties steadily mounted. Many of the wagons were holed by the cannon-balls and the herrings spilled on to the ground. If this bombardment had been persisted in there could have been but one outcome— the ignominious surrender of the English army. And it would have constituted the first occasion in military history when guns had brought victory in the field.

But the unpredictable happened. In the French army was a Scottish contingent, small in size. Its commander was Sir John Stewart of Darnley, the Constable of the Scots in France.[1] Clermont's orders were that the whole army (less the gunners and crossbowmen) should remain mounted, but Stewart disregarded this order; he not only dismounted his men but, not waiting for the artillery bombardment to take effect, advanced impulsively to the attack. It encountered the deadly fire of the English archers, and suffered a bloody repulse.

The French men-at-arms then essayed a mounted attack, but this also was disastrous. A Burgundian writer describes how

---

[1] He had been wounded in the eye and captured by the English at the battle of Cravant six years before, and subsequently released.

the French cavalry spurred their horses on to the stakes that the English archers had stuck into the ground in their front, how the horses were impaled on them and how their riders were pitched forward over their ears. Just what one might have expected to happen! The same writer says that when the Scots saw the outcome of this affray they fled. I doubt this: I think it occurred a little later in the battle.

For the time had come for the counter-attack. Sir John Fastolf now ordered his men-at-arms to get mounted, the archers at the openings made way for them, and two torrents of English cavalry poured out of the leaguer and put the crowning touch to the victory. The Franco-Scottish army was scattered to the winds. The battle of the Herrings, or of Rouvray, was won. Sir John Fastolf delivered his precious supplies to the army in triumph, and returned to Paris for more. The spirits of the English were raised; the hearts of the French drooped to their very nadir.[1] The relieving army had quite unexpectedly been broken into smithereens, and all hope of relief must now be abandoned. Negotiations for surrender were, therefore, put in hand.

But the course of history is inscrutable; even unpredictable. Suddenly there appeared a portent in the west, a comet in the sky: another relieving army was approaching, and at its head, incredible though it sounds, marched a Maid.

JOAN OF ARC AT ORLEANS

Joan of Arc was a peasant girl, about 17 years of age.[2] In her early girlhood she heard what she called her "Voices". The exact nature of these voices is, fortunately, outside the province of this book to examine or pronounce upon. All we are concerned with is the practical effect they had upon her and the practical effect she in turn had upon the military operations.

First the effect upon herself. The Voices convinced her, to the very depth of her being, that it was the will of the King of Heaven

---

[1] Professor Lot writes (op. cit., p. 37): "This stupid defeat had a disastrous influence on the morale of the French captains. They were firmly convinced of the impossibility of further resistance at Orleans."

[2] There is doubt about her exact age, but Eugène Deprez lends the weight of his great name to the statement that she was born on January 4, 1412.

that the English should be thrown out of France and that she was in some way to be instrumental in their eviction. This developed into the belief that, as a first step, the Dauphin must be anointed with the holy oil at Rheims, after which the English would not be able to stand against the powers of the King of Heaven, wielded terrestrially by the new king, Charles VII. Joan's own first step was therefore obvious: she must impart to the Dauphin the message given her by her Voices. On February 23, 1429, just a fortnight after the battle of the Herrings, she set off from her home on the eastern border of France to seek out the Dauphin in his castle at Chinon, 25 miles south-west of Tours. The ultimate upshot of the interview that she obtained with Charles, in spite of the opposition of la Trémoïlle his chancellor, was that he fitted out a fresh army for the relief of Orleans, placed the duke of Alençon in command of it and allowed Joan, resplendent with banner and a full suit of armour, to accompany it.

On April 27, 1429, the army, about 4,000 strong, set out from Blois, along the south bank of the river. The march was uneventful materially; spiritually it was one of the most important and exciting marches ever made by an army. For that army was spiritually transformed, and it was all the work of the Maid.

Whether they regarded her as a saint or a mascot, the simple credulous French soldiers took heart of grace from her presence among them, and unquestioningly, as far as we can gather, obeyed her behests as to behaviour. And they were exacting and unpopular behests: swearing was to be abolished, loose women were not to be tolerated, and everyone must attend Mass and make his confession. A large body of priests marched at the head of the army chanting psalms. The atmosphere was one of elation, almost of ecstasy, as the troops set out on the gay adventure on which, they knew, Heaven was smiling. In military parlance, their morale was high, and it had been raised by precisely the same means as those employed by Archbishop Thurstan before the battle of the Standard, by Henry V before Agincourt, and by Oliver Cromwell before Dunbar.

Before setting out, Joan dictated a letter to the English, opening with a sentence so astonishing as almost to take the breath away:

"King of England, and you Duke of Bedford . . . render up to the Maid who is sent by God, the King of Heaven, the keys of all the good towns that you have taken and violated in France."

Well might Bedford raise his eyebrows and rub his chin when he received such a missive. It has been averred that terror was struck into the hearts of the English army, but there is no satisfactory evidence that the troops in the English camp, except the leaders, were even aware of the Maid's existence on her arrival outside the city on April 28.

With the army came a convoy of supplies for the city. There were two possible means of getting them into the town without having to risk a battle, to which the French were naturally averse. One was to make a wide circuit to the north through the forest, and approach through the gap between forts Paris and St. Loup; the other was by barge from Chezy five miles upstream, landing them at the Porte de Bourgoyne on the eastern face of the city. This was rendered possible owing to the neglect of the earl of Suffolk to stretch a chain across the river—a laxity that would have horrified Henry V. The count of Dunois[1] who was in command in the town, but in communication with Alençon without, no doubt reported this absence of river barrier and suggested the possibility of this route for the convoy. Thus it was that Alençon led his army by the southern bank of the Loire, contrary to the wish of the Maid that they should follow the northern bank. Why she, being ignorant of the topography, should have any views on the point is not clear. Alençon, for some reason, kept his plan secret from Joan.

To carry out the plan numerous barges were required, but Chezy could not supply them. There were, however, a sufficient number lying idle and empty under the walls of the city. The plan concocted between Alençon and Dunois was therefore as follows. When the wind should be favourable the empty barges

[1] Generally known thus, though he was not created count till 1441.

were to sail upstream to Chezy, and meanwhile the army would halt opposite the city, while the convoy marched on to Chezy. There the supplies for the city would be transferred to the barges which could then slip downstream, whatever the direction of the wind.[1] In order to distract attention during the downstream journey Dunois arranged a demonstration against Fort St. Loup. It was no doubt this demonstration, coupled with the fact that St. Loup possessed few cannons, that ensured the success of the project.

The wind changed in the nick of time, and all went according to plan. Joan with a small escort also crossed over the river at Chezy and entered the city overland, next morning, April 30, amid the rejoicings of the populace.

The action of the escorting army was puzzling. It did not cross over the river and enter the town by the unguarded Porte de Bourgoyne, as one might have expected, but immediately returned to Blois, and a few days later set out again for Orleans with further supplies, but this time on the northern bank. The usual surmise is that only a portion of the convoy could be escorted on the first trip, and consequently the army had to return for the other half. It is not easy to see why it should not all have travelled with the first expedition; nor, even if unavoidable, why the previous route which had proved so successful was not again followed. There is, as a matter of fact, evidence contained in the town accounts that some wheat did reach the garrison by water on May 4, so it is just possible (though I have never heard the suggestion advanced) that the army marched by the north bank with the specific object of distracting attention from the convoy which marched in on the south bank.

The relieving army entered Orleans on the morning of May 3. Up to date it would seem that the English had practically ignored the Maid–assuming that they were even aware of her presence. But that was their mistake, and they were soon to

[1] The belief, sponsored by Bernard Shaw's play *St. Joan*, that the problem was merely to cross the river into the town but that this could not be done unless the wind was favourable is of course absurd.

realize it; for later that day, while another attack was being made on Fort St. Loup (probably intended only as a diversion to cover the entry of the wheat), Joan galloped out of the town, joined the attackers and inspired them with such enthusiasm and military zeal that they actually captured and burnt the fort.[1] Probably both sides were equally surprised at this unprecedented occurrence. The fact that Fort St. Loup was so dangerously isolated was evidence of the supreme disdain that the besiegers had for their enemies at this time. However, Talbot, finding that the attack was actually being pressed home, moved round from his headquarters in Fort St. Laurent, picking up a few troops from each fort as he passed, with the intention of going to its relief. But the French, spotting his intention from the walls, sent out a covering force to engage him. The two bodies clashed outside Fort Paris, and at the same time Talbot saw the smoke rising from St. Loup. He realized that he was too late, and had no option but to fall back inside his own lines.

The capture of St. Loup was the turning point of the siege, and in a sense the whole war. What followed in the next few days is highly dramatic, but is already well known and does not raise many problems, so it may be passed over briefly. The next day was Ascension Day, and to show how chroniclers contradicted one another, some assert that Joan refused to fight that day, while others assert the exact opposite, that she wished to attack but was restrained by Dunois. So the attack took place on May 6, and it was directed with sound judgement on the part of Dunois against the Tourelles. The striking force for this task crossed the river by boat to the Isle of St. Aignan, and thence by a short bridge of two boats to the south bank. Why the garrison of the Tourelles allowed this bridge to be constructed does not appear. There is an obvious gap in the narrative at this point, and one man's guess is as good as another's. Mine is that the advanced party crossed by boat and kept the garrison engaged while the bridge was being

---

[1] The so-called fort appears to have been little more than the church of St. Loup put into a state of defence.

built (the small observation post of St. John le Blanc had been evacuated). The fight for the Augustins fort was a homeric affair. The English were hopelessly outnumbered. Anatole France calculates that no fewer than 4,000 French were concentrated against the work, with 500 English in it and the Tourelles. After an all-day struggle, and several repulses, the fort was at last captured, thanks to the resolution and stimulating influence of Joan. The next morning the attack was resumed, this time against the barbican. The previous day's history was repeated and even intensified. Guns, scaling ladders and mines were brought up; even a fire-ship was rigged out and floated down beneath the drawbridge, which was thus set alight. The retreat of the garrison of the horn-work was thus threatened, and as they fell back into the Tourelles across the drawbridge it collapsed and the gallant Glasdale, waving aloft the banner of the Black Prince's great captain Chandos, was cast into the river and drowned. Last of all, the powder for the cannons failed, until the charge was so small that the cannon-balls merely dribbled out of the muzzles and fell harmlessly into the water. At the same time, the garrison of the town had extemporized the equivalent of what is now known as a Bailey bridge, with which they spanned the broken arches and attacked from the north simultaneously with the attack from the south. This was the last straw; the small remnant of the garrison, that had fought as gallant a fight as is recorded in our annals, surrendered, and the Maid of Orleans three hours later proudly rode her charger across the bridge into the acclaiming city. And well did she deserve her triumph. For there had been no sign of crumbling morale on the part of the English garrison, some of whose names should be rescued from oblivion. Here they are: John Reid, William Arnold, Walter Parker, Matthew Thornton, William Vaughan, John Burford, Pat Hall, Tom Sand, John Langham, Tom Jolly, George Ludlow, Black Harry, Bill Martin, Davy Johnson and Dick Hawke. (Tom Cobley's name does not appear.)

The English leaders had now to make a cruel decision. Their

16

great advantage over the enemy–the superiority of their morale
–had vanished in a couple of nights, and they were left with an
impossible military position. Heavily outnumbered and out-
gunned, one half of their position–patiently built up in the
course of the previous six months–had crumpled up, the town
walls were as intact as ever, the garrison was indeed increased,
and supplies could be admitted at will; finally, the morale had
passed to the enemy's side. Look where they would, the English
commanders could see no single redeeming feature, and I thnik
they showed their good judgement by bowing to the logic of events
and abandoning what was now shown to be a quite impossible
enterprise. But one action still was open to them, one proud
gesture to show that the English leopard had not got its tail
between its legs. On the morning of May 8, the whole army was
marshalled in battle array and advanced into No Man's Land
opposite the ramparts, where it silently stood, challenging the
French to come out and engage it in open battle. After waiting
for some time, and the French making no indication of desire
to engage, the army quietly filed away to the north "en bon
ordre", as the French chroniclers are forced to admit. There was
no attempt at pursuit. As in the case of Sir Richard Grenville:

> "They dared not touch us again
> For they knew that we still could sting."

Thus did the Maid and the Bastard of Orleans triumph over
the English Achilles.

OBSERVATIONS ON THE SIEGE

To those readers who have obtained their knowledge of the
siege from biographies of Joan of Arc, the above account may
be scarcely recognizable. The Maid herself hardly seems to
come into the story, yet surely she was the central figure in it?
An explanation is obviously required. In the first place, it is
natural that biographies of the Maid should concentrate on her
rather than on the general history and military aspect of the
siege. This tends to give a distorted impression of the course and
importance of events. In the second place, statements made by

contemporary fellow-countrymen may be, consciously or unconsciously, biased. The most reliable statements are those given by
eye-witnesses at the *Procès de Rehabilitation*. But even these must
be treated with reserve. As M. Edouard Perroy has observed:

"The testimony (of the Procès) relates memories already distant
and, so to speak, hazy with legend. It comes from those same
countrymen of hers legitimately and sincerely anxious to clear her
memory. . . ."[1]

In the third place, testimony from the English side is almost
completely lacking, and few writers seem to have made allowance for this. I except M. Boucher de Molandon, whose
L'Armée Anglaise vaincue par Jeanne d'Arc (1892) is the most
thorough investigation into this aspect of the subject that I know.
M. de Molandon, after pointing out that a great deal has been
written about the raising of the siege, adds:

"But it is evident that, in the absence of any English chronicle
giving in detail the general idea and the methods of attack, much
remains to be said."[2]

But it is not easy to say it. For we are in the realm of conjecture.
A contemporary poem was given the title *Le Mystère d'Orléans*,
for the raising of the siege did appear to Frenchmen at the time
as a divine mystery. To Englishmen it appears a mystery of
another nature. How, they may well ask, came it about that at a
time when English military prowess and prestige were at their
height could their commanders make so many apparently
egregious errors and act in so supine a way as they apparently
did? So far as this is true I think it can legitimately be laid at
the door of the earl of Suffolk (though Bedford is to be blamed
for not troubling to visit the scene of action throughout the
siege). Much of the supposed mystery has, it is to be hoped, been
cleared up in the preceding narrative. The more complex case
of the failure of the besiegers to reinforce the Tourelles in the
final attack will be dealt with in an Appendix.

The general conclusion that is forced upon us is that the
English commanders, though faced with a tough proposition,

[1] *The Hundred Years War*, p. 280.   [2] Op. cit., p. 69.

were making headway with it till the apparition of the Maid, and that this was mainly due to the moral ascendancy they had obtained after 14 years of almost continuous victory. Only four days before the capture of St. Loup a French attack upon Fort Paris was frustrated by what Andrew Lang calls "the dread Hurrah of the English", and years afterwards Dunois testified that prior to the coming of the Maid "two hundred Englishmen would put to flight eight hundred or a thousand Frenchmen". But once the French morale had attained to, or even approached that of the English, the result was almost a foregone conclusion and can be accounted for on purely military grounds without having to invoke the direct intervention of the King of Heaven. There was thus no reason to retail the many stories that attached themselves to the Maid, the "miraculous change of wind", or the rather rude conversations she is said to have had with the English across a No Man's Land 700 yards wide (where sharp eyes on the one hand and strong lungs on the other must have been required). Joan's contribution to the victory was that she roused the fighting spirits of the French, which had lain dormant for so long. This contribution was decisive, and we may say that the main credit for the raising of the siege rests upon that glorious creature, the Maid of Orleans.

APPENDIX

THE SITE OF THE BATTLE OF THE HERRINGS

The situation of the battle of the Herrings is as inaccessible as that of Cravant is accessible. The little village of Rouvray, to give the battle its alternative name, lies away from main roads and railway. To a visitor staying at Orleans and not possessing a car it is practically essential to hire a taxi. And, arrived in Rouvray, it is hard to pick up local knowledge and tradition. It is however available, as will be seen presently. Co-ordinating the various sources it can be stated that the battle took place somewhere between Rouvray and Janville. As these places are nearly six miles apart something more is required. Here

I must have recourse to what I call I.M.P. Let us put ourselves in the shoes of Sir John Fastolf on the morning of the battle. The evidence implies that his army had either just set out or was on the point of setting out when his patrols rode in with the news of the approach of the French. We can picture him riding out along the Janville road in search of a position. He would not have far to go, for the ground was open (as it still is) and the *glacis* smooth. It would take some time to construct a leaguer with as many as 300 wagons, so no time was to be lost. At the first suitable spot outside the village, therefore, the leaguer would be made. At just under a mile outside the village the ground seems eminently suitable, for there is a good unimpeded view in all directions. The road runs along the top of a very slight ridge and at 1,600 yards from the village there is now a small copse–a mere wind screen. On my visit I took some photographs of this spot considering it the most likely locality, and returned to the village–to learn from a *cultivateur* that the locality I had just fixed on was called *le camp ennemi*. I know of no other *ennemi* than the English who have fought in those parts, and if we may assume that the *ennemi* was in fact the English it seems to go far to put the coping-stone on the investigation and to allow us to claim that the copse marks the site of the battle.

A further indication that the battlefield was near the village is the fact that after the battle the villagers issued from their shelters and regaled themselves with the herrings that had been spilt on to the ground from the wagons damaged by the French cannon-balls. Indeed, it was a red-letter day for them, and no wonder they speak, not of the battle, but of the DAY of the Herrings.

THE FAILURE TO REINFORCE THE TOURELLES

The most puzzling problem to some is why Talbot (assuming that he was responsible) failed to reinforce the garrison in the Tourelles. Here we are of course in the realm of conjecture. In the first place, though we know that Dunois planned a holding attack on Talbot's main force at St. Laurent to cover the attack

246 THE AGINCOURT WAR

on the Tourelles (just as he had twice previously done against
St. Loup), no mention is made of this attack being actually
carried out. Historians have concluded that it was not carried
out. But this assumption is unwarranted. All eyes were centred
on the dramatic events unfolding at the Tourelles, and it is quite
natural that the local diarist on whom we largely rely should
have omitted reference to such an apparently unimportant affair
as the holding attack. But as no mention is made of a change of
plan, and as it is inherently probable that Dunois should have
stuck to such a sound and indeed obvious plan, I cannot accept
silence as an indication of cancellation. Now, if this attack took
place as planned it would go far to explain why Talbot could
not sally forth to the relief of the Tourelles.

In the second place, how could Talbot expect to render effective aid to the Tourelles? Consider the situation. A glance at
the map will show that to approach it he would have to cross over
the Isle of Charlemagne, and land opposite the Fort St. Privé.
Now the garrison of this fort had evacuated it after the fall of
the Augustins. This was, I hold, the first sign of the demorali-
zation caused in the English ranks by the magic of Joan's name.
(The idea that Talbot may have *ordered* the evacuation before
ever the Tourelles was attacked seems preposterous. Oh, for
that English account of the siege!)

The landing on the south bank would thus be opposed, for
Dunois was bound to take the elementary precaution of
watching the crossing with some of his unemployed troops (only
a handful at a time could be employed in the actual assault).
Such an opposed landing, improvised as it must be, would
present even greater difficulties than those of our troops in
Normandy on D Day. Talbot can thus, I think, be absolved of
bad leadership on that fatal May 7, 1429.

THE ENGLISH LINES

The most casual glance at the sketch-map of Orleans will
bring out the extraordinary lay-out of the English *bastilles* or
forts on the north side of the river. The point had been lightly

touched on in the narrative, but it deserves some further treatment for those interested in the subject.

On the west side we have a line of five forts, about 400 yards apart, with a double line of circumvallation and contravallation connecting them, whereas on the east side there is a single isolated bastille, on the river bank with a gap of over one and a half miles between it and its neighbour the Fort Paris. Through this gap the enemy could and did often penetrate. There are two explanations. The first one becomes obvious directly one approaches Fort St. Loup. The terrain between the city and this fort is flat, but the fort itself is on a hill, 100 feet high, overlooking the river. Clearly its *raison d'être* was not to complete the girdle of forts but to command the river approaches to the city from the east, and also to form a look-out post in that direction. Owing to the intervening flat ground some species of signals, probably smoke, could be employed to give warning of an attack from that direction. There were, however, two weak points about it: a large island lay under the near bank of the river, thus deflecting the main channel some 700 yards to the south. Even with a numerous force of cannons it would be difficult to hit an enemy moving fast downstream with the current – a fact that Dunois duly appreciated. The second weakness was that the extensive forest of Orleans reached within a short distance of the fort on the north side, thus providing an attacker with a covered line of approach.

The second explanation of this large gap is a simple one: there were insufficient troops to man the other forts adequately and at the same time to construct such a long defensive line, complete with forts (without which it would be valueless at night time). The weakness was not lost upon the English leaders and, after the more vital works on the west side were completed, work was started on the east side too, with a single fort midway between St. Loup and Fort Paris. But the defection of the Burgundians seems to have slowed up the work, if it did not put a a complete stop to it before it had got far enough to be effective. The authority for this is a single sentence in Jean Chartier's

Histoire de Charles VII, and it was overlooked by M. Jollois when he wrote his standard history of the siege and consequently continues to be overlooked in most accounts. Unfortunately, the ground is now a built-up area and all traces of the earthworks or connecting fort have vanished.

Fort Fleury. Nearly two miles to the north of the city there is an old earthwork which Victorian writers ascribed to the English. By any tenets of I.M.P. this claim must be suspect, quite apart from the lack of documentary evidence in support of it; but in any case it has since been established that the earthwork belongs to a quite different period.

A NOTE ON SOURCES ETC.

The primary source for the siege is the *Journal du siège d'Orleans*. As a result of an exhaustive examination made in 1913 by Felix Guillon entitled *Etude Historique sur "Le Journal du siège d'Orleans"*, it is now possible to state that the author of the *Journal* was G. Cousinot, Chancellor of Orleans, who was present throughout the siege and kept the journal from day to day. It was afterwards borrowed largely from by both Berry the Herald, and Jean Chartier (whose books have already been cited), and by Cousinot himself in his *Chronique de la Pucelle*. It is not therefore necessary to cite any other sources.

On the English side there is practically nothing. The period is an arid one as anyone will realize who studies Kingsford's *English Historical Literature in the 15th Century*. We are now well in the 100 years gap between the death of Walsingham, about 1422, and the appearance of the Chronicles of Polidore Vergil and Edward Hall.

The standard history of the siege was written by J. Jollois in 1827, but much more useful for our purpose are the two books by Boucher de Molandon, *L'Armée Anglaise vaincue par Jeanne d'Arc* (1892), and *Première Campagne de Jeanne d'Arc* (1874). Also valuable is *Le Compte de l'armée Anglaise au siège d'Orleans* (1892) by L. Jarry. These two authors have studied the composition of the English army at the siege much more thoroughly than any Englishman. For the early part of the campaign the best account is *"Campagnes des Anglais dans l'Orleanais . . . "* by A. de Villaret (1893). No Englishman has published a detailed study of the campaign or siege.

The battle of the Herrings. The most useful sources are: *Chronique de la Pucelle, Waurin, Le Bourgeois de Paris, Jean Chartier,* and for the Scottish contingent, *Liber Pluscardine.*

N.B.—Sources for Joan of Arc are dealt with in an Appendix to the following chapter.

CHAPTER XV

JOAN OF ARC'S CAMPAIGNS

THE siege of Orleans was over—a siege which the Abbé Dubois described as one of those events on which depend the fate of empires. The news came as a great shock to the duke of Bedford, but he set about scraping together a new army. As for the besieging army, Suffolk stupidly dispersed it, taking about 700 men to Jargeau, while Talbot took the remainder to Meung and Beaugency. On the French side, the count of Dunois followed Suffolk to Jargeau but was repulsed and fell back to Orleans, while the Maid rode off to Tours to announce the glorious news of Orleans to her king.

Charles held some earnest war councils debating the next step. Joan was for raising another army and proceeding with it to the capture of the Loire towns still in English hands, preparatory to marching to Rheims for the sacring and crowning. But Charles and La Trémoïlle were hesitant. The news had reached them that Fastolf was approaching with a new army, and Fastolf was now a name to inspire legitimate fear. Ultimately the persuasive Maid had her way, the duke of Alençon was despatched with an army to Orleans, with Joan in company. Arrived at Orleans, Dunois's garrison was added to it and the whole marched along the south bank of the river to the capture of Jargeau. It was a well-found army, well equipped for a siege and it is said to have been nearly 8,000 in number.

On approaching the town a war council was held to decide whether to proceed with the enterprise. There are two notable points about this council. In the first place it seems extraordinary that, with a powerful army at their back, the resolution of the leaders should have weakened to the extent of contemplating the abandonment of the enterprise before ever it had started.

This can only be put down to the fear of the English military prowess, which could not be dissipated in a night or in a single siege; the captains were looking over their left shoulders wondering what the formidable Fastolf was up to. (There were indeed rumours of his approach.) The second point of significance is that, unlike the procedure at Orleans where the leaders did not usually trouble to call Joan to their councils, on this occasion she attended them all, as if by right. This is good evidence as to the prestige that already attached to the name of the Maid of Orleans.

At this council Joan's voice was raised clamorously in favour of proceeding with the project, and her voice prevailed. The army resumed its march up to the walls of the town, and after a skirmish in which Joan distinguished herself, they drove an English sortie back into the town. Joan that evening approached the walls and uttered the following unforgettable challenge: "Surrender the town to the King of Heaven, and to King Charles, and depart, or it will be the worse for you". Suffolk took no notice of the ravings of this witch, but he did enter into negotiations with Dunois, which, however, came to nothing. Next morning, Sunday, June 12, the besieging artillery were placed in position and the bombardment commenced. With only three shots the great mortar *La Bercère* demolished one of the chief towers, and great damage was done.

After some hours of bombardment another war council was held, and the question was debated whether to go straight to the assault or to await events. Again the voice of the Maid was raised uncompromisingly in favour of immediate assault, and again it was listened to. Scaling ladders were brought forward, and Joan herself mounted one of them. The town was entered and captured, and the escape of the English over the bridge was blocked. The earl of Suffolk, with his brother John, was captured on the bridge. Of his captor he enquired anxiously whether he was a knight. On the Frenchman confessing that he was only a squire, Suffolk knighted him on the spot and, honour being thus satisfied, formally surrendered to his captor.

The whole English garrison, except the nobles who were ransomed, were put to the sword, and the church which had been used by the English troops was looted.

Two towns on the Loire, Meung and Beaugency, remained to be captured before the way would be sufficiently safe to conduct the reluctant Charles to Rheims. This time the French generals acted promptly, for was not Fastolf on the war-path? Jargeau fell on the Sunday (June 12) of a week destined to become memorable. On the Monday the army returned to Orleans, and on the Wednesday resumed its march along the south bank to Meung and Beaugency. The bridge at Meung was reached at nightfall. It was defended by the English, who had made a small bridgehead on its southern end.[1] That night the bridge was won and a small guard was left on it. No attempt was made to take the town, which was separated from the bridge by a meadow.

The army continued along the south bank to Beaugency, where it was found that the English were holding the bridge and château, just as the French had held them in the previous year. The train of siege artillery that had been so effective against Jargeau was soon brought into action and opened on the bridge and château; some of the guns, in order to shorten the range, being floated by barges to a spot opposite the château. But their cannon-balls cannot have had much effect upon the gaunt, grim 12th-century keep of the château (which today looks as if it would never fall). However, the bombardment was kept up all next day (Friday) and that night the defenders, led by Matthew Gough and Richard Gethin, feeling themselves hopelessly out-powered and despairing of relief, compounded with Alençon to quit the town next morning, taking their arms and belongings with them.

On Saturday morning at dawn, therefore, they filed out of the town as agreed, little dreaming that Fastolf's relieving army had been halted within two miles of them on the previous day, and was now preparing to come to their relief along the south

---

[1] No signs remain of this earthwork.

bank. To explain how this astonishing situation arose we must go back to the English side.[1]

On June 5, the army commanded by Sir John Fastolf had marched out for the relief or reinforcement of Jargeau, and any other threatened towns. Its strength is usually given as 5,000, a suspiciously round figure. It is impossible to accept this figure. Less than twelve months previously Bedford had the greatest difficulty in finding about 2,000 men to complete Salisbury's army. In the following February he had been able to find only 1,000 English troops for Fastolf's relief army, and in the intervening four months no reinforcements had arrived from England. It is unlikely that at the second scraping the barrel would produce more men than had the first. As on that occasion, there must have been a considerable addition of *milice* or "Faux Français" who had taken service under the Anglo-Burgundian banners.[2] Even so, it seems improbable that the total can have attained to 3,000.[3] All the best and most active soldiers from the Normandy garrisons had already been taken, and the quality of Fastolf's new army must have been poor. The fact cannot have been hidden from the experienced eye of Sir John–which may explain much of what is to follow.

Marching after depositing a convoy of supplies, for some reason, at Etampes (25 miles south of Paris), Fastolf reached Janville about June 13, only to learn that Jargeau was besieged by a powerful French army. Considering it hopeless to attempt relief, Fastolf turned his eyes towards the twin towns, Meung and Beaugency. On the 16th he was joined by Lord John Talbot with a tiny force of 40 lances and 200 archers, say 300 men in all. He had come from Beaugency, which had been his headquarters since the siege of Orleans, in order to strengthen the relief army that he heard was approaching.

Talbot arrived in the morning, and Fastolf visited him at his

---

[1] Here I have followed Waurin's account. Gruel makes the date of the surrender the Thursday night, which is impossible, for in that case Fastolf would have heard of it in Meung. Moreover Count Charles of Clermont supports Waurin's dating.
[2] Two French sources mention the presence of these "Faux Français".
[3] The earliest French source only makes it 3,500.

lodging for *déjeuner*. Over the meal they discussed plans, and it soon became apparent that they were hopelessly at variance. Talbot, the less experienced soldier of the two, but a man possessed of ardent fighting spirit, argued hotly in favour of an immediate advance, as the Loire towns were obviously threatened, but Fastolf demurred. He knew, better than Talbot, that a poor spirit pervaded his own ranks, and that the efficiency and even loyalty of the French contingent was questionable. He had, moreover, learnt that Bedford was again planning to send reinforcements – probably more were expected from England – and Sir John was in favour of falling back and maintaining a defensive attitude till they arrived. To this Talbot raised violent objection, declaring that he at any rate would go to the relief of Beaugency (which he had just quit!) even if no-one else followed him. This forced Fastolf's hand, and he consented to march next day with his whole force. Early next morning, Saturday, June 17, while the French siege guns were hammering at the château of Beaugency, the English army paraded. But once again Fastolf made an effort to avert what he believed would result in disaster. A war council was held, while the troops, standing fast, must have suspected what was happening, and when at last the word to advance was given it was an army infected by the disharmony of its leaders, that moved off.

The march was, however, carried out fairly speedily, Meung being the first halting place. From here the army necessarily marched along the northern bank of the river, Meung bridge being still held by the French. About two miles short of Beaugency the road mounts a slight ridge, and from its summit another ridge can be seen crossing the road about 800 yards away. On this second ridge a French army was being drawn up in battle order, evidently intending to offer fight. On seeing this, Fastolf took the traditional English action: he halted his army, deployed it for battle in the usual formation; the archers planted their pointed stakes in their front, and all awaited the oncoming French. But nothing happened. The French having completed their dispositions sat firm. Something must be done to stir them to action, and Fastolf sent forward heralds with the proposal that three knights from each should fight out the issue in the space between the two armies. This was a slight variant of the usual challenge, so much favoured by Edward III, of a single combat between the two leaders. But now, as in practically all cases, the French ignored the challenge – and still they did not stir. Fastolf had no intention of taking the offensive himself, the French position appeared too strong for his weak army. He therefore bethought him, in all probability, of the tactics of the earl of Salisbury in a somewhat similar situation on the eve of Cravant: and he took the same course. That is to say, he fell back to Meung, intending to cross the river there, and approach Beaugency from the south side where the bridge was still in English hands. The army accordingly withdrew that evening to Meung, and immediately made preparations to capture the bridge. Cannons were put into position, and during the night they maintained a fire against the defenders on the bridge – one of the earliest recorded cases of "night firing" by artillery.[1]

Saturday, June 18, dawned with the bridge still in French hands. At about 8 a.m. the English assault party were providing themselves with improvised shields from doors, etc., when a galloper arrived with the disturbing news that Beaugency was in the hands of the French and that they were now advancing towards Meung. This settled the matter; the little English army now found itself between two fires north and south of the river; retreat was the only possible course, and with a heavy heart it set out on the return march to Janville. This was the first step, had the troops but known it, in a retreat which was to last with fluctuations for 24 years.

We now return to the French camp. On Friday morning Alençon had received an unexpected and indeed unwelcome

---

[1] The most recent French life of Joan, *Jeanne d'Arc* by Lucien Fabre, states that the bridge was attacked in order to capture the town. This is to put the story upside-down. The bridge could not be attacked until the town was occupied. The real reason why the English attacked the bridge was because they wanted to get to the other side. In war the simplest explanation is usually the correct one.

accession to his strength. Arthur of Richemont, Constable of France, marched into the camp at the head of 1,000 Bretons. Since we last met him fighting in Brittany he had been at the Dauphin's court engaged in a bitter and prolonged struggle for power with La Trémoïlle. In the upshot he was worsted and driven from the court in disgrace. Moreover, Charles forbade Alençon to receive him. The meeting therefore was an embarrassing one. And Count Arthur did not make it less so. He had an awkward manner and unprepossessing appearance – like that other distinguished Breton, Bertrand Duguesclin – being short of stature, dark and thick-lipped.

As soon as he had dismounted from his horse, Joan embraced him around the knees, to receive the gruff response: "Whether you are sent by God I know not; if you are I do not fear you, for God knows that my heart is pure. If you come from the Devil I fear you still less." This undoubtedly authentic utterance throws a useful light on the puzzled attitude of Frenchmen towards the Maid at this period of her career.

Joan acted as peacemaker between the two soldiers, and her task may have been eased and hastened by the abrupt news that Fastolf was approaching at the head of a powerful army. Danger makes good bed-fellows of enemies. Thus it came about that when Alençon started off in pursuit of the English the Constable and his contingent were included in his ranks. The army that set off may have been as high as 6,000 in number.

THE BATTLE OF PATAY (June 18, 1429)

Joan's campaign had started on Sunday at Jargeau. It was now Saturday, the last day of an unforgettable week. The English had suspended the attack on the Meung bridge and had retreated towards Patay, 18 miles away due north. On hearing this news the French leaders exhibited their usual indecision. "You have spurs," exploded Joan, her eyes ablaze, "use them!" They did. Selecting the best mounted men for the vanguard, Alençon ordered a vigorous pursuit. Rapidly the French vanguard gained on their opponents whose pace was necessarily regulated by the speed of the baggage-train. Thus, when the English army had reached the vicinity of Patay, the French vanguard was at St. Sigismund, four miles to the south. Here

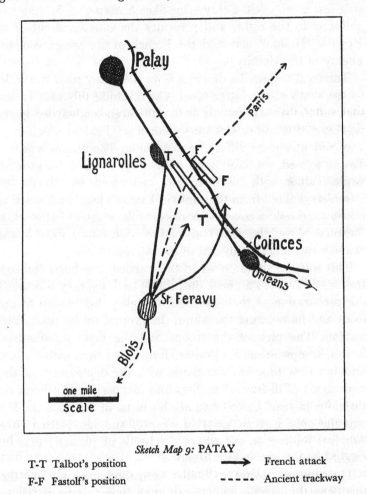

Sketch Map 9: PATAY

T-T Talbot's position   ⟶   French attack

F-F Fastolf's position   - - - - -   Ancient trackway

the French army halted at noon for their mid-day meal, and resumed the journey two hours later. Hitherto they had not obtained touch with the English army. Patrols were now sent out in all directions. Presently word was received that by a happy chance the English had been located halted just to the south of Patay. It had happened in this way. Advancing northwards along the Patay road leading patrols had set on foot a stag just north of St. Feravy (see Sketch Map 9). The stag had galloped to the right, and presently the raucous shout of an English "Halloo" had told the French of the presence of the enemy in the vicinity.

The road to Janville diverges from the Patay road two miles to the south of the latter town. On reaching this spot Fastolf received the news from patrols that the French advanced-guard was close on their heels. A hasty council was held, at which there was evidently some difference of opinion. The upshot was that Fastolf agreed, probably with reluctance, to stand his ground, while Talbot with his own 300, reinforced by about 200 "archiers d'élite" from the ranks of Fastolf's host, undertook to occupy and hold a covering position to the south of Patay while Fastolf deployed the main body on the ridge, now marked by the railway two miles south-east of the village.

This was the situation when the startled stag burst through the line of Talbot's archers. Suspecting nothing, they continued the preparation of their position, bringing their stakes to the front and hammering them into the ground in the prescribed fashion. The pick of the troops and the best commanders, Scales, Rempston and Sir Walter Hungerford, were with Talbot, and but slow progress was made with the deployment of the main body of ill-trained soldiers and inexperienced officers on the ridge in rear. Fastolf had not his heart in the business. His was the only English army in France, and he realized (like Admiral Jellicoe on the eve of the battle of Jutland) that he might lose the war in an afternoon.

The position selected by Talbot seems to have run along the road from Lignarolles to Coinces, at the point where it crosses the old Roman road from St. Sigismund to Janville. This point is near the bottom of a slight dip in the ground, which however was calculated to form a suitable locality for its purpose, being a few hundred yards in front of the ridge that Fastolf would hold.

The ground was much enclosed with small copses and hedges, and there was probably a hedge along the road that the archers were to line.

The French army was advancing in the following order. The advanced-guard was composed of specially selected men all well mounted, under the command of La Hire and Poton de Xantrailles, comrades in arms in many an operation. The main body was led by Alençon and Dunois, and with the rear-guard were the Constable de Richemont and Joan of Arc, who was much peeved at being kept back in this way.

Contact with the English rear-guard was obtained shortly after two o'clock in the afternoon. The battle that ensued reached its decision in a matter of minutes and can be described in a few sentences. The French advanced-guard, on topping the slight rise from St. Feravy to Lignarolles, saw the English drawn up in the dip in front of them. Inspired by the *élan* imparted to them by the Maid, and led by the best cavalry commanders in their army, the French horsemen swept impetuously down the slope in a wild avalanche on top of the 400 English archers, who were not ready for them and were taken by surprise. Moreover, the line was turned on each flank and almost before they had realized what was happening they found themselves surrounded. Archers, like gunners, can defend their own front, but are helpless against attack from the flank. They were helpless. Most of them fell. A few managed to get away to the rear, and running back over the ridge added to the confusion that was already affecting Fastolf's heterogeneous collection of soldiers. For the French attack was made in such large numbers and was so closely followed up by the main body, that Fastolf found himself overwhelmed before he could take any effective steps to oppose this surprise attack. It was all outside the experience of any Englishmen in the field. Previously a French antagonist had approached a position held by them with circumspection, even trepidation. But this attack had the unhesitating thrust of a Thomas Dagworth, a Robert Knollys, or indeed of a John Talbot. The Joan of Arc yeast had worked; the loaf was leavened and transformed. The Maid of Orleans, who, with the rear-guard did not see a blow struck–except on an English prisoner[1] –had won the battle of Patay.

Lord Talbot was captured, taken near a prominent bush in his front line, mounted but spurless: evidently a horse had just been brought up for him and he was about to make a dash for it. His was already a name to conjure with in the French army, and his capture was a great morale-raiser in the French ranks. That night he spent in a lodging in Patay, situated in a road which still goes by the name of the Rue Talbot. Next morning the Duke of Alençon who had himself been captured at Verneuil (and had only recently been released) could not resist the temptation of gloating over his prisoner–to receive the dignified response that "it was the fortune of war", a sentiment that seems to have so much impressed the hearers that it was deemed worthy of permanent record by the French Chroniclers.

Lord Scales and other leaders had also been captured, but Fastolf managed to get away and also to save something out of the wreck, though he lost his baggage and guns. He retreated to Janville, 18 miles away. Arrived there he found the gates shut in his face. There was nothing to be done but to continue the weary march to Etampes, another 24 miles, making no less than 60 miles covered that day and night. A terrible journey it must have been for the old warrior, his only consolation being that he could say "I told you so!" But he still had a stout body of English archers around him. They made a firm face to every attack by their pursuers, and when they had exhausted their arrows they attacked their opponents with drawn swords.

*   *   *

When the news of the disaster reached the English and French capitals the reaction was significant. In London a fund was at once raised for the ransom of Lord Talbot. In Paris the wretched Sir John Fastolf was, it is said, deprived of his Garter.[2] He had, it would seem "lost the war in an afternoon".

[1] There is a window depicting this incident in Patay church.
[2] It was later restored to him, and he served again in command in Maine.

The dazzling campaign of a week had ended for Joan in triumph. General Lemoine, after pointing out that this was the only campaign made entirely under the inspiration of Joan, adds admiringly:

"She knew but one method–force, and one argument–battle. . . . Therefore the humble Maid of Domrémy takes her place among the very great generals."[1]

* * *

It might have been supposed that Joan's Voices would have now councilled an immediate advance on Paris, on the well established principle of "striking while the iron is hot". And the prospects of such an advance were rosy. But Joan's eyes were set on Rheims, and the sacred anointing of Charles as the legitimate king of France. As a matter of fact the reverse of Patay had the unexpected effect of a rapprochement between the Burgundians and the English; the duke himself visited Paris and steps were taken to strengthen the defences of the city. He contracted to raise more troops.

Meanwhile Charles was at last on his way to Rheims. By dint of continually pumping courage and confidence into her Prince, Joan ensured that the march should be speedy and almost unopposed. Charles de Valois entered the city of Rheims on July 16, 1429.[2] Next day the anointing and coronation took place, and Charles the Dauphin must now be described as Charles VII. The mission of Joan of Arc was accomplished. It would indeed have been well for France and for England if she had contrived to get killed in the very next engagement. But it was not to be.

* * *

There followed the most bloodless and almost farcical campaign (if it can be called a campaign) of the war. Joan, set upon attacking Paris, dragged a reluctant monarch in that direction. But he kept edging off towards home, till on August 5, the army

[1] *Jeanne d'Arc, Chef de Guerre*, p. 53.
[2] The writer had the luck to be present at the celebrations in Rheims on the 500th anniversary of the historic entry into Rheims.

approached Bray, intending to cross the south bank of the Seine there, and thence back to Bourges. But the duke of Bedford who had not only been reinforced, but had received an undertaking from the unpredictable duke of Burgundy to enter upon active operations in support of his ally, now approached the newly crowned French king, intent upon crossing swords with him. His first step was to post a strong force at Bray to head Charles off that crossing place, whilst he himself advanced with his army to Montereau, 25 miles to the west. Charles, seeing that his project was baulked, turned in his tracks and marched north to Crépy, 40 miles north-east of Paris. To this place Bedford sent a message of studied insolence, that might well be calculated to sting the most phlegmatic coward into aggressive action. It looked for a moment as if this challenge was having its effect, for Charles advanced some 12 miles to Dammartin (20 miles north east of Paris), and there found the English army drawn up to oppose him. A day of skirmishing ensued, and in the evening the French army fell back again. Bedford then advanced to Senlis (12 miles further north) and on August 16 the two armies were again face to face. Bedford drew up his army, blocking the road to Paris, but again the French declined to attack, and their king fell back once more to Crépy.

Seeing that the French had no intention of risking a battle, Bedford took his own army back to Paris, disturbing news having reached him from Normandy. The Constable de Richemont had advanced from Maine and was threatening Evreux, only 25 miles from Rouen. Bedford accordingly took the major part of his army to that region, leaving the Burgundians with a sprinkling of English troops to hold the capital. He had taken stock of the French king and of the danger to be expected from that quarter.

Meanwhile King Charles was finding it more pleasant and profitable to receive the surrender of Burgundian towns such as Compiègne without a blow being struck, than to undertake the hazards of war against the English–a policy in which his evil genius, La Trémoïlle, concurred. All this time he was negotiating with Duke Philip who however proved altogether too dexterous for him. For the time being the lot of this cold and calculating Prince lay with the English party.

Joan was naturally dispirited, but she did not cease to hope. At last her king was induced to quit Compiègne and move forward to St. Denys, (only four miles north of Paris) which had been evacuated by the Burgundians. He arrived there on September 7, Joan and the advanced guard having preceded him by several days. An attack on the capital was planned for the next day. While Alençon watched the Porte St. Denys (from a distance) Joan with her party assaulted the Porte St. Honoré. The Maid exhibited her usual bravery and intrepidity under fire, and the outer ditch was successfully crossed. But it was too late; the defences had recently been strengthened and the attack on the inner ditch failed. Joan was wounded in the leg by a crossbow shaft, and left lying in the open till dark. Alençon held his hand all day and the king did not quit St. Denys. The Maid of Orleans had been deliberately left in the lurch. The evidence is clear enough, although it might appear almost incredible. La Trémoïlle was probably "the villain in the piece".

King Charles now showed his hand; he marched off to the south, ordering Joan to follow. Crossing the Seine at Bray—now undefended—he was on September 21 safely ensconsed at Gien, the point of departure for his march to Rheims.

The Maid had failed. It was her first failure; still she had failed, and it was bound to react upon her prestige. But worse was to follow. For nearly two months she was kept inactive at court, and when eventually allowed to take the field again, after a preliminary success in capturing St. Pierre on the upper Loire, she failed for the second time at La Charité. After besieging this town (also on the upper Loire), for a month in bitterly cold weather, and after failing to receive further supplies from the court, she was obliged to abandon the siege. Winter then put an end to operations.

*   *   *

We have reached the year 1430. During the early spring, operations languished; indeed Burgundy had arranged a local truce with Charles. But in April he took up arms once more, possibly influenced by the knowledge that a new English army, led by Cardinal Beaufort, with the boy king Henry VI included, was about to land at Calais. Duke Philip now assembled his army at Montdidier (30 miles north-west of Compiègne) and advanced to the recapture of that town. Hearing this, Joan slipped away from the court, then at Sully, with a handful of followers and made her way by stages to Compiègne, which she entered on May 13, three weeks after Henry VI landed at Calais.

The duke of Burgundy was nominally besieging the town, but it was not even as complete an investment as that of Orleans had been. Compiègne lies on the south bank of the river Oise, and the attackers were confined to the north bank. Included in Duke Philip's army was an English detachment under Sir John Montgomery. During the next ten days the Maid took part in some rather petty and abortive manoeuvres on the south bank, but on May 24 she made a sudden sortie with about 500 troops, to the north of the town. Crossing a long causeway her troops surprised and scattered the nearest Burgundian post. But it happened that John of Luxemburg was at the time reconnoitring on a hill in rear. He witnessed the attack, and sent for reinforcements. When they came up a hot fight took place, in which the Maid particularly distinguished herself. While thus engaged, Montgomery's troops attacked her party in the rear. Most of them fled into the city while Joan herself with a tiny band was driven off the causeway and her retreat to the bridge was cut off. She was in fact driven by the English into the arms of the Burgundians and by them she was captured.

Assessed in cold military terms, it seems to have been a happy piece of co-operation between the two allies and there is no need to impute treachery on the part of the French garrison or of members of Joan's party.[1] It was a spirited end to a dazzling and

---

[1] Most history-books state tersely that Joan was captured by the Burgundians. As the above account shows, there is a *suppressio veri* in this statement. It was essentially a combined operation.

utterly unique military career, and one can but regret that the Maid had not the fortune (which she had prayed for) to be killed in an engagement. It would have been better for France and for England, for no person, English, Burgundian or French comes out of the sorry sequel with credit – except that nameless English soldier who dashed into the flames to hand the Maid a rude wooden cross. . . .

At this point, therefore, we take leave of the glorious Maid, for there is no need here to relate the story – more widely known than any other story of medieval times – of how she was sold by the Burgundians to the English, condemned by the French Church and executed by the English army. In passing, one may wonder why the English leaders should have been anxious to take the life of a prisoner whom they deemed no longer an adverse influence to their cause. It may indeed be that they were not particularly anxious, and that there is basis for the story that the earl of Warwick had offered Joan her liberty provided she would promise not to take up arms again.[1]

*   *   *

Be that as it may, we come back to the two questions with which we approached the appearance on the scene of the Maid. What military influence did her Voices have upon Joan, and what practical influence did she have upon the course of the war?

The first question has perhaps been answered inferentially in the preceding pages. No-one pretends that Saint Margaret and Saint Catherine were well-versed in military strategy or that they always guided her aright – for example in her advocacy of an attack on Paris or the relief of Compiègne. Indeed, Joan herself never made such a claim, once her king had been anointed. But what the Voices did do was to inspire her with a burning faith in her mission to rid France of the invaders and in the equally firm belief that this must be accomplished by aggressive action – by the sword. Further, that in order to temper and sharpen that sword the morale of the troops must be raised by a

[1] Scurrilous writers have suggested a different proviso.

living faith in victory akin to her own. This achieved, everything else followed the well established war principles of offensive action, the maintenance of the objective–whatever the set-backs and disappointments that had to be encountered–the taking of risks, and the application of speed and surprise. These simple but fundamental military virtues had long lain dormant in the French ranks; it was the Maid, and the Maid alone, who roused them into action.

This leads us on to, and indeed overlaps, our second question and suggests the answer to it: what practical influence did the Maid have upon the course of the war? This question could be answered with greater assurance had the war ended with the death of Joan. But it continued for another generation, indeed the tide turned and for a time seemed to flow quite perceptibly in the opposite direction–as will shortly appear. A further difficulty is that we require to know, not only what practical effects she had upon the fighting capacity and spirit of the French troops but also upon the English troops, and we have very little data to go upon. There is an almost complete silence on the subject of the Maid in contemporary English records, and when all the evidence comes from the enemy's side it has to be treated with caution. Indeed, there is really only one single contemporary English document that bears on the subject. But that is an important document and must therefore be examined closely. I refer to the famous letter written by the Duke of Bedford to the English Council in 1433.

"At the whiche tyme [The Siege of Orleans] there felle by the hand of God, as it seemeth, a greet strook upon your peuple that was assembled there in grete nombre, caused in grete partie as I trowe of lakke of sadde [sound] beleve, and of unlevethefulle [unbelieving] doubte that thei hadde of a disciple and lyme [limb] of the Feende, called the Pucelle, that used false enchauntments and sorcerie; the whiche strook and disconfiture nought only lessed in grete partie the nombre of youre peuple, there, but as welle withdrowe the courage of the remenant in merveilleus wyse; and couragiged youre adverse partie and enemies to assemble them forthwith in grete nombre."[1]

[1] Rymer, IV, p. 408.

This seems pretty clear, though two things must be remembered. First, the letter, though written three years after the capture of the Maid, refers to the effect she had upon the English soldiers during her campaign which was not necessarily a permanent effect. Second, Bedford was naturally looking for a scapegoat, attributing all the evils of the period to the Pucelle, and none to himself or the English leaders. But it is as good evidence as we could wish for that the Maid "started the rot", and in so doing changed the course of military events. Nor is it relevant to remark that she appeared at a fortunate moment, when the Burgundians were tiring of the struggle and when it would seem that the pendulum of fortune was bound to swing back, if not at once then on the death of Bedford, after which the Burgundian alliance could not be expected to endure. All this is of course true, and there were in fact to be (as I have said) some oscillations of the pendulum in the course of the 23 years that supervened after the capture of Joan before the English were finally driven out of France. But all the credit for starting the pendulum in its backward swing, and for starting it in no uncertain manner, must go to that marvellous soul, the pure and peerless Maid of Orleans.

APPENDIX

RECONSTRUCTION OF THE BATTLE OF PATAY

It has been particularly difficult to reconstruct the battle with any degree of confidence, for the sources are obscure and in places conflicting, so that considerable recourse has had to be made to I.M.P. Yet there were two eyewitnesses present who afterwards wrote about the battle: on the English side that ubiquitous Burgundian Jean Waurin, on the French side Guillaume Gruel, a Breton who followed the banner of the Constable de Richemont and afterwards wrote his *Chronicle*. Yet Waurin's account is so confused that one suspects the author had himself a confused notion of what really happened. In at least one passage he wrote *avant-garde* when he must have meant *arrière-garde*. One cannot therefore place as much credence in his story as one

would wish, though most writers appear to accept every statement of his. He marched in the main-body under Fastolf and he
seems more concerned to defend the flight of himself and his
unnamed "capitaine" than to give an explicit account of the
sequence of events.

*   *   *

The first thing is to establish the site of the battle.[1] The
sources are in general agreement that it was:

(a) Near Patay. (b) To the south of the village.

Other villages mentioned in this connection are St. Sigismund,
St. Feravy, Lignarolles and Coinces. Taking the mean of all
these indications, the site should lie fairly close to Lignarolles.

The English were retreating from Meung towards Janville.
What road would they take? Here local knowledge comes in,
and there is little doubt that it must have been along the old
Roman road that runs between St. Sigismund and St. Feravy
and leaves Lignarolles 1,000 yards on its left. The road Lignarolles–Coinces is also an old track. Next, we may assume that
Talbot's position was astride the road by which the army was
marching i.e. the Roman road. This further narrows the search
for his position.

When selecting a position in a hurry, such as in a rear-guard
action, the simplest and easiest position to take up is the one
usually adopted, such as the line of a road. Talbot may thus
have selected the line of the Lignarolles–Coinces road where
it crosses the Roman road. How does this position stand up to
the requirements of the situation? It stands up fairly well. It is
not an ideal position for it crosses the dip; the ridge linking
Lignarolles to St. Feravy would be a stronger position, but not
so easy to take up in a hurry.[2] Moreover the earliest French

---

[1] There is no general agreement as to the site and local information is hard to
come by. Indeed Owen Rutter in his delightful *Land of St. Joan* writes, "The
memory of that field of battle seems to have passed from the memory of man.
At least we could find no-one who could direct us to it, and we returned to Orleans."
[2] Talbot may have purposely left this ridge for Fastolf's force.

source states that the position was not well selected. Finally, a region of hedges would probably have a hedge alongside a road, and according to one account the line was along a hedge. I believe this was the position occupied by Talbot. It is said that the earl was captured close to a prominent bush. His command-post would naturally be in the centre of his line, *i.e.* where it crosses the Roman road. Now it happens that at this spot there is a solitary prominent bush and it will assist the imagination of the visitor to the field to picture Talbot being taken when sitting his horse alongside the bush. We may even go one further and dub it "Talbot's bush". *Le Buisson de Talbot.* There is no monument or memorial on the battlefield. This would be a suitable spot on which to erect one.[1]

SOURCES FOR THE BATTLE OF PATAY

The three earliest sources are the three best. The first takes the form of a letter written in Latin only five weeks after the battle, by Jacques de Bourbon, Comte de la Marche, to the Bishop of Laon. It was not published till 1891 (too late for use by Ramsay). It is included in Charpentier's edition of the *Journal du Siège.* Though it contains some obvious errors, there is a solid core of information in it, and many of its details ring true. Thus it contains the description of La Hire's no doubt rather disorderly charge as "un pêu pêle-mêle". Waurin's account, which should be the best, is confused and probably misleading: Monstrelet copies and improves upon it slightly. The third source is Guillaume Gruel's *Chronicle d'Arthur de Richemont.* Though Gruel was present, his master took no active part in the battle; consequently Gruel did not either, but his account is good as far as it goes. The other French sources add but little to the above three. On the English side there is, as is usual for this period of the war, no chronicle whatever.

I know of no modern work, French or English, that takes into account the topography of the battle.

---

[1] In 1950 the then Curé indicated to the author this dip in the road as the site of the battle; but he gave no reasons for his belief.

SOME SUGGESTIONS FOR FURTHER READING ON JOAN OF ARC

Fortunately a bibliography of Joan of Arc would not be appropriate for the purposes of this book. Fortunately, for the number of works on the subject is well-nigh legion: there is in Orleans a library of several thousand volumes devoted exclusively to the subject of the Maid. We are merely concerned with works of assistance to military students. And here we are at once struck by the dearth of books by English military writers. General Fuller, it is true, has some arresting things to say about the Maid in his *Decisive Battles of the Western World* but they are necessarily strictly condensed, whilst Fortescue cannot find any space for Joan. French soldiers are of course better represented, but they tend to be rather uncritically panegyrical. General C. Lemoine however has some useful observations in his *Jeanne d'Arc, Chef de Guerre*. Professor Edouard Perroy in his admirable *La Guerre de Cent Ans* is balanced but rather noncommittal. In spite of the fact that many lives of the Maid have appeared since it was published in 1908, Andrew Lang's *The Maid of France* increases rather than diminishes in stature. It is understanding, sufficiently detailed and quite useful from the purely military aspects. The same applies to Owen Rutter's sympathetic *The Land of St. Joan*.

The two latest books at the time of writing (1955) are M. Lucien Fabre's *Jeanne d'Arc* and Regine Pernoud's *The Retrial of Joan of Arc*. The former is too violently nationalist and Anglophobe to inspire confidence in a military historian. For example the author delights in dubbing Henry V "The Cut-throat King" and he is at pains to discount the tributes paid to the Duke of Bedford by contemporary Burgundian chroniclers. Madame Pernoud's book on the other hand may be truly described as "filling a long-felt want", for she translates into French (here re-translated into English) the Latin of portion of the *Procès de Condamnation et de Rehabilitation de Jeanne d'Arc*, which was published by Jules Quicherat in 1841 and partially translated into French in 1868. I agree with the author that it is strange that this document has been so neglected. Many years ago I enquired of it in a high-class bookshop in Rouen – *in Rouen!* The shopkeeper's face was a complete blank; he had never heard of the book. Though the military detail contained in it is only incidental, it is worth study, if only for the full transcript of Dunois' testimony.

CHAPTER XVI

THE TREATY OF ARRAS

ON May 30, 1430, the sentence on Joan of Arc pro-
nounced by the French ecclesiastics was carried out by
the English soldiers. But long before this event the
tide of war had begun to turn back in favour of England. Once
the Maid was in captivity her influence over the English army
evaporated. It was now clear that she was not infallible, and
in the eyes of the soldiers she must be a witch–a view that was
to be confirmed next year when the church condemned her to
be burned. Thus within a month of her capture the strong
castle of Château Gaillard had been retaken, to be followed
in the succeeding months by the recapture of several towns to
the north, east and south of Paris. In fact the situation improved
to such an extent that it was deemed safe to convey the young
King Henry from Calais to Rouen.

The Burgundians however were not so successful in their campaign; the siege of Compiègne dragged on, the earl of Huntingdon replacing Sir John Montgomery and John of Luxemburg
replacing Duke Philip. The latter had gone to take over the
province of Brabant which had fallen to him on the death of his
cousin. In January 1431 Bedford returned to Paris from Rouen.

Best of all, the redoubtable Poton de Xantrailles had been
captured by the earl of Warwick in a brilliant enterprise. With a
force of 800 men Xantrailles had set out from Beauvais on a
raid towards Rouen. The earl of Warwick got wind of it and
hastily collected about 600 men, and advanced rapidly to intercept him. The two forces met in the open at Savignies near
Gournay, 20 miles west of Beauvais. It was a one-sided battle,
the French putting up very slight opposition; they were utterly
defeated and pursued all the way back to Beauvais, while
Xantrailles himself and several other knights were captured.

Among these prisoners was a young shepherd whom the Archbishop of Rheims had designed as a successor to the Maid. The
Archbishop, who knew Joan well but had received the news of
her capture with some complacency, declared that the youth
"talks just as well as Joan ever did".

A further notable success was the recovery in the autumn,
after three months siege, of Louviers. All was now in order for
Bedford's long planned design—the coronation at St. Denys of
Henry VI as king of France. This coronation took place on
December 16, with due ceremony though without the presence
of many notable Frenchmen. But the Paris populace gave the
young king a warm welcome, evidently expecting some favours
from him—which they did not receive.

The year 1432 followed the general pattern of 1431 except
that there were no spectacular English successes, and indeed
there were two distinct setbacks. The first was that Chartres
fell to the French in March; the second was the siege of Lagny.
The duke of Bedford had made this the most important item in
the summer campaign. But the French put up a spirited defence,
the weather became unbearably hot, and Bedford himself over-
exerted himself in the heat and suffered some permanent ill-
effects. Eventually Dunois brought up a relieving army, and
Bedford regretfully abandoned the siege. He also suffered the
loss of his wife, Anne of Burgundy, sister of the Duke Philip; thus
a link and an important one, in the entente between England
and Burgundy was snapped, for there were no offspring of the
marriage.

The year 1433 was chiefly marked by successful campaigns in
the eastern theatre of the war, mainly undertaken by the Burgundians under Duke Philip. The Duke had become addicted to
making short local truces with the Valois, whilst allowing his
troops to continue fighting under the English banner for
English pay—an economical method of waging warfare. French
incursions while the truce was still in operation had however
stung him into action. Over the rest of the war-theatre there
were alternate gains by each side, which it would merely con-

fuse the reader to recount in detail. A political event of importance however cannot be passed over in silence. The worthless
but all-powerful La Trémoïlle fell at last – assassinated in his bed
at Chinon as the result of a "Court plot", in which his rival the
Constable de Richemont had a hand. His place was taken by
the Queen's brother, Charles of Anjou. It is however difficult to
trace any immediate change in the direction or course of the
war.

The year 1434 opened propitiously. The earl of Arundel conducted a very successful campaign in Maine and Anjou, eventually extending his conquests to the banks of the river Loire.
Unfortunately he was mortally wounded and captured by La
Hire and Xantrailles on the estuary of the Somme next year. A
still more notable commander was however to step into his
shoes. Tremendous efforts had been made in England to raise
the enormous ransom demanded for Lord Talbot. The capture
of Xantrailles therefore came at an opportune moment, for an
exchange between the two warriors was quickly arranged. Talbot landed in France in the Spring, bringing with him 800 men.
He soon made his presence felt. He carried out extensive operations in the area to the north of Paris. He recaptured a large
number of towns, some of which surrendered incontinently on
the mere news that the great Talbot was approaching. Gisors on
the eastern border of Normandy soon fell, and Creil, Clermont
and Crepy in the Oise watershed quickly followed. St. Valery
also was recovered among other places.

The duke of Burgundy was again having successes within his
own borders to the south, and all this time the French reaction
was distinctly and increasingly weak. Charles VII has been
blamed for failing to raise a field army with which to attack the
allies. But the simple truth is that he had not the financial means
to support an army that could do anything effective in face of an
English army in the field. His cause seemed to be in a poor way.
Moreover, throughout the area of the war all semblance of law
and order was vanishing, and brigandage, reminiscent of the
Free Companies of the previous century, was springing up. It

became increasingly difficult to get food into Paris, and the inhabitants sent a despairing appeal to London for reinforcements with which to drive the enemy further from their gates. In Normandy also there were peasant risings, caused more by economic than national or Francophil motives. These were however easily repressed.

But in the late autumn a surprising development and change came over the scene. Duke Philip had recently concluded one of his local truces with the Valois king and negotiations for a possible peace began to appear likely. In January 1435 Philip met at Nevers the heads of the Valois government, and next month preliminaries of peace were signed. But Philip still felt he could not ratify any peace terms without the consent of his ally, so England was invited to be present at a second meeting to be held at Arras in July. The English consented, though without enthusiasm for they had their misgivings. It seemed to them that this was the worst possible time to treat for peace. The king of Bourges seemed to be nearing the end of his tether.[1] A little perseverence, a few more pulls on the rope, and the tug of war would be over. The unknown quantity was the duke of Burgundy; he must at all costs be retained in the alliance, and as much to humour him as for any other reason English plenipotentiaries appeared at the conference chamber at Arras at the appointed time.

The story of the protracted negotiations and bargainings that took place cannot fail to be of interest to the present generation, brought up as it has been on a series of international negotiations of a somewhat similar nature. But we can only summarize them here. The Pope appointed Cardinal Alvergati as his legate and he presided throughout at the conference. The chief English delegate was Cardinal Beaufort.

Scarcely had the proceedings commenced than they were interrupted by an event calculated to wreck the whole conference. La Hire and Xantrailles–the Castor and Pollux of the

---

[1] "The Valois kingdom was not merely out of breath; it was at the end of its strength." *The Hundred Years War* by Edouard Perroy, p. 290.

Valois army–selected this critical moment to make a raid into Burgundian territory from Beauvais. They crossed the Somme at Bray, and worked west towards Corbie. This disturbing news reached Arras, only 30 miles to the north, while the duke of Burgundy was dining the French envoys. He instantly turned out a force, to which English and even Valois knights attached themselves, to repel the invader and disturber of the peace. The "Heavenly Gemini" were encountered near Corbie, but thanks to the Valois knights, blows were avoided and the raiders were allowed to return to their own territory, minus their booty and prisoners. The conference then proceeded.

Each side received secret 'maximum' terms that it was authorized to offer if need be, but each side opened up with proposals very far apart. Gradually the differences were whittled down, concessions of territory being made, chiefly on the part of Charles's party. It soon however became evident that the negotiations would split on the rock of Henry's title to the throne of France. On this point the English envoys were adamant. Duke Philip exhausted his utmost powers of persuasion on this issue with Cardinal Beaufort who, for his part, became so worked up that the perspiration streamed down his face. It was all of no use, the negotiations broke down and on September 6 the English took their departure.

The French delegates, evidently upset and alarmed by the peremptory departure of the English envoys, sent after them a fresh proposal that the question of Henry VI's renunciation of his title as king of France should hang over till he became of age, on condition that they should at once evacuate all ceded territory. But this last-minute concession was of no avail. Feeling in London ran high, the mob attacked French domiciles and the unfortunate messenger, none other than the famous chronicler Le Fèvre (who relates the story) received the following remarkable reply from the Lord Chancellor:

"The King of England and France, my master, has seen the letters and offers that you have brought him, which have much displeased him, and not without reason, for which things he has assembled those of his blood and Lineage for advice on the subject; and you can now return across the sea."

And that was all.

Seeing that the duke of Burgundy had now shown his hand and was obviously resolved upon an accord with his old enemy, whether the English were agreeable or not, it may be considered that the unbending attitude of the English Government was unreasonable and mistaken. Without the Burgundian alliance the "dual monarchy" could hardly persist indefinitely, and the sensible course was to relinquish the claim to sovereignty, as Edward III had done, and be content with the minor sovereignty of Normandy and Gascony. But in the eyes of the proud and obstinate English people Henry VI was the lawful king of France, Charles having been disinherited by his own father.[1] Mistaken or not, one cannot withold a certain admiration for the pertinacity thus exhibited by the English people—a pertinacity that was to become a part of the national character—the pertinacity that refuses to abandon a struggle or relinquish an aim that it has once embarked upon—as exemplified by the long struggle with Philip II of Spain, Louis XIV of France, Napoleon Bonaparte, Kaiser William and Adolf Hitler of Germany. . . .

*　　　*　　　*

The duke of Burgundy made his peace with Charles. By what processes of casuistry he salved his conscience in breaking unilaterally his alliance with England, sworn to at Troyes, we are not here concerned. The all-important fact is that the alliance which both Henry V and the duke of Bedford so clearly realised to be essential to the endurance of the "dual monarchy" had snapped. John, duke of Bedford, a sick man, saw his life's work crumbling in ruins. His heart was broken; he turned his face to the wall and died.[2]

Of this splendid English prince, a man in advance of his time, who had nursed farseeing projects for the unification and better-

[1] This point is conceded by Professor Perroy, op. cit., p. 292.
[2] He was buried in the chancel of Rouen Cathedral—a pilgrimage to the grave of this great Englishman is therefore easy.

ment of two great nations, it will be sufficient to quote only the tribute of a Frenchman. The Bourgeois of Paris described him as:

"Noble in birth and worth; wise, liberal, feared and loved."

While the peace talks had been going on, military operations had not ceased. In the summer Lord Talbot and the Burgundian leader L'Isle Adam, had carried out successful operations in the Isle de France, retaking many strong places that had fallen into French hands. And early in September he had taken the field with Bedford himself in an attempt to recover St. Denys, which also had been for some time in Valois hands. He had amassed an army 6,000 strong, and the attack was conducted with vigour. After a heavy bombardment an assault with scaling ladders, through the waters of the moat neck-high, was attempted. It failed. But shortly afterwards the garrison despairing of relief, surrendered at discretion.

Some Burgundian troops had assisted in this siege. It was their last cooperation with their allies. A few weeks later they were to be found fighting on the side of the Valois. Duke Philip had offered to remain neutral after the signing of the Treaty of Arras, but the English, infuriated with the "false, forsworn Duke" rejected his offer with contumely, and proudly set about the formidable task of opposing Burgundians and Valois combined. But the defection of Burgundy was fatal to the English cause. The Burgundians in Paris, hitherto faithful to the alliance and to Henry VI, fell away, and when a French army under the Constable de Richemont appeared before the gates on April 13, 1436, they were opened to him. The English garrison was allowed to depart unmolested, but "it was amid the hoots of the burgesses who had once hailed it with delight".

The English cause in France seemed lost.

CHAPTER XVII

THE ENGLISH RECOVERY

THE English cause in France was lost. Or so it must have seemed to most Frenchmen. But they had overlooked two things: the stubborn pride of the English nation, and the presence at the virtual head of their army in France of John, Lord Talbot. But at the outset of this new phase of the war there came a surprising turn of events. Instead of a combined Valois-Burgundian army invading Normandy, such as might have been expected, the fighting was done, not by Armagnacs or Burgundians but by the old allies of England, the Flemings.

It came about in this way. Duke Philip had been piqued by the contemptuous spurning by England of his offer of neutrality, and he conceived a violent hatred of his old ally—a hatred that was reciprocated, for there is no wrath like that of ancient friends who have quarrelled. The English had always regarded Charles with quiet contempt; now they regarded Philip with loathing. The Burgundian resolved to strike back. How could he hurt his old ally with least expense and effort to himself? Calais was the obvious answer. Whatever other possession in France England might be obliged to relinquish, the loss of Calais—a veritable "pistol pointed at Paris"—would hurt her pride the most. Now the Flemish border ran adjacent to the Calais "pale", and the Flemings were his subjects. If he could only persuade them that it was their own (trade) interest to turn the English out of Calais he might utilize them to do the turning out. It was a bright idea, with logic and sound reasoning behind it. Duke Philip tackled the task deftly and successfully. If the Flemings would attack the town on the land side he would blockade it from the sea; relief would be impossible; its fate would be

sealed and the English wool duties would be abolished. The
Flemings were won over by these cajoleries; they collected a
large army, and exuberantly advanced to the attack. But the
English had had warning and counter-measures were taken; a
nation-wide appeal was made for recruits, reinforcements and
supplies were poured into the town, and the duke of Gloucester
was named as the commander of the garrison.

The Flemings duly opened the investment, but things did not
go well for them. The defenders were resolute and even aggressive. As casualties mounted up, the enthusiasm of the Flemings
for the fight diminished—especially as there was no sign of the
promised Burgundian fleet. They complained loudly to their
duke, who responded with excuses, and more promises and
blandishments. With difficulty he prevailed upon the Flemings
to continue the siege. Eventually the fleet did appear, and four
block-ships were fitted out to block the channel leading into the
harbour. One of them however was sunk by gun-fire before it
could be got into position,[1] and the remaining three were run
ashore in the wrong place. At low tide they were high and dry,
and the exultant garrison rushed out, broke them up, and used
the wood for fuel. The Burgundian fleet then sailed ingloriously
home. This was altogether too much for the Flemings; they
were on the point of open revolt, and despite desperate efforts at
pacification on the part of Duke Philip, they broke up their camp
and retreated hastily on Bruges. The garrison pursued them as
far as Gravelines, and made large captures. The duke of Gloucester landed in Calais in time to see his victorious troops re-
enter the town.

Duke Humphrey then conducted a nine days almost bloodless campaign, pushing rapidly into Flanders, burning Bailleul
and Poperinghe, and threatening St. Omer. He then paid off
his army and returned to England. For this critics have blamed
him, suggesting that he might have advanced into Picardy and
captured Arras, the duke of Burgundy's headquarters. But his
army was not fitted out for a field or siege campaign, but solely

---

[1] One of the earliest instances of ships being sunk by artillery.

for the defence of Calais, and an attack on Arras without a
siege train would have been futile.

*   *   *

Whilst the fate of Calais, that "precious jewel", as English
chroniclers lovingly called it, lay in the balance all eyes in
England were turned in that direction, little interest being
taken in the war with Valois. Indeed the duke of York, who was
now sent out as regent was authorized to enter into negotiations
with Charles VII, (though nothing came of this). But with the
victory over Burgundy at Calais the original war could be
resumed with increased vigour. Matters had begun to improve.
The panic created by the apparition in the field of the "Limb
of the Fiend" had long passed away and the same old resolute
spirit of England was reasserting itself. This spirit was incar-
nated in John Talbot, who soon began to make his presence felt.

THE ENGAGEMENT OF RY

In January 1436 the twin gadflies, La Hire and Poton de
Xantrailles had penetrated right up to the gates of Rouen with
1,000 men, hoping to be admitted by French sympathizers.
Baffled in this they fell back ten miles in an easterly direction
and halted in the village of Ry awaiting reinforcements. Talbot
got news of this; hastily collecting a force of 400 men, including
Lord Scales and Sir Thomas Kyriell, he galloped out of Rouen
in a whirlwind swoop. The little town of Ry lies in a hollow
beset on every side by woods. Half a mile to the west, in the
direction of Rouen, there is a well defined ridge, over which
the Rouen road runs. The top of the ridge is hidden from the
village by a screen of trees. The French outposts on this hill were
thus invisible to the troops in the town. When Talbot swept
down on the outposts, therefore, the surprise was complete. As
the outposts came running down the hill panic overtook the
troops in billets in the town. La Hire did his best to rally his men
in the market square, in the main street, but in vain. He himself was wounded and swept out of the town in the general stam-

pede. Talbot's troopers galloped through the main street in hot
pursuit of the fugitives, who fled to the east, leaving a number of
high-born knights as prisoners in Talbot's hands, and all their
baggage was captured. The victory was complete. Though the
numbers engaged were small, the significance of the engagement was great; for the old dash and supremacy in the field of
an English force against one over twice its size was once more
demonstrated; and the two most famous and skilful French
generals had been ignominiously defeated.

*   *   *

John Talbot now looked round for a fresh quarry to attack,
and an obvious one came to mind. Pontoise had returned to its
French allegiance along with the other towns of the neighbourhood, and its commander was none other than L'Isle Adam,
Talbot's comrade-in-arms in the capture of St. Denys two
years previously. This acceptance of a key post by his old friend
was not appreciated by Talbot and he decided to teach the rene-
gade, as he regarded the Burgundian, a lesson.

We shall have a good deal to do with Pontoise, so it will be
well to visualize its aspect and situation. As its name implies, it
is the site of a bridge over the Oise, here nearly 100 yards wide.
It is on the direct road from Rouen to Paris, and being the
lowest bridge on the river was of particular strategic importance,
for the Oise in its lower reaches is wide and unfordable. It was
the gateway to Paris from the north, and it is not surprising
that it had become a military fortress of the first order. Anyone
crossing the railway bridge on his way by train to Paris from
Dieppe, will realize the significance of the lay-out at a glance,
for, towering over and dominating the bridge stand the ruins
of the castle, on a rocky cliff—the end of a narrow ridge running
north from the river, on which the town lies. A lofty wall, much
of which can still be traced, girt the town. Altogether Pontoise
was a formidable obstacle, well stocked with military stores and
supplies and adequately garrisoned.

Such was the town that John Talbot elected to attack,

although he had only 400 men available for the task and it was the depth of winter – and a very hard one too. Perhaps this very fact encouraged the English general to select that season, for it would favour the element of surprise.

On February 12, 1437, hard on his success at Ry, Lord Talbot set out from Rouen. Making a dash worthy of Sir Thomas Dagworth, he reached the vicinity of Pontoise utterly unexpected. The weather was so hard that the river Oise was frozen over and we are told that Talbot crossed over the ice. This is at first sight puzzling, for the river is on the far (that is the Paris side) side of the town, so he should have had no occasion to cross it at all. The clue seems to lie in the poem of Martial d'Auvergne. He describes how a party of English troops disguised as villagers and carrying hampers and baskets of food, as if on their way to the market, entered the town without exciting suspicion. This they could hardly expect to do unless they approached from the French side, i.e., from across the river. Thus it seems that Talbot utilized the ice to get this party across. It is true that Martial says they were dressed in white, but I fancy he must be mixing it up with the other party in the operation, namely the scaling party. Now snow lay deep on the ground, and Talbot clothed his storming party in white in order to conceal them in their approach to the walls at daylight next morning. This stratagem was also completely successful; and the stormers were able to place their ladders against the walls without attracting attention. All was quiet and peaceful in the sleeping town, and L'Isle Adam was in bed, when suddenly a great shout rang out inside the city: "The town is ours! St. George! Talbot!" This was the prearranged signal made by the "market men". The stormers mounted the ladders, entered the now awakening town and rushed to the gates to open them for the remainders of Talbot's force. The surprise and the success were equally complete. L'Isle Adam and his men fled from the town without striking a blow, leaving all their belongings and an immense quantity of stores behind them. Thus the gateway to Paris was captured with the loss of scarcely a man.

But that was not the end of the exploit. Talbot, like the true soldier he was, appreciated the advantage of "striking while the iron is hot". He decided to make practical and instant use of the "gateway". Despite the minute proportions of his force he resolved on attacking Paris itself. Whether this was a mere act of bravado, or whether it was a "calculated risk" on his part we do not know. John Talbot, like all generals of the period, was more proficient with sword than with pen, and his motives and thoughts throughout his campaigns have to be divined from his acts. Whatever the motive, this splendidly audacious action had some initial success. His handful of men penetrated right up to the walls of the capital, crossed the moat over the ice, and made preparations to climb the walls. But the task was beyond them. Assailed by powerful artillery and by crossbow shafts and lances, they were forced to abandon the enterprise and to fall back in good order and good heart to Pontoise.

*   *   *

The English recovery was almost at full flood. Though the duke of York himself had some successes in winning back a few towns in Caux, such as Dieppe, the main credit must go to the triple blow delivered in the winter of 1437 by John, Lord Talbot. Six months later Talbot was again on the warpath. The English still held the two bastions, as it were, on each side of the Somme estuary—St. Valery and Le Crotoy. The Burgundians were besieging the latter in a half-hearted way, and, making no progress, they appealed to the duke of Burgundy for reinforcements. The duke called on John of Luxemburg to supply them, but one Burgundian chief at least remained loyal to his old comrades-in-arms. John stoutly declined to cross swords with the English, and Philip was reduced to conducting the operation himself. Le Crotoy was the nearest coastal town to Calais still in English hands and it would not do to let it fall. The earl of Warwick, now 58 years of age, had just reluctantly succeeded the duke of York as king's lieutenant in France. Recognizing the importance of Le Crotoy he despatched Talbot with an army estimated at 5,000 men, to its relief. The Burgundians are given as 10,000 strong, but both figures can probably be halved. Talbot, with Kyriell as his chief lieutenant, marched from Rouen to St. Valery. On this occasion he changed his strategy, making no attempt to conceal his march, and indeed issuing a challenge to Burgundy to a fight in the open. Duke Philip did not respond to this but he took alarm, and went in person to Abbeville to strengthen its defences. Whilst he was still there the English resumed their advance. Abbeville being firmly held by the enemy, Talbot resolved to follow the example of Edward III (and the intention of Henry V) and cross the Somme by the famous ford of Blanche Taque. Here history was repeated, for the tide was partly up and the far side was strongly held by Burgundian infantry and artillery. Undeterred by this contretemps, Talbot impulsively plunged into the water at the head of his army–up to his chin, it is said (but need not be believed)–struggled across the mile-wide estuary on the narrow causeway, and dispersed the enemy on the far bank with trifling loss to his own army. This was a truly remarkable performance –one that would have been quite impossible against staunch troops. Talbot must have had evidence of the poor quality of these defenders, no doubt local levies, who had no heart for the fight, especially when they learnt the name of the English commander. On reaching the far bank Talbot did not turn at once against the besieging army. It had secured itself in a "bastille" or field work similar to those built by the English at Orleans. Talbot's object was to entice them out into the open and in order to do this he started ravaging the surrounding country, penetrating almost to Hesdin, 25 miles to the east, Duke Philip's northern capital. Practically no resistance was offered to the English troops wherever they went or whatever they did. The Burgundian chroniclers are bitter in their contempt for the sorry display exhibited by their men. Talbot then returned towards Le Crotoy. On his approach the garrison of the bastille fled in panic leaving all their artillery and immense quantity of stores. The garrison of Le Crotoy pursued them, according to Monstrelet "shouting after them as they would have done to a ribald mob". The English army returned to Rouen, heavily laden with booty, and well pleased with themselves and with their commander. And well they might be, for Talbot had shown his versatility. His was no one-track mind; his methods had been entirely different to those employed heretofore; he had sized up his opponents correctly—one of the marks of military genius—and had achieved his aim with a minimum of bloodshed.

Eighteen months after Paris had fallen Charles VII deemed it safe to enter his capital. On November 12, 1437, he entered the city amid the plaudits of the populace. But three weeks later he left it again and fell back to his beloved Loire country. The weakness and supineness of the French king at this period has been much criticized by French historians. It is indisputable that Charles had little stomach for the fight—less even than had the preceding Valois kings—but his difficulties at the time, with an uncertain and recently cemented concord with Burgundy, an impoverished treasury, and a state of semi-anarchy due to the French freebooters running riot through the land, were enough to daunt a Churchill. His inactivity immediately after sealing the concord with Burgundy may have also been due in part to the expectation that England would now throw up the sponge.[1]

*　　　　*　　　　*

In 1438 the war languished in the north, partly owing to the famine and plague that affected both France and England. But in the far south it flared up. Ever since 1377 the boundary between English-held Aquitaine and France had been static till 1420. During the next few years the local levies had driven the French back a short distance, recapturing St. Macaire, La Réole and other towns. Thereafter calm descended once more on the scene till this year 1438. There had been no need to call in English troops to defend Gascony, nor even to take part in the 1420 advance, for, as Sir Charles Oman points out:

[1] Adolf Hitler's inactivity in July 1940 was due to a similar miscalculation.

"The English dominion rested, not on the spears and bows of an aline garrison, but on the willing obedience of the whole population."[1] This is scarcely surprising when we remember that Aquitaine had been an appanage of the English crown for nearly 300 years, and had been governed in an enlightened spirit. However, Charles VII now considered that an opportunity presented itself to drive the English out of Aquitaine, and he collected forces in the south for the purpose. The campaign that ensued was of some military interest strategically, as the French for the first time endeavoured to concert operations by several columns working on exterior lines, in a manner reminiscent of Edward III. But Charles was to learn, as Edward had done, that such operations were beset with difficulties in an age when communications were in a primitive state. The columns were to advance inwards, concentrating for the final assault on Bordeaux, the capital. But co-operation between the columns was bad, indeed almost non-existent, and the successes attained fell far short of what had been planned and expected. Next year the English government sent out an army nearly 3,000 strong, under the earl of Huntingdon, which had little difficulty in driving the French back practically to their starting line.

*   *   *

Both nations were by now growing increasingly weary of the war, but the tragedy was that the English could only obtain peace by renouncing the claim of their king to be the legitimate king of France—an admission that would imply that their 23 years of war had been unjustified—while the French could not be expected to acknowledge the jurisdiction of a second king in their domains whilst they had one who had been anointed with the sacred oil of Rheims in actual possession of the capital. Nevertheless peace was in the air and Cardinal Beaufort, the leader of the peace party in England (the war party being led by the duke of Gloucester) entered into tentative negotiations in the autumn. The upshot of these was that a peace conference was fixed for the following summer. The venue was Calais and the confer-

[1] *Political History*, p. 328.

ence assembled at a spot midway between Calais and Gravelines on July 6, 1439. Memories of the treachery on the bridge
of Montereau were uppermost in the minds of both parties, and
the most elaborate arrangements were made to safeguard
against a repetition of anything of the sort. Cardinal Beaufort
led the English party, and for some reason, the duchess of Burgundy led the French party. The proceedings were protracted,
but we can see in retrospect that they were doomed to failure;
as always, they were shipwrecked on the snag of "the renunciation of the title" of king of France by Henry VI. All that came
out of the conference was a local truce for three years between
England and the duke of Burgundy in the Calais area.

While the peace negotiations were taking place the war was
proceeding. Meaux was now the only town to the east of Paris
in English hands. In July a strong army was fitted out for its
reduction, liberally supplied with siege artillery under one Jean
Bureau. The course of the siege that resulted was singularly
similar to that of Henry V; that is to say, the defence was obstinate, and when the pressure on the town became too great the
garrison crossed the river into the Market. Meanwhile attempts
at relief were being made. Talbot led thither an army of 3,000,
accompanied by the earl of Somerset, and Lord Scales.

Marching straight for Meaux the army arrived in the vicinity
three days after the evacuation of the town. Moreover, the
Constable de Richemont, the French commander, had withdrawn all his troops into the town on hearing of the approach
of the dread Lord Talbot. The latter was intent on a fight
with the Constable, the man to whom he largely owed his
capture at Patay, exactly ten years before. He sent the Frenchman a formal challenge, to which he received no reply. He then
marched his army backwards and forwards in front of the town,
but all to no purpose. His arrival had had an astonishing effect
upon the besiegers, who had now practically themselves become
the besieged garrison. But Richemont did not trust his troops
and would take no risks. His biographer, Dr. Cosneau, frankly
admits the fact.

"The English and their captains, above all Talbot, had a well-established reputation for superiority, Richemont knew them better than anyone."[1]

The supine but correct attitude adopted by Richemont allowed Talbot to pass into the Market fresh stores, and reinforcements. This was accomplished by means of leather boats that had been carried by the army for this purpose. Talbot went further than this. The besiegers had erected a number of bastilles round the town including at least one on an island between the town and Market. Talbot must have felt rather frustrated and disappointed at not being able to inflict much damage on the Constable. To carry the town by assault was out of the question for no siege train had been brought, nor supplies for a long siege. One thing however was possible and that Talbot did. The bastille on the island was too close to the Market to be comfortable. Talbot decided to take it. This he did with speed, killing or capturing the whole of the garrison on the island without let or hindrance from the French troops in the town, only a short distance away, and within easy bow-shot. It was as if the French were hypnotized by the very name of Talbot.

However, in spite of this signal success there was no more that could be done, and, Talbot having "refreshed" the garrison of the Market, took his army back to Rouen. Richemont thereupon resumed the siege and not long afterwards the garrison surrendered on terms. So it would seem that the Constable's rather inglorious procedure was on the short view the correct one.

*   *   *

AVRANCHES

Lord Talbot led his army back to Normandy and proceeded with the recovery of towns in the Pays de Caux (between Rouen and Dieppe) which had been lost five years before. The Constable de Richemont, as soon as his army was set free by the surrender of Meaux, made no attempt to go to the help of the threatened towns in Caux, but decided to undertake the siege of Avranches, on the borders of Brittany. It has been supposed

---

[1] *Le Connétable de Richemont*, p. 294, n.

that he expected help from his elder brother the duke of Brittany. But the latter had signed an agreement with England at Calais, and, so far from playing the turn-coat, he promised to support the English cause.[1]

Avranches is picturesquely situated on an isolated hill half a mile to the south of the little river Sée, and four miles from the sea. The tidal waters are fordable in places, and there are occasional fords above the town. In late November Richemont appeared before the town, bringing with him a reinforcement under the command of the duke of Alençon. As soon as Warwick heard of this attack he sent help to the threatened garrison, under the inevitable John Talbot. The French army was about 6,000 strong, and the English decidedly smaller.[2]

In mid-December the English approached from the north and took up position along the north bank of the river Sée facing the town.[3] For some days there was bickering and skirmishing between the sides, whilst Talbot evolved his plan. The main body of the French army was camped between the river and town, and was thus between two fires (much as had been the case at Cravant). Much of the army consisted of ill-disciplined mercenaries, most of whom were in the habit of trickling away when it got dark and sheltering in the nearby villages. Talbot evidently became aware of this and decided to profit by it. He had discovered a ford over the river away to a flank (apparently up-stream) which was either unguarded, being unknown to the French or inadequately guarded at night. On the night of December 22/23 the attack took place. The ford was seized by the English and crossed without difficulty; the attackers then swung inwards parallel to the river and assaulted the French camp. The outposts were all captured or put to flight, and the English penetrated into the sleeping camp. There seems to have been but little resistance, and panic set in. The whole army decamped and dispersed in confusion except a tiny remnant of

[1] Cosneau, citing *Preuves de l'histoire de Bretagne.*
[2] The *Bourgeois de Paris* gives the French as 40,000 and the English 8,000.
[3] Ramsay makes them approach from the south, but Jean Chartier's account (the best) leaves no doubt on the point.

about 100 lances under the Constable. Eventually he also was compelled to retreat, while the English army entered the town in triumph.

The French had retreated in a westerly direction, across the border into Brittany, and the flight was continued without respite as far as Dol, 20 miles to the west. As for the Constable, he made his way as best he could to Paris, minus his army. Here he had an interview with the king, which can scarcely have escaped being stormy; for he told Charles in no uncertain terms that he could do nothing with such an undisciplined rabble as his vanished army. The interview had important results; it strengthened the king in the steps he had already put in hand to reorganize and improve his army. We shall hear more of this later on.

In the early part of the following year, 1440, the English lost a good opportunity for attacking while France was distracted by civil strife. The leaders of the revolt were the dukes of Bourbon and Alençon, the count of Dunois and, of all people, the 16-year-old Dauphin, Louis (later Louis XI), who is described by Ramsay as "a cool astute youth, embued with a profound contempt for his father."[1] It was not till July that the English Government gave orders for the siege of Harfleur, by which time Charles VII had got the revolt under control. It was certainly high time Harfleur was retaken; it had been for five years in French hands, and had become a thorn in the side of the English. The leaders appointed were the earls of Somerset and Dorset (his younger brother), and Lords Talbot and Fauconbridge. Thus the curious and unsound medieval custom of not nominating a supreme commander was followed. In practice Somerset took command of the naval portion of the force and Talbot the land portion. The siege opened in August.[2] The garrison appealed to Charles VII for help and he responded by sending a large army under Richemont and La Hire, (where was Xantrailles?) to its relief. The English army was only 1,000 strong, but they set about their

---

[1] *Lancaster and York*, II, p. 29.
[2] Ramsay follows Monstrelet in dating it April.

work energetically and thoroughly, constructing double lines of circum- and contra-vallation. Deep continuous ditches and stockaded ramparts were built, instead of the isolated "bastilles" favoured by the French. In addition a defensive line was thrown up along the shore to prevent relief by sea. This was indeed part of the French plan, which comprised a double land attack from two sides together with a simultaneous landing in the estuary.

Some of the French ships must have succeeded in running the gauntlet of Somerset's protective squadron for they were able to approach the town but failed to effect a landing owing to the English shore defences. Both land attacks failed dismally, the English archers causing heavy casualties to the assaulting men-at-arms. This must indicate that they reserved their fire to point-blank range for plate-armour was now fully developed and arrows could only penetrate at the shortest range. The French accepted defeat, and in October fell back to Paris. Shortly afterwards the town surrendered at discretion. A curious incident that ocurred during the French retreat illustrated the fundamentally divided state of the French nation. On the outward march the army had passed through the lands of the duke of Burgundy in the valley of the Somme. They started to retrace their steps along the same route, only to be met by a peremptory demand from the incensed duke that they should keep clear of his domains as they had wrought it so much damage by pillage on the outward march. Count John of Luxemburg also made difficulties about allowing them passage. He was living in retirement, having resolutely declined to take up arms against his old comrades the English in spite of all that Duke Philip could do by threats and cajolery to persuade him. Next January this good friend of the English died, faithful to them to the last.

That same autumn the duke of Orleans, who had been a prisoner in England ever since the Battle of Agincourt, was released; the motive of Henry VI was purely humanitarian; those of his government more calculating; it was hoped that his presence and influence in France would further the English cause, and the duke undertook to do his best in the interests of peace.

THE SEINE ET OISE CAMPAIGN

The chief event of the following year, 1441, was the siege of Pontoise, described by the French historian Du Fresnes de Beaucourt with pardonable exaggeration, as "a veritable siege of Troy". The strategical importance of Pontoise has already been made apparent. While held by the English, only twelve miles from St. Denys, it was a standing menace to the capital. Encouraged by the capture of Creil, thanks largely to Jean Bureau and his artillery, Charles VII decided to attempt the reduction of this key fortress. He was now taking increasing interest in the military operations. He had "witnessed" the siege of Creil from Senlis, some six miles away. This time he led his army in person to the attack on Pontoise, approaching it from the eastern side of the Oise. On June 6, he took up his residence at the Abbey of Maubuisson, two miles short of the river, and opened the siege. The bridge spanning the river was in English hands, with a work forming a barbican (or bridgehead) on the far end of the bridge. It was the lowest bridge on the Oise, which joins the Seine at Conflans six miles to the south. A bridge obviously had to be constructed by the French and this was thrown across the river a short distance down-stream, opposite St. Martin's Abbey. A large bastille was then constructed enclosing the Abbey, and the Dauphin Louis was placed in command of it. There were not sufficient troops however to construct continuous lines of circumvallation round the town, and so (as at Orleans), there was a big undefended gap to the north and east.

The strength of the French investing army may be put, at a very rough guess, at about 5,000. Nearly all the leading French generals, including La Hire and Xantrailles (for the last time together) were present. The Constable was in active command, with Admiral Coëtivi as his second-in-command. The artillery, again under Jean Bureau, was numerous and powerful and it showed its prowess early in the siege. The southern end of the town could not be approached as long as the bridge remained in English hands, and Bureau was set to work on the destruction of the barbican. This he was successful in doing in a few days, together with the destruction of the first three arches of the bridge – a questionable policy, for the attackers would be obliged to repair it themselves before they could make use of it. The first attempt to storm the barbican was defeated with heavy loss, but the second was successful. A powerful battery of guns was also transported across the river and the bombardment of the town commenced in earnest. Several breaches began to appear, but each morning it was seen that the walls appeared as intact as ever; the garrison had been at work on repairs during the night. Sorties were also made from time to time.

While this was going on, Lord Talbot in Rouen had not been idle. He was busy collecting a relief force, complete with food, supplies and ordnance stores for the garrison. Assembling them at Elboeuf, eight miles south of Rouen, he on June 16, marched along the northern bank of the Seine to the relief. Approaching the town from the west, his road took him close past St. Martin's Abbey. The French, as they had done at Meaux, withdrew inside their bastille, and offered no impediment whatever to the entry into the town of the relieving force. This was the direct order of the king: the Constable did not agree with it. Talbot was thus able to replenish the garrison, exchange some worn out soldiers for fresh and strengthen the high command by leaving in it Lords Scales and Fauconbridge. Then he returned the way he had come as far as Mantes, 20 miles distant, where he immediately began collecting a second supply train. With this train Talbot again marched to Pontoise and again he delivered the goods without the French attempting to cross swords with him. It was now becoming obvious that the king had decided on a policy of "non-aggression".

And now a newcomer was to appear on the scene. The earl of Warwick had died in 1439 at the age of 58, and the duke of York, who had held the office for a short time in 1435, was appointed in his stead. After long delays he landed at Harfleur with some reinforcements in June. Arrived at Rouen he set about collecting further supplies for the besieged town, and in the middle of July he set out, Talbot commanding the vanguard. The army was this time on a bigger scale, but there is little indication as to its actual strength. It clearly was much inferior to the French in numbers: the *mot* was shortly to be heard in Paris, "Whenever the French find themselves in a superiority of three to one they immediately retreat." If we assess the English at between 2,000 and 3,000 we shall not be far out.

On the approach of the relieving army, Charles this time withdrew his army across the river, leaving a garrison in the St. Martin's Bastille, under Admiral Coëtivi. Thus York was able to enter the town unmolested, and deliver his supplies.

But this was to be only the beginning of a campaign which possesses an interest – and indeed a humour – seldom surpassed in the war.[1] The leading spirit, if not the architect of the whole operation, was of course John, Lord Talbot. The duke of York opened the proceedings by informing the French king, quite in the style of Edward III, that he intended to cross the Oise with his army whether Charles of Valois liked it or not. The effect of this braggadocio was that Charles extended his troops in a long defensive line along the river from its confluence with the Seine to Creil, a frontage of over 30 miles. York (or shall we say Talbot?) countered this in a way that smacks of the duke of Marlborough of a later era.[2] First he withdrew his army nearly ten miles to the north, well out of sight and touch of the French. From there he marched rapidly to a point on the river near Beaumont, 15 miles upstream from Pontoise. This sector was defended by the Count de la Marche, who had a detachment in Beaumont. The town was attacked, but it was merely a feint; which succeeded in attracting attention and drawing defenders to that point. Meanwhile, the main body was pushing on still further north to opposite the abbey of Royaumont. Here the river (nearly 30 yards wide) was unguarded. A small boat was rowed across, a rope was then stretched across the stream, and the pontoon bridge, made of portable leather boats, specially

[1] Sketch map 10, on page 297, if studied closely, will be found to give an epitome of the campaign, step by step.

[2] In his crossings of the Geet and of the Lines of Non Plus Ultra. But it is unlikely that Marlborough consciously adopted Talbot's method.

brought up for the purpose, was rapidly constructed. The whole army then crossed by this bridge without a blow being struck in its defence. Looked at from any point of view it was a brilliant achievement.

When the startling news reached headquarters at Maubuisson abbey, the Constable de Richemont, a vigorous practical soldier, jumped on to his horse, collected what troops were to hand and galloped to L'Isle Adam, ten miles away upstream, to verify for himself the report. It was all too true. Richemont hastened back and either he or the king decided on a curious step. St. Denys and Paris were obviously threatened, and a portion of the army was at once despatched to St. Denys for its protection. But there was a further danger–the king's own person was in jeopardy. Only a few days before, the army had crossed the Oise from west to east to put the river between themselves and the English. Now the process was reversed, but with the same object: the English were to the east of the river, therefore the French must cross to the west bank, even though it took them away from their base, the capital. Stores were packed up in a hurry and the king and his army made their way across the Oise, while the English army was marching down the left bank of the river, and approaching Maubuisson abbey.

Talbot took possession of the abbey, 24 hours after Charles had quit, with much of the king's belongings and stores still there, for the French had departed in such haste. It seems that they had broken down the Oise bridge after crossing it and York halted for four days whilst repairing the bridge and constructing another at Neuville near Conflans. The English army then crossed and turned south in pursuit of the French king.

Meanwhile Charles, after leaving a strong garrison in the St. Martin's Bastille again under the mis-named Admiral Coëtivi, had retreated still further, in a southerly direction. Not until Charles had placed another river, the Seine, between him and the English did he feel tolerably safe. He took up his residence at the abbey at Poissy, on the south bank of the Seine, some 15 miles south of Pontoise. The inhabitants of Paris

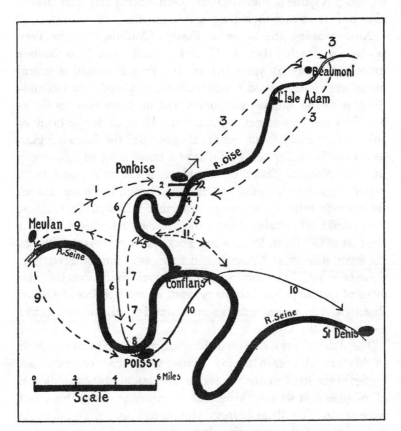

Sketch Map 10: THE SEINE ET OISE CAMPAIGN

--→ English marches
—→ French marches

1. English enter Pontoise
2. French cross the Oise
3. English cross the Oise
4. French recross the Oise
5. English recross the Oise
6. French retreat to the Seine
7. English pursue to the Seine
8. French cross Seine
9. Talbot crosses Seine
10. French recross Seine
11. York tries to intercept the French

viewed this game of hide-and-seek with disgust and were beginning openly to rate their king as a coward.

After crossing the Seine at Poissy, (doubtless by the very
bridge by which Edward III had crossed during his famous
march to Crecy 95 years before) the French posted a strong
guard at the bridgehead which was soon engaged in hot skirmishing with the English vanguard. The problem now confronting York was how to get at the enemy. Here the fertile brain of
John Talbot came to the rescue. He proposed the following plan
to his chief. He himself would take a small force of 1,000 men
back to Mantes. There he would cross the Seine, and by a
rapid night march would surprise the French in Poissy and set
them off in retreat once more towards St. Denys. To reach it
they would presumably recross the Seine by a bridge slightly to
the east of Conflans. Meanwhile York was to recross the Oise to
the eastern bank at Neuville and lie in wait for the French at
their crossing. Thus they would be driven by Talbot into the
arms of the main English army, and, in the opinion of Bishop
Basin (who alone records the operation in full) nothing could
have saved the king.

The duke of York accepted the plan, and Talbot marched off
to Mantes. Accurate timing between the two disconnected
bodies of the English army was of course essential for the success
of the plan and we may assume that arrangements to this effect
were made. The distance from Mantes to Poissy is 17 miles. As
the success of the operation largely depended upon surprise,
Talbot decided to make the march by night. To do 17 miles in a
single night, whether with or without the aid of the moon is to
ask a lot of the troops. But Talbot asked for it—and received it.
They reached Poissy early in the morning and the surprise was
so complete that when Talbot entered the abbey, where the
king had slept, "his bedclothes were still warm".

King Charles, the reader may not be surprised to hear, was
crossing yet another river, or rather the same river—the Seine—
in the reverse direction, as before. But where was the duke of
York and the main English army? The answer is that they had

been too slow in re-crossing the Oise at Neuville so that the French got across the Seine and back to St. Denys before the duke's army had put in an appearance. They were only in time to see the French marching across their front from a hill, probably just to the north of Herblay (two miles north-east of Conflans).

A curious incident is related by Gruel of this campaign. As soon as the king reached Poissy he had sent off a supply column to Pontoise under the Constable. Xantrailles commanded the vanguard on the outward journey, and the rearguard on the return. On that day the English were throwing their bridge across the river Oise at Neuville, midway between Pontoise and Conflans, so there might be danger from the eastern flank. On the return journey Xantrailles represented this danger to Richemont, strongly urging him to take the roundabout route via Meulan, ten miles down the Seine from Poissy. The Constable agreed and did so. But Xantrailles hung back till the main body was out of sight. He then marched straight for the Poissy bridge, thus arriving well before the main body. He then declared to the king that Richemont had not dared to take the direct route but that he himself had done so. On Richemont's arrival Charles naturally taxed him with this, whereupon the Constable explained the true facts and gave Poton de Xantrailles a good dressing down in the presence of the king. This story illustrates the degree of disharmony and jealousy that reigned in the French army. Indeed the count of St. Pol, a Burgundian, was so disgusted with the turn of events that he marched away with his detachment. And deserters from the army were numerous.

The king of France was now safely back in his capital, at the cost of raising the siege of Pontoise, and at the loss of considerable prestige. Not unnaturally the French were put out of countenance by this unedifying exhibition of the Royal army of France, running away, not once nor twice from a smaller English army. What was to be done about it? Charles held a war council at St. Denys to consider the matter. The problem was partly solved for him by the actions of the duke of York who returned with his army to Rouen. This seems a tame ending to a truly brilliant if short campaign. But logistics are inexorable, and it seems that his army was now practically starving; in fact when they got back to Rouen the haggard appearance of the soldiers was generally remarked on. Moreover, the duke had seen the French army crossing a river four times within 14 days in order to get away from him, and it seemed time to give up such a wild-goose chase.

Charles VII now rose to his full stature as a king, for the first time in his reign. He would listen to no defeatist councils. Perhaps rumours had reached his ears of "cowardice" and he was put upon his metal. *Coute que coute* he would persevere with the siege of Pontoise. The English army had disappeared; his own artillery had already made visible marks on the defences of the town; let the good work continue, and success would crown their efforts! Thus reasoned the king, and, turning a deaf ear to the timid councils of some of the staff, thus he ordered. The bridges were once again repaired, the guns were brought out of the shelter of the St. Martin's Bastille, the town was again invested, this time on all sides, and John Bureau again got to work.

So did the other John. The indefatigable Lord Talbot collected yet another train of provisions at Elboeuf, and on August 16 he advanced with it along the direct road to Pontoise. Richemont got news of it, and this time reversed his policy of refusing battle. Instead he collected a field army from the besieging forces and advanced resolutely down the road to meet the English. The two armies met that evening head-on at Vigny, nine miles west of Pontoise. The Constable did not attempt to attack, but neither did he refuse battle. Talbot's object was to conduct his supply column to its destination, his "army" was a mere escort, and it was not his game to attack the French in position. Both forces therefore sat watching each other during the daylight. As soon as it was dark Talbot lit camp-fires and left them burning while he withdrew his troops silently to the rear, then turned sharp to the north, and marched away across the Viosne river, some two miles to the left and then turned

straight for Pontoise. The besiegers having been denuded to
form Richemont's field force, the English were able to penetrate
the French lines in the northern sector, replenish the garrison
and return to Rouen, before the Constable could do anything
about it. The river Viosne separated the two armies, and though
Richemont could see the English approaching the town he
could not get across the river to attack them. (Talbot's manoeuvre closely resembled that of Prince Rupert in relieving
York in 1644 and was equally sparkling.)

On August 28, Talbot again made a reconnaissance towards
the beleaguered town, and took advantage of it on September 6,
to make yet another successful relief–the fifth in all–of the
town.

But Jean Bureau was now getting his fangs into the defences.
On the 16th he took the church of Notre Dame, in a suburb to
the west of the town, where he established an observation post,
and three days later the general assault was made. The orders
for this assault, issued by Admiral Coëtivi, still exist. They show
that the walls were assaulted at a large number of points on all
sides, in a simultaneous attack. Evidently the necessary breaches
had been made. Thanks to the excellent work of the guns, the
assault was successful, and after two hours resistance Pontoise at
last fell. King Charles himself rode into the town while the fighting was still proceeding, if we are to believe a curious story that
Bishop Basin declared he heard from the king's own lips. It was
to the effect that an English armed soldier ducked under the
belly of the king's charger for protection, and whilst in that constricted position he carried on a fight with his opponents, despite
the efforts of Charles to make them desist.[1] As a natural result
his unfortunate horse received several sword cuts in the belly.

The capture of Pontoise was a sore blow for the English, after
the brilliant campaign that had preceded it. It is also important
as marking a distinct step in the evolution of siege artillery.
Cannons had recently increased considerably in size and power

[1] The author once had a wild boar under his horse's belly and could do nothing
about it for the moment, so he can sympathize with King Charles in his predica-
ment.

in the French army, and a man had arisen who understood how to apply their power.[1]

About 500 English soldiers were slaughtered in the garrison, the remainder being put to ransom, including their commander Lord Clinton.

Note. It is pleasant to be able to record that both sides exchanged poems at the opening of the siege, both of which were reproduced by Jean Chartier. The English sent the first, full of braggadocio and challenge. The French poet had rather the best of it in his reply. It is interesting to note that he addressed it to "Vous Anglais et Normans". He is aware of the approach of the duke of York (duc d'Iort): the only other Englishman named is Talbot.

*   *   *

Meanwhile the duke of Orleans had not forgotten his promise to further the cause of peace, and in the spring of 1442 he did his best at a conference at Nevers to produce some accord, but without avail. The real interest of the war now lay in Gascony whither King Charles himself led an army in the summer, and met with a fair amount of success. In taking St. Sever he also captured the Seneschal of Gascony, Sir Thomas Rempston, who thus disappears from our pages. St. Sever was later recaptured, as were many other towns. The whole campaign in fact resolved itself into a series of sieges, and constant changes of ownership, in a rather bewildering fashion. There was however one very notable siege, that of the much-captured La Réole.[2]

The town of La Réole soon surrendered but the very strongly situated castle held out all through the autumn and winter, which was a very hard one. The French in their trenches suffered much from the rigours of the climate and our old friend La Hire literally "met his death of cold". Ramsay describes him as an "utter Free Lance", but we must admit that most of his exploits were achieved under the banner of Charles. He became a national hero and his visage still adorns the Jack in a French pack of cards.

*   *   *

[1] The English also had some powerful cannons, notably the two "Michelets" with which they attempted unsuccessfully to reduce Mont St. Michel. These cannons now lie inside the fortress; they have bores of 15 and 18 inches diameter. But a glance at the strength of that fortress will explain why they failed to breach it.

[2] I calculate that in the course of the Edwardian Wars this town changed hands no fewer than seventeen times.

While the Gascony campaign was dragging on Talbot had returned to England, where he received an enthusiastic welcome – as well he might – and an earldom. Henceforth we should call him the earl of Shrewsbury, but it will be convenient to keep to the name by which he is always remembered. (The French complain, not without reason, of our frequent change of names.) French writers delight to call him "The English Achilles".

Talbot on his return to France in the summer of 1442 captured Conches in Normandy, and in the autumn laid siege to Dieppe, the only port of any size remaining in French hands between St. Valery and Harfleur. Talbot swooped on the place in his usual style, surprising and investing it before the garrison could take effective action. His force, only 1,000 in all, was much too small to invest it completely by land, so he contented himself with constructing a large bastille, in the fashion of the times, on the Pulet Hill to the east of the town, and commanding the harbour. Here he left a garrison on being recalled to Rouen, where he took up the duties of Constable of France. Profiting by his absence the French made several attempts to overrun the bastille, which was in reality more besieged than the town it was nominally besieging. The English however made a gallant and prolonged defence, and it was not till August 1443 that the Dauphin and Dunois, who had been specially sent for the purpose, succeeded in taking it. One of the prisoners was Henry Talbot, a natural son of the earl.

*　　　*　　　*

Meanwhile political events at home were obtruding increasingly on the war. The duke of Gloucester was in semi-retirement, his wife having been convicted of intriguing against the king. His loss was Oxford's gain, for it resulted in the formation of the Bodleian Library, built up round good Duke Humphrey's collection of books. The Beaufort party were now supreme and as if to mark their success they arranged for the duke of Somerset, eldest nephew of Cardinal Beaufort, to obtain the command of an army destined for the defence of Gascony, with the title of captain general of Guienne (or Gascony). This appointment was a slight to the duke of York, who was the king's lieutenant for the whole of France. (This was the first rift between the two branches of the House of Lancaster which eventuated in the Wars of the Roses.)

In August 1443 Somerset's army set out. It was about 7,000 strong. But instead of making for Gascony, Somerset for some reason landed at Cherbourg in Normandy. Possibly he shunned the risks of the long sea voyage to Bordeaux. He was ailing in health, and was not pining for unnecessary hardships. From Cherbourg he marched south along the border between Maine and Brittany, and with what appears criminal and almost incredible stupidity, captured La Guerche, a town inside Brittany, 25 miles south-east of Rennes. Stupidity–for Brittany was now in treaty with England. The account of the affair given by the Breton historian Lobinau, writing in 1707, however, puts a different complexion on the matter. He states that the inhabitants were taken by surprise, in view of the treaty made with the late duke, but he adds mildly that circumstances had since changed. He makes no mention of pillage, but says that Somerset set free all who were favourable to the régime, and imprisoned the others. Finally he writes:

"The duke [of Brittany] having given some sum of money to the duke of Somerset, the latter handed back La Guerche and returned into Normandy."[1]

The duke of Somerset then wandered aimlessly through Maine. When his captains asked what his plan was he replied with a frown, "I do not divulge my secret to anyone. If even my own shirt knew my secret I should burn it." Bishop Basin, who tells the story, adds maliciously that it was doubtful whether he knew his own secret. That winter he returned to England without effecting anything–and shortly afterwards he died.

Disappointment at the lack of success of Somerset's expedition was natural, but the government took an over-despondent view

[1] *Histoire de Bretagne*, I, p. 623.

of the matter. After all, the French had had ample forces available to oppose the invasion for operations elsewhere were at a standstill; yet for four months Somerset had been able to roam whither he wished without let or hindrance – as in the days of old. There was no real cause for discouragement; even Edward III had found it difficult to compete with an enemy who refused to fight, and if the government selected a second-rate and ailing commander, as they had done, they had only themselves to blame. The fact is, they were heartily sick of the war and clutched at any straw to get out of it without loss of prestige. The ever-helpful duke of Orleans provided the straw; René, duke of Anjou, was the brother-in-law of Charles VII, and he had an unmarried daughter, Margaret. If Henry VI would take her to wife, the duke argued, a bond of amity and peace between Lancaster and Valois might be knit. The English government embraced the idea, and the earl of Suffolk – that William de la Pole who had been captured on the bridge at Montargis, and afterwards released – was selected to conduct negotiations for peace.

In March 1444 he crossed over to France, and a peace conference took place on the Loire. But difficulties arose; this time the point at issue was no longer the English claim to the throne, for Suffolk was prepared to barter that for the absolute possession of Normandy. It was instead the old question of homage, which had lain dormant for 84 years. Suffolk showed such anxiety to obtain peace that Charles naturally raised his terms, supposing that the English must be negotiating from weakness, always a fatal thing to do. Charles demanded that homage should be done for Gascony and Normandy, and on that the conference broke down. A two years truce was sealed, and Suffolk negotiated the marriage of Margaret of Anjou to Henry VI.

APPENDIX

SOURCES FOR THE SEINE ET OISE CAMPAIGN

Easily the best account is that of Guillaume Gruel, the faithful servant and scribe of the Constable de Richemont. He himself took part in the campaign as a soldier, and his story, though sometimes confused, is first hand, and may be presumed to be reliable. Next come two histories of Charles VII, one by Jean Chartier and the other by Guillaume le Bouvier, the latter being the more detailed of the two; otherwise it is difficult to differentiate between them. Chartier's *Chronique de Charles VII* was published by Vallet de Viriville in 1858, but for Le Bouvier's *Les Chroniques du feu Roy Charles*, one has to go back as far as 1661 when Godefroy incorporated it in his *Histoire de Charles VII*.[1] Incidentally, the name of the author is rather confusing. He is often cited as Berry, or Berry Heraut, or Le Roi Heraut, having served in that capacity to Charles VII. I mention this because he is going to be useful to us.

The fourth source is *Histoire de Charles VII* by Thomas Basin, Bishop of Lisieux. Written in Latin it has fortunately been recently translated into French by Samarin (1933). Basin was not present, but he later became the confidant of the king and much of his account is at least second hand.

Waurin gives what he can pick up from the Burgundian side and borrows from the Armagnac writers, while Monstrelet as usual copies Waurin.

On the English side there is precisely nothing. It is a thousand pities that Talbot did not have his Gruel. We might then have obtained some reliable insight into his mind, while his account might have presented the English achievements in an even more favourable light than do the enemy chroniclers.

Admittedly, it is not easy to piece it all together, in particular the final phase, which is my own construction of a rather obscure and isolated passage in Thomas Basin.

But even as it is, this Seine et Oise campaign can claim to be one of the most remarkable bloodless campaigns of the Middle Ages, and it is astonishing that so little attention has been paid to it by modern writers.

[1] Joseph Stevenson in his *Loss of Normandy* published long extracts from it.

CHAPTER XVIII

THE END IN NORMANDY

GLADLY would I pass over in silence the five next years, the two-years truce of Tours – twice extended. For it constitutes one of the most discreditable periods of our history where relations with other countries are concerned. The focus of the whole sorry affair was one matter and one man. The matter was the cession of Maine to France: the man was the earl of Suffolk.

Cardinal Beaufort having retired to his diocese of Winchester, and Somerset having died, the Beaufort power in the government now passed to Suffolk. He started badly; the truce of Tours, in the words of Edouard Perroy "set the seal on the recovery of the Valois and confirmed his conquests".[1]

But worse was to follow. As the price of an extension of the truce Suffolk promised to return Maine to France, and withheld the knowledge as long as he could from the English people. When the news got abroad, a fury of indignation against the earl arose; the people were not as tired of the war as was their government; it had not hit most of them personally and their national pride was touched. There appeared to be no military necessity for the cession. The greater part of Maine had for long years been firmly "in the English obedience". Its capital, Le Mans, was held, and its inhabitants were to all appearances friendly or at least resigned to the English cause. The valley of the Sarthe between the capital and Alençon was studded with English-held castles, and over the rest of the county an English army had recently wandered at will. And all that the nation had received in return was a foreign queen! Suffolk made matters worse for him-

[1] *The Hundred Years War*, p. 311.

self in the eyes of history[1] by bowing to the storm and initiating a pitiful policy of prevarication and procrastination in order to get out of his obligations.

In the midst of all this, Suffolk became still more powerful – and therefore still more unpopular – owing to the death in 1447 of the two men who between them had practically ruled England since the death of Henry V. Cardinal Beaufort died in his palace of Wolvesey, the greatest, proudest and richest prince-bishop of England in medieval times, not excepting Cardinal Wolsey. Though for many years the leader of the peace party, he had at the same time conducted the war with sagacity, and during his régime the English cause prospered. His rival, Duke Humphrey of Gloucester, predeceased him by six weeks. As leader of the war party and heir presumptive to the throne, he was naturally the enemy of Suffolk and of Queen Margaret, who as yet was childless. Suffolk and the queen in practice ruled England, for poor Henry VI, though now 23 years of age, was a puppet in their hands. Suffolk hatched a vile conspiracy against his rival and had him arrested on a trumped-up charge. Three days later Gloucester died, under circumstances that looked black for Suffolk. He gave out apoplexy as the cause of death. It matters little whether that be the truth, for one cannot arrest the heir to the throne and ever release him. One is in the position of a snake that has its fangs in the throat of a rival; it dare not leave go. Gloucester would never again have been a free man.

Many opprobrious adjectives can be cast at the good duke with some justification – impulsive, irresponsible, rash, self-centred – but over and above all this he was, in his later years, genuinely concerned for the good of his country. He held a passionate belief in the justice of his country's cause, which he had inherited from his eldest brother, a brother whom he revered and whose wishes he ever regarded as commands.

---

[1] Recent research is however veering towards less harsh judgement on the earl, especially as regards his initial responsibility for the cession of Maine. But this is no excuse for the shiftiness that he displayed.

[2] See *Humphrey, Duke of Gloucester*, by J. H. Vickers. The author, after thorough examination opines that Gloucester was murdered by a slow poison.

Henry VI was in his eyes the legitimate, duly elected king of France. It was a simple faith; and in that faith he died. And in so doing he had, so far as one can see, the feeling of the nation behind him.

Suffolk had already practically banished his only possible living rival, the duke of York, by appointing him lieutenant of Ireland for ten years. Now there was no enemy left who could harm him–or so Suffolk thought. Being now all-powerful, he made himself duke of Suffolk, and he made Edmund Beauchamp, earl of Dorset, duke of Somerset and king's lieutenant in France.

Meanwhile the shifts and subterfuges by which Suffolk sought to wriggle out of his undertaking to hand over Le Mans to France by a specified date, continued with wearisome evasions, till at last Charles VII lost all patience and decided on a resumption of the war.

The king of France had been steadily increasing the efficiency and strength of his army during the truce whereas Suffolk had been whittling down the English armed forces, fondly supposing that he could obtain a favourable peace by friendly gestures such as the cession of Maine, and the marriage of Margaret. He seemed oblivious to the fact that good peace terms have, throughout history, only been obtained through strength and bargaining power. He had deliberately reduced his bargaining power by the needless cession of Maine. Worse still, though the balance of military power had now swung to France he continued to act and talk in the lordly manner of Henry V. The French king, on the other hand had at long last realized that battles do help in ridding a country of an invader, and he was becoming in a sense almost fond of war–that is, on its strategical and planning side. The study of it was no longer repellent to him, he busied himself in logistics, and found that he rather liked them.

All this changed state of affairs on both sides of the line was hidden from Suffolk, who instigated some semi-freebooter English troops to sack the town of Fougères in Brittany, and declined to give redress, though strongly pressed by both the new Duke Francici and by King Charles VII. A resumption of the war was thus inevitable, and indeed Charles may be praised for his patience and forbearance–unless it be that an earlier declaration of war would not have "suited his book".

The king of France had by this time completed the formation of what may be called his "new model" army. It was constituted somewhat on English lines; that is to say, the feudal element had almost disappeared, and its place had been taken by a paid professional army, at least as far as the mounted portion was concerned. It had a fairly definite organization in which the constitution of the "lance" becomes clearly defined. This consisted of six mounted men, the man-at-arms, one swordman, two archers, one *valet aux armes* and one page. Ferdinand Lot says that the latter two were unarmed, but they carried at least a dagger each, and though useless for offensive action they would be useful for the defence of the wagon lines, etc., as were English pages. The latter were included in the number of the retinues, so for the purposes of comparison we should perhaps reckon a French lance at six men.

Now for the first time in the Hundred Years War we get some reliable figures regarding French strengths. Professor Lot has collected them with great care, but there remain so many *lacunae* that we are still rather in the dark. The following basic figure seems at least established. In the king's pay were 1,500 lances, or 9,000 mounted men. To this must be added 1,500 lances, in Languedoc, making a total of 12,000 mounted men on the king's pay-roll. There were other lances called "petites ordanances" which might bring the total up to 15,000. Of dismounted troops–almost exclusively crossbowmen–there was an unknown number. They constituted a paid militia, somewhat after the English model. Lastly, there were the permanent garrisons of defended towns, principally archers, whose numbers it is quite impossible to compute. From the above we must deduct the troops required in Gascony–again impossible to compute, but we must add the armies provided by the duke of Burgundy for operations in eastern Normandy, and the duke of Brittany who now came out openly on the side of Charles.

Looking at the matter as a whole, it seems impossible to pare down the total numbers available for field operations against Normandy much below 30,000. Against this total, what had the English to show? As the reign of Henry VI advances it becomes increasingly difficult to estimate numbers in France, largely because we have no figures for wastage. Under this heading come deserters, who towards the end of the war became a considerable item. In the palmiest days early in the reign it is doubtful if the army in France ever topped 15,000, and nearly all these were normally employed on garrison duties. When a particular effort was planned in the field the bulk of the army for the operation was usually sent out from home. Moreover, of latter years Suffolk had cut down the numbers, and been backward in providing pay, though parliament must share the blame for this. It therefore seems safe to assert that no field army could be provided without depriving the garrisons and leaving them dangerously weak. This will help to explain why in the operations about to be described we hear little of English armies in the field.

Early in July, Charles had sent to seek the advice of the duke of Burgundy as to whether he should go to war. But before receiving the reply, and indeed before issuing his ultimatum, two of his columns commenced operations. The campaign that ensued is singularly lacking in military interest. The reason is not far to seek. The English having no field army, field operations could not take place; consequently the war devolved into a succession of sieges. Most of these were short, almost "token" sieges leading to speedy surrenders on easy terms. Now one siege – still more one surrender – is much like another, and it would be tedious to relate each in detail – even if we possessed those details. It did however possess a certain strategical interest, though even this was somewhat illusory. Charles was, as we have said, beginning to fancy himself as a strategist, and he determined to apply the strategy followed by him in Gascony (and so loved by Edward III); that of exterior lines. He stationed no less than four columns round the circumference of Lower Normandy, and gave them orders to advance inwards and simultaneously. Now the successful application of exterior lines strategy depends, as we have seen so often, on the possession of good communications between columns, and also on resolute commanders. It would seem that the French possessed neither of these for they advanced with circumspection and with an absence of any detectable co-operation between columns. This however did not much matter in the absence of an opposing field army which might strike at one of the isolated columns.

Somerset employed a method that looks supine but which in reality was the only feasible procedure–that of "sitting and suffering". Each town in turn was summoned to surrender, and the smaller ones usually did so. Isolated, with no prospects of relief, often with a Norman commander, always with a partially Norman garrison, and sometimes with an English commander married to a local Norman lady, there was little inducement to hold out long. Any such inclinations were speedily stifled by Jean Bureau's guns.

It is difficult to be certain as to the real feelings of the population. French chroniclers naturally depicted them as burning to escape from "*le joug Anglais*" and to return to their beloved and native France. But this over-simplifies the matter. Normandy was not yet a fully fledged part of France; it had been in English occupation for a third of a century,[1] and it must have appeared to the average inhabitant that they were now permanently linked to England. His attitude was perhaps akin to that of the townsman in the Great Civil War–anxious to be upon the winning side. As it became more and more evident that France would be the winner, adherence to her cause became ever more popular. The rapid fall of one town effected and led to the still more rapid defection of its neighbours. It was like a river approaching a waterfall; the current becomes ever more rapid, till at last nothing can prevent the water falling into the abyss below.

[1] Not to mention the whole of the twelfth century.

The invasion of Normandy can be likened to a boy nibbling round the edge of a biscuit. Four armies converged on the duchy from east, south and west. King Charles attached himself to the eastern one, commanded by Dunois, and directed on the capital. It arrived before the gates of Rouen on October 16, 1449, and Dunois endeavoured by a stratagem to scale the walls. He nearly succeeded, but Talbot rushed to the rescue in the nick of time and the French were driven out. There followed an unexpected event. At that moment a deputation of inhabitants was in England appealing to the king to send English troops to defend the city against the invaders. But the inhabitants were divided in their loyalties, as I have suggested was the case elsewhere. Next day portions of the mob so worked upon Somerset that he weakly allowed the archbishop to negotiate for a surrender. What John Talbot's feelings were we do not know. King Charles took up his residence at the monastery of St. Catherine overlooking the city whilst the parlies proceeded. But they were protracted, and on October 19 the mob seized the gates and opened them to the French. Somerset fell back to the citadel (where Joan of Arc had been imprisoned) and after further negotiations, a treaty on honourable terms was signed. Eight hostages were selected including Talbot, and Somerset marched out with the remainder of the army to Caen.

In December, Harfleur was besieged and Jean Bureau's artillery made short work of it. Next month, January 1450, Honfleur followed suit. All that was now left of Normandy was the central area including Caen, Bayeux, Falaise and the Cherbourg peninsula.

Meanwhile in England there was a storm of fury; and naturally it was centred on the head of Suffolk. The bare possibility of losing Normandy had never crossed the mind of anyone, least of all the ineffable government, who throughout the twelve months preceding the invasion had sent no reinforcements or supplies to the threatened duchy. An army was hastily raised, fitted out and placed under Sir Thomas Kyriell. Now that Talbot had gone, Kyriell was the most experienced commander left, if we exclude Sir John Fastolf, who had long been restored to favour and to the Garter, and had for some years been acting as military advisor to the great council–a post apparently akin to what we might now call director of military operations.

The army consisted of a mere 2,500 men. It was collected at Portsmouth during the autumn, was land-bound for a long period by adverse winds and did not set sail until March 1450.

Kyriell's orders were to land at Cherbourg (which was still in English hands) and march straight to the relief of Bayeux, which was now threatened. He landed at Cherbourg on the 15th but departed from his orders at the request of the local authorities to retake Valognes (in the middle of the Cherbourg peninsula) before pushing on to Bayeux. Not only did he accede to their wishes, but he requested the duke of Somerset, the governor of Normandy, to send reinforcements to him. This Somerset weakly did, scraping together 1,800 men from Bayeux, Caen and Vire. This brought Kyriell's army up to slightly over 4,000 men and enabled him to capture the town of Valognes, though not without considerable casualties. Valognes fell on April 10, and the army resumed its advance to Bayeux two days later, having already consumed nearly four weeks.

The situation when Kyriell landed in France was that, in addition to Rouen, most of the towns in the eastern and southern parts of the duchy had fallen into French hands, and the king was slowly advancing west on Caen. The four weeks delay had also given time for various French columns in Western Normandy to work towards Cherbourg, hunting for the English army. Chief among these was the army of the count of Clermont, the young son of the duke of Bourbon. His headquarters were at Carentan, 20 miles west of Bayeux and 30 miles south of Cherbourg.

At Coutances, a further 20 miles south-west of Carentan, lay some 2,000 men under the Constable de Richemont. These two columns, if they could join hands, would make an army about

5,000 strong, sufficient to confront Kyriell with. Thus, when on April 12 Kyriell set out from Valognes with some 3,800 men,[1] Clermont was only six miles from the route he must take, while Richemont was about 25 miles from it.

Clermont could, of course, easily intercept Kyriell single-handed – if he dared – but Richemont could not expect to get there in time. Valognes and Coutances were, however equi-distant from Bayeux, and by marching thither on the direct road through St. Lô, Richemont ran a good chance of getting there first. He accordingly set out for St. Lô. This was sound military judgement.

The direct road to Bayeux for the English army crossed the estuary of the river Vire by a causeway four miles long. It was only passable at low water and Kyriell must have had an anxious time waiting for the tide to fall, being aware of the presence of Clermont's army at Carentan, only six miles away. The picture of Edward III's crossing of the Somme before Crecy must have come into his mind.

But Clermont sat as tight as a badger. He refused to be drawn by the clamour of the inhabitants of Carentan, who eventually surged out on their own and engaged the English rearguard as it waded through the water waist-deep. The English army continued on its way unmolested, and camped for the night beside a little stream ten miles further on, being still ten miles short of Bayeux. It was the 14th of April. That night Richemont billeted at St. Lô, 19 miles to the south-west, while Clermont remained motionless in Carentan, 15 miles west of Kyriell. The latter had only to continue his march next morning and by mid-day he should be secure in Bayeux.

THE BATTLE OF FORMIGNY, APRIL 15, 1450 (Sketch Map 11, page 321.)

As the sun rose on that fateful mid-April day, the little army of Sir Thomas Kyriell might be seen grouped in the shallow valley in which the tiny village of Formigny nestled. It was a

---

[1] Allowing for the casualties at Valognes.

pleasant spot surrounded by orchards, fruit-trees and gardens, now in full April bloom. A handy brook supplied the necessary water, and a good direct route, the "grand chemin", provided an easy connection and communication with Bayeux.

It was no place to dally in, but Kyriell was an experienced soldier. Why then did he not continue his march, in compliance with his orders, to the safety that Bayeux could provide? History is silent on the point, but I fancy the clue to the problem can be found in the actions of Sir Matthew Gough, the commander of the reinforcements. The troops were not tired; they had only marched 30 miles in three days – an average speed for that period. While the army was sitting motionless round Formigny, Gough was speeding into Bayeux, ten miles in rear. For what purpose? The strong presumption is that Kyriell had a plan of his own, which would not entail continuing the march to Bayeux, and that he had sent Gough in order to obtain approval of it, and possibly reinforcements wherewith to carry it out. What was this project? Again the natural presumption is that Kyriell, who was of course aware by this time of Clermont's column in Carentan, believed he had an opportunity of falling upon it while it was still unsupported by any other column, for it is unlikely that he was aware of Richemont's march to St. Lô the previous day. No contemporary English account of the battle exists, and the French chroniclers cannot have known what the English plan was. My conclusion is thus mere conjecture, but it is in accordance with IMP.

Thus, the morning of April 15 saw the English army stationary, whilst its opponents were hour by hour drawing nearer to it and to each other.

The previous evening the count de Clermont had sent word to the Constable de Richemont at St. Lô of the movements of the English, with the request that he would come to his support in an attack on them the following day. What reply Richemont sent we do not know, but his actions make its purport pretty clear; for he set off up the road to Formigny. Was this a lucky shot, or had definite information of the enemy's position at

Formigny come in during the night? It is impossible to say; which is a pity, for if the Constable was acting merely on an intuition it stamps him as a great general, and confirms my opinion that he was not only the most experienced, but easily the most skilful French general living.

Clermont had the shorter distance to cover and the better road; he was, therefore, the first to gain contact with the enemy. This happened in the early afternoon. Kyriell had, of course, on the previous evening, posted outposts on the low ridge covering his rear, *i.e.* facing west. The slope is gentle and the ridge-top only 50 feet above the valley bottom. The top of the ridge is 800 yards from the little brook that winds down the valley, and astride the road on the ridge-top we may safely locate the line of outposts. Preparations to man it would have been put in hand during the morning, and when the enemy was signalled approaching, every available man was put to work completing it. Kyriell had at his command nearly 4,000 men and Clermont something over 3,000. (See Appendix on numbers.) Kyriell had originally only 425 men-at-arms and if we add 500 from the Gough contingent and allow for casualties at Valognes, sickness etc., we may put the number at about 800. It is important to assess this figure, for thereby we can compute the approximate length of the line. Let me explain.

Kyriell formed up his battle line in a strikingly similar manner to that employed by Henry V at Agincourt. That is to say, it consisted of a thin line of dismounted men-at-arms, interspersed by three clumps of archers, which projected like bastions in front of the spearmen's line. Also as at Agincourt, the number of men-at-arms was so small that no reserve was possible, nor indeed could they form more than a single line and it had to be supplemented by a second line of archers and a third line of billmen. (Billmen had only recently made their appearance in battle.)

The line of men-at-arms was thus about 700 yards in all, and if we allow 80 yards frontage for each archer clump, which I reckon is about right, we get a total length of front of slightly under 1,000 yards, or say 450 yards each side of the road.[1]

Kyriell's headquarters was no doubt on or near the stone bridge, which existed even in those days, alongside which the memorial chapel was afterwards erected. As was usual, the archers planted stakes in their front and, as at Bannockburn and later in Brittany, holes and short trenches were dug all along the front of the line to impede the hostile cavalry. We are often left wondering as to how the troops obtained entrenching tools. In this case we are specifically informed they utilized their swords and daggers. This was doubtless the normal method.

A slightly higher ridge runs eastwards on the south side of the road. This ridge was crowned by a windmill and from it a good view could be obtained southwards over the valley of the river Aure and warning could be obtained of the approach of any enemy from that direction. A small detached force seems to have been posted on this ridge–a sensible step.

It was about 3 o'clock in the afternoon. The French army approached, marching straight up the road. On getting near the position held by the English they deployed in three lines to right and left of the road, in a parallel line to that of their opponents, and distant from it "two bow-shots", *i.e.* about 600 yards.

A pause now ensued, during which the English improved their defences. This pause was to allow Clermont to confer with his officers. He was young and inexperienced and, though he wished to attack, his officers, who had a wholesome respect for an English army in position, and who could not forget Agincourt and Verneuil, tried to dissuade him. The English, they pointed out, were probably superior in numbers and it would require a two to one superiority on the part of the French to defeat them. Better wait till the Constable came up. Such was the advice given, but the headstrong Clermont, probably

[1] Sir James Ramsay, who has a curious propensity for placing the line askew to the natural front and sometimes even perpendicular to it, does so in this case, and his beautifully coloured map–the only one I know of in this country–shows the position running along the Bayeux road, facing south instead of west.

supported by the younger officers who had grown to manhood since Agincourt and who were sick of hearing the word mentioned as an excuse for inaction, took the bit in his teeth and ordered his troops to the assault.

The French men-at-arms for the most part dismounted and advanced "impetuously" on foot. But the English line stood firm behind their stakes and pot-holes and the attackers made no impression. The archers exacted a heavy toll, enfilading the line of pot-holes at short range and from the two flanks. Mounted attacks on the flanks met with the same reception. The action went on for two hours, with no result. Then the French remembered their guns. Two "culverins", heavy field guns, were dragged out in front of their line and galled the English position. This proved too much for the archers who broke their ranks and with headstrong initiative charged forwards straight upon the offending cannon. The French gunners were all dispatched or dispersed and the triumphant archers, not knowing how to spike the guns, began to drag them back into their own lines. Here the accounts are hopelessly conflicting and we cannot be sure whether they succeeded or whether the French recaptured them. It matters not; the incident is picturesque and consequently has been seized upon by all writers, but it is of trifling importance. What matters is that the French had by this time suffered so heavily that they began to melt off the field. One of their leaders, Pierre de Brezé, distinguished himself by rallying many of the fleeing archers. The French had plainly shot their bolt and it has been conjectured that, if Kyriell had "plucked the golden moment" and launched a general counter-attack, the enemy would have been completely routed. But two things happened, or rather one thing happened and a second did *not* happen. Kyriell did *not* attack, but sat motionless in his position, while from the south, in the very nick of time for the French, the army of the Constable appeared over the skyline.

Of the details of Richemont's approach march we unfortunately know nothing, but it is probable that the sound of the culverins firing reached him and told him what he wanted to know:

the English must be standing at Formigny. By this time the Constable had reached the village of Trevières, one and a half miles due south of Formigny, on the banks of the river Aure.

Climbing the steep slope to the north of it, Richemont reached the windmill on the summit, and tradition asserts that he climbed it to get a view of the battle. Likely enough, if the ground was as thickly timbered as it is to-day. Otherwise he could have taken in the situation at a glance from ground levels and the spectacle was enough to gladden his heart. For the English were heavily engaged, fighting with their flanks and backs to him. What an opportunity! But the Constable was a cautious man. He could also see signs of the French rout. It would take some time to get up his own army on to the ridge-top and deploy it for the attack. What if by that time Clermont's troops had disappeared completely off the battlefield? He would then be left to face a victorious and greatly superior English army single-handed.

Richemont decided to get in touch with Clermont before committing his own army. He accordingly rode forward, crossed the brook by a ford (probably the one marked on my sketch-map) and managed to find Clermont. A hasty consultation was held and it would seem that Clermont placed himself under the orders of the older man. At any rate an agreement was reached: Clermont would rally his army and return to the attack, engaging the northern half of the hostile line, while Richemont attacked the southern half.

Richemont returned to his own army, which he deployed on top of the ridge by the windmill. He then advanced down the hill towards the English left, being careful to extend his left across the brook, so as to contact Clermont's right flank.

By this time Kyriell had become aware of the approach of the Constable's army. Whether or not he had contemplated turning to the attack of the defeated enemy in his front, (which seems likely) such a thing was now out of the question. He must form front to the new enemy, and that quickly, for the windmill was less than a mile from his nearest flank, and the enemy could approach rapidly down the hill.[1] There being now signs that Clermont's troops were now rallying, Kyriell's course was obvious. While still holding a front against the old enemy he must form a second front to face the new one. This could be done partly by refusing the extreme left of the line, and partly by

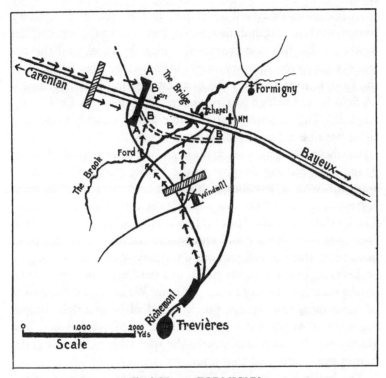

Sketch Map 11: FORMIGNY

A-A English position phase I   O.M. Old monument
B-B English position phase II   N.M. New monument

withdrawing troops from the old line and extending the flank with them. This was a difficult and complicated manoeuvre to carry out without previous warning in the heat of battle, but there was no alternative for he possessed no reserve. It was done,

---

[1] The situation was strikingly similar to that at Waterloo when the Prussians appeared on the field—as had also been the previous strategy.

after a fashion, but the confusion and disorder must have been fearful. However, a French chronicler pays tribute to the courageous way the English faced up to the new emergency–"They held themselves grandly" he writes. Their line was now bent back into a right angle or rough semi-circle, with the bridge as centre.

As Richemont's attack developed in full view of Clermont's troops, the latter, thus enheartened, returned to the attack. The weakened English line crumbled under the shock and the defenders gave ground everywhere. Step by step they fell back to the bridge, round which the heaviest fighting now developed. (A field by the bridge was until recently known as Le Champ Anglais.) The pressure of the double attack steadily increased, till it became a case of "Sauve qui peut!".

Matthew Gough, who had been hurriedly recalled from Bayeux in time to take part in the battle, managed to cut his way out with a portion of his men and to regain Bayeux. Kyriell was not so fortunate; he was surrounded and captured. The English were now split up into small packets, each of which fought on individually and stubbornly. Little quarter seems to have been asked or offered and one party of about 500 English archers fought it out to the death in a garden by the brook-side, selling their lives dearly to the last man. We know not the names of these men, but we are put in mind of Newcastle's famous regiment of White Coats, on the field of Marston Moor, 200 years later. No memorial marks the spot where these nameless heroes stood and died to a man.

The battle was over; the English army was practically wiped out; Normandy was lost for ever.

*   *   *

COMMENTS

This battle contained a strategical feature almost unique in medieval warfare. That is to say, two armies operating on exterior lines effected a concentration on the battlefield. The concentration of Wellington and Blücher on the field of Waterloo was not more timely and more effective than that of Clermont and Richemont on the field of Formigny. In both cases the operation that Napoleon was never tired of warning against was carried out successfully. The question naturally arises, how much did this happy result owe to luck and how much to good management?

It is impossible to answer this question with any assurance, for the records fail us. The difficulty of bringing about concentration on the battlefield, before the advent of modern inventions had improved communications out of all knowledge, was extreme; this accounts for the rarity of successful undertakings of this nature and for Napoleon's reiterated warning. Unfortunately there is no space here to go into this fascinating subject, but I think that, however great the luck in this case, we must salute Arthur of Brittany for his courage and tactical skill in carrying out what luck may or may not have put in his path.

The powerful influence of one battle on another was perhaps never more strikingly shown than in that of Agincourt on Formigny. Agincourt in its turn was influenced by Crecy and Poitiers, and Crecy in its turn by Halidon Hill and Dupplin Moor.

Of the soldierly qualities of the Englishmen of that day, the battle is an eloquent witness; of the leadership displayed it is more difficult to make an estimate, mainly because no English combatant had the heart to write, or even talk, about the battle and consequently our Chronicles were reduced to copying the French accounts. If we knew more we might condone Kyriell's actions. He was a veteran of the war, with a good record. We must be content to give him the benefit of the doubt. We should however have been better pleased if he had met his death in the field as did the great Talbot three years later at Castillon. Instead he ended on the traitor's scaffold, 21 years later. The sole contemporary English criticism of Kyriell that I have found is contained in a memorandum submitted to the great council by their advisor, Sir John Fastolf, shortly after the battle. He writes of Kyreill as "negligently tarrying in Normandy, and sped him not to go spedly to [Somerset]".[1]

THE FINAL PHASE

The news of the complete destruction of England's last army came as a thunder-clap to the government and people. Fastolf set about raising another army 3,000 strong, but events in Normandy moved too fast for him. Instead of advancing straight on Caen, the French turned south to Vire. Six days sufficed to capture it with its commander Lord Scales, who thus passes out of these pages. There were now but half a dozen defended towns, but all had strong garrisons. Clermont and Richemont here parted company, the former to Bayeux, which soon fell, the latter to assist Duke Francis of Brittany in the siege of Avranches. This outpost of Normandy had acquired a great reputation, having valiantly sustained the siege of 1439, as we have seen. The heroic wife of its captain, John Lampet, donned the trousers to rally the garrison, and when all hope had gone, resumed the skirt in order to conduct negotiations with the duke. Francis fell in love with this amazon, but fell ill and died shortly afterwards. John Lampet, according to the contemporary, "List of Cities . . . taken from the English. . . . "

"come to England and died of grief."[2]

The time was now ripe for the siege of Caen. No less than four columns concentrated against it—the fruition of the strategic plan of Charles VII. In it was the remnants of the main English forces in Normandy, under the duke of Somerset (who had his wife and children with him). The "List of Cities . . . " gives the French as 100,000 strong, and they may well have been up to one fifth of that number. The siege followed somewhat similar lines to that of Henry V. The town was surrounded by troops, the two great abbeys were occupied and a vigorous bombardment opened by Jean Bureau on June 5. But there was no

[1] *Collections of William of Worcester*, printed in Stevenson's *Letters and Papers*, II, Part 2, p. 595.
[2] Stevenson, op. cit., II, p. 633.

storm; after standing three weeks bombardment the English came to terms. The "last straw" was a cannon-ball which penetrated the ducal nursery, the duchess being in the room at the time. The duke of Somerset was granted a free passage to England, the prospect of which he did not relish. Instead he got himself conveyed to Calais.

But all was not over yet. Falaise, the appanage of the captive earl of Shrewsbury, was now besieged by Xantrailles, and an early surrender was negotiated in return for the the liberation of its lord. Thus John Talbot once again became a free man, and promised (so it is said) not again to put on armour against Charles VII.

Last of all came Cherbourg. To the Constable and Clermont, who were by now a firm combination, was granted the honour and triumph of the final siege. They were accompanied by Jean Bureau, who now surpassed himself. The most advantageous site for his battering artillery was on the sands, which however were submerged by every flood-tide. But Bureau was equal to this. Just before each tide rose he had the guns plastered in tallow and hides (thus "waterproofing" them in a manner unconsciously copied nearly 500 years later). There they were left till the tide fell again, when the bombardment was resumed. The English garrison under Thomas Gower, as if conscious of the historic nature of the occasion, put up a splendid resistance and stretched the great French besieging force to the full, exacting a heavy toll in killed and wounded, including that gallant sailor, Admiral Coëtivi. But the end was inevitable, and on August 11, 1450, the English rule in northern France came to an end.

Seven days later John Paston's servant wrote to him wistfully:

"This morning was it told that Shirburgh is goon, and we have not now a foote of londe in Normandie."[1]

THE LOSS OF NORMANDY

It was of course inevitable that Normandy should eventually be completely absorbed by France. A tract of the earth's surface

[1] *Paston Letters*, I, p. 139.

of the size and shape of modern France, almost surrounded by water and mountains was bound by the process of inter-marriage and inter-communication to become a single political entity in the long run. The English had had only a short run – a mere 30 years – one tenth of their dominance in Gascony. Nevertheless there was no overriding political reason why the inevitable should happen so suddenly in 1450. It is true that the Maid had stirred and stimulated the sense of patriotism and nationalism in France proper. But it is at least doubtful if she had had much influence in Normandy; all that the Normans knew about her came from the English garrison or the Church; from both sources they heard that Joan was a witch – a limb of the devil – and it would be surprising if they did not believe it. Though England and Normandy had been bad neighbours, being rivals on the sea, there were still some historic and blood links between the two countries and as long as the people were better governed and more secure in their persons than their neighbours in metro-politan France, they had little inducement to try to upset what was beginning to look like a permanent connection with the people *outre la Manche*.

It would seem then, that the sudden overrunning of their country must be assigned to other than political, social or economic causes. In fact, the whole course of events can be explained on purely military grounds and on no other. It can be expressed in a single sentence: so long as England was able to put and maintain in the field a more effective striking force than her opponents, she was able to maintain her position indefinitely; but when the balance of military power passed to the other side, her dominion in France was doomed. When we enquire WHY the balance of military power veered from one side to the other we at once find ourselves in the domain of politics, economics, and social history – factors which it is outside the scope of this book to examine.[1]

It only remains to record with a satisfaction that I will not

[1] They have been well set out by Professor Edouard Perroy in his book *The Hundred Years War*.

attempt to disguise, that the duke of Suffolk was arraigned by
the Commons, banished by the king, captured by some English
ships (including one of the king's), beheaded on a boat gunwale
and his headless body cast on to the sands at Dover. Sir Charles
Oman thrice describes him as "the shuffling Suffolk". If we add
the adjective "shifty' that will suffice for his epitaph. And now
let us try and forget the man.

APPENDIX

THE NUMBERS

Numbers in a medieval battle are usually the most controversial item. This is not surprising; records were few, and sometimes altogether absent; estimates as to numbers were wild and
often biased; our checks on their veracity, where they do exist,
are scanty. The result is that most conflicting estimates as to
numbers are still being made by historians. Formigny is no
exception, although the degree of difference is not nearly so
wide as that of the other great battles of the war.

The French chroniclers and the official bulletin all assert
that the English outnumbered the French. This might be due
to patriotic pride; indeed a French writer suggests that the
French claim to absurdly few casualties was due to an attempt
to make the result appear due to Divine interposition. Modern
French writers accept the old figure unquestioningly. The last
to do so is Professor Ferdinand Lot.

His figure for the English (slightly under 4,000) need not
detain us, for I arrived at the same result (though not for precisely the same reasons). M. Lot, who is the exponent of small
numbers in medieval war, accepts the figure given by the
official bulletin of 3,000 for Clermont's army, though it had
every motive to minimize the French numbers. At the same
time he rejects the statement (again likely not to be exaggerated,
to say the least) made by Jean Chartier that Richemont besides
his lances had 800 archers. (Blondel also confirms the presence
of these archers.) This Ferdinand Lot will not allow, on the

grounds that to take dismounted archers would be "extremely perilous". The professor may think so, but count de Richemont may not have shared this opinion; and in any case, why should Chartier and Blondel expressly state the fact if there were no dismounted archers present? By this arbitrary reasoning M. Lot is able to show that the French had rather fewer men than the English. My own computation is as follows. To the official figure of 3,000 for Clermont I think we must add some hundreds. The number of Richemont's lances is variously given as 200, 220, 250 and 300, the last being the usual figure. Accepting this and counting only four armed men per lance, we get a minimum of 1,200, plus 800 archers, total 2,000. The grand total of the two armies can thus safely be placed at something over 5,000.

It may be objected that the figure 4,000 for the English is too low seeing that the number of dead alone is given as 3,774 in the official bulletin. The exactitude of this figure is at first sight impressive, but on second thoughts it becomes suspicious. We know that the English were buried in 14 grave-pits extending over a fairly wide area. The corpses would be stripped and thrown into these pits simultaneously, since the whole army which did not pursue, would be available for the purpose. Was there a clerk at each pit narrowly counting the corpses? And were no dead French bodies included in the pits? A naked French body would look much like an English one. I think it more likely that the figure 3,774 was deliberately fabricated for propaganda purposes, in order to enhance the measure of victory, and underline its miraculous nature.

CLERMONT'S DEFEAT IN PHASE ONE

The official bulletin spoke of a "skirmish", not a genuine attack, by Clermont, and this word has been accepted by most modern writers, including Sir Charles Oman and Sir James Ramsay, the only two modern English historians to devote attention to the battle. Unfortunately for the official bulletin, Admiral Coëtivi, one of Clermont's senior captains, "spilt the beans" in a letter written only four days after the battle. After relating the English defeat he adds:

"But, to tell the truth, I believe that God brought us M. le Constable, for if he had not come at the time and by the manner that he did, I doubt if, *entre nous*, [*sic*] . . . we should have got through the battle without irreparable damage for they were half as strong again as we were."

THE ENGLISH POSITION IN PHASE TWO

It is here that the chroniclers are most obscure and most at variance. I have had to draw largely on I.M.P. in order to resolve the matter to my own satisfaction. The reader must judge whether the course of events as described above seems a natural one. Both Ramsay and Oman disagree with me and with each other and Lot (as always) is more interested in the relative numbers engaged than in the course of the battle. As for other writers I can find nothing of note in the French language since about 1900 when the 450th anniversary of the battle produced a number of papers on the subject. No two exactly agree, and the one which goes into the matter the most thoroughly, providing a number of maps, is unfortunately guilty of inventing a valley which does not exist (thereby rendering my investigation on the field unduly difficult and prolonged – till I discovered his error).

SOURCES FOR FORMIGNY

The main, in fact practically the only, English source for the battle is the "List of cities . . . " under the heading *William of Worcester's Collection*, edited and translated in J. Stevenson's *Letters and Papers*. . . . Incidentally, these *Letters and Papers*, though they add little to our knowledge of military operations, become increasingly useful for the logistical side of the war; (but they are clumsily edited; to ascertain the provenance of many of the letters and papers in Vol. I and Vol. II, Part 1, it is essential to have by one Vol. II, Part 2).

On the French side the sources are naturally plentiful, though, as mentioned in the text, they copy one another to a large extent. Charles Joret, in his *Bataille de Formigny* (1903) gives no less than 15 sources and transcribes the relevant passages from most of them.[1] His book is the best published on the battle. The chief chroniclers are, Jean Chartier, Berry the Herald, Robert Blondel,[1] Guillaume Gruel, Thomas Basin, all of whom have already been cited in these pages. A brief allusion to some modern works has also been made and need not be repeated here; but to them should be added Du Fresne de Beaucourt's *Histoire de Charles VII.*

[1] J. Stevenson in his *Expulsion of the English from Normandy* prints the original Latin of Blondel's *De Reductione Normanni* and Berry's *Le Recouvremont de Normandie* in the original French from his *Histoire de Charles VII*, and also an English translation.

CHAPTER XIX

CASTILLON

NORMANDY having been regained, Charles VII turned his attention to Gascony. But he made his usual thorough preparations and it was not till nearly a year later that he was ready to strike. The Count de Dunois then led a large French army into Gascony.

Few English troops remained in the duchy, and the Gascons were much too weak to offer effective resistance. On June 30, 1451, the French entered Bordeaux, and all seemed over. But the unexpected happened, as it so often does in our history. The French may have regarded themselves as liberators, but the inhabitants of Bordeaux looked upon them as conquerors. Not for 300 years had the streets of Bordeaux seen a French soldier. In addition, there were economic and commercial reasons – the wine trade, above all – for their preference for the English, which we need not go into here. Suffice it that the king of France himself admitted that the Gascons preferred the English as their masters. "Everyone knows", he wrote six years later to the king of Scotland, "that it (Gascony) has been English for 300 years and that the people of the region are at heart completely inclined towards the English party."

The burgesses of Bordeaux, therefore, did not settle down quietly under their new masters, and in March, 1452, some of the leading citizens sailed to London to entreat Henry VI to send an army of deliverance. In spite of the domestic troubles that were developing, Henry not only complied but appointed to the command the foremost captain of the day, John Talbot, earl of Shrewsbury. He had literally grown grey in the service of arms, for at his last battle he was reputed eighty years of age. Though according to my calculations he cannot have passed his seventieth year, that was a great age for his or any other period.

His fame had become so great, and the French dread of him so deep, that mothers could be heard to quieten their fractious offspring with the threat that "Tal-bote" would have them. (In this respect Talbot must be bracketed with Marlborough and Napoleon.) Later, we shall see an equally striking example of the hold that he acquired over the imagination of the people of France.

The English expeditionary force was about 3,000 strong— rather a small army, one would say, for the reconquest of a dominion. Small or not, however, it appeared sufficient. Talbot landed in Gascony on October 17, 1452, and Bordeaux ejected the French garrison, joyfully opened its gates to him, and hailed their deliverer as "Le Roi Talbot". Most of western Gascony followed suit, and the few towns occupied by a French garrison in the Bordelais which did not capitulate were taken by force.

So the winter passed, while Charles VII did not stir. The English, it seemed, had come back to stay. But the king of France, who did nothing in a hurry, began in the spring of 1453 to collect an army. This time there was to be no mistake about it: an overwhelming force should be assembled, nothing less would suffice against Le Roi Talbot. By mid-summer, 1453, Charles was ready to strike. The strategy he adopted was similar to that which had proved successful in Normandy three years previously: it was that of operations on exterior lines. Three armies were to approach Bordeaux simultaneously, one from the south-east, one from the east and one from the north-east, while the king himself held his reserve well to the rear. The French were in overwhelming superiority, though probably no one army by itself outnumbered the Anglo-Gascon army that the earl of Shrewsbury could put into the field. Reinforcements under his favourite son, Lord de Lisle, had arrived, but the total at Talbot's disposal cannot be exactly estimated owing to scanty Gascon records. It may have been as much as 6,000.

The French advanced slowly and cautiously, and by mid-July the centre army had reached Castillon, a small walled town 30 map miles east of Bordeaux. Meanwhile, Talbot sat tight in the capital, waiting for the French armies to advance closer so as to enable him in a single rapid march to swoop on the nearest of them and defeat it before the other could come to its assistance. This was the best answer to the strategy of Charles.

Unfortunately for Talbot's strategy, the inhabitants of Castillon, which was of course in imminent danger, did not see any attractions in it. They objected to being "thrown to the lions", and clamoured for help. In this they were backed up by the burgesses of Bordeaux. Talbot explained to them as patiently as he could the nature of his strategy, and assured them that he was only biding his time and would strike in due season. The burgesses were inclined to disbelieve him and he lost much of his phenomenal popularity and prestige. The earl was deeply hurt by this disbelief in his good faith, and eventually, against his better judgement, he yielded to the clamour and decided to go at once to the help of the threatened Castillon.

The army that was about to lay siege to the town had been collected from many parts of France, including Brittany, and had at least six commanders who seem to have acted as a committee. This was a very unsatisfactory arrangement, but it was alleviated by the fact that a chief of staff (as we should now call him) had been appointed, and the actual dispositions were left to him. The person in question was that stocky little Frenchman, Jean Bureau. He had graduated in the English service in his youth, but had afterwards transferred his allegiance to the Valois king. When Charles decided on a campaign for the recovery of Gascony he had commissioned Bureau to construct a great park of siege and field guns for the purpose. Of these no less than 300 cannon, great and small, accompanied the centre army if we are to believe the chroniclers, though the number is probably exaggerated. The men-at-arms and archers numbered something between 7,000 and 10,000.

On arrival opposite the walls of Castillon, Bureau who seems to have been the *de facto* commander adopted what may appear curious procedure. Instead of constructing lines of circumvallation round the town, with possibly a line of contravallation

facing the direction whence Talbot's relieving army might be
expected to approach, Bureau set to work to construct an en-
trenched camp for the bulk of his army. Nor did he site it to
the west of the town, so as to cut it off from reinforcements, but
on the east side, and 2,000 yards distant, well out of range of the
town's guns. Why did he take this curiously defensive step? It is
true that he had done something of the sort on occasion in Normandy, but I fancy his main motive was one of fear–fear of
Talbot. If he sited his camp to the west of the town he might
find himself caught between two fires, the town garrison on the
east, the relieving army on the west. Whatever his motives,
Bureau set 700 pioneers to digging and building. For four days,
July 13th to 16th, they worked night and day, and at the end of
that time a deep continuous ditch backed by a palisaded rampart surrounded his camp on three sides. This camp (Sketch
Map 12, page 339) was 700 yards long and on an average 200
yards wide, situated with its long side parallel to and abutting
the river Lidoire. The main entrance was on the south side, and
a footbridge probably spanned the river on the north. Along the
north side, the camp perimeter followed the river bank which,
being ten feet high and almost perpendicular, acted as a rampart, with the river as ditch. No digging was therefore required
on this side.

The camp was, as the map shows, of a most extraordinary
shape.[1] Its area was nearly 30 acres–and its shape was exactly
as shown on my map, for its lines can still be traced on the ground.
(The grounds for this remarkable assertion are given in the
Appendix.) Roughly, it was designed to afford the artillery a
maximum of oblique and enfilade fire, and the hand of an artilleryman is discernible in its planning.

The guns were placed round the perimeter of the camp and,
if there were as many as 300, they must have been almost wheel
to wheel in an unbroken line–a fact that makes me doubt the
accuracy of this figure. In addition to the troops encamped in

---

[1] Its shape has, however been plausibly explained by Major J. L. Nicholson,
O.B.E., R.E., in an article in *The Royal Engineers Journal* (1949, p. 290).

the new work, Bureau (or the committee) stationed 1,000 archers in the priory of St. Lorent, 200 yards north of the town (the site is now occupied by the railway station), to act as an outpost against the approach of the English army; and also a force of 1,000 or more Bretons in the woods on the high ground to the north of the camp. All was now ready to commence the siege works, or to resist attack by Talbot, should he accept the challenge.

We must return to Bordeaux. But prior to narrating the movements of the relieving army I must warn the reader that, as was almost always the case in our infrequent defeats of medieval days, no English participant seems to have troubled to tell his story to our chroniclers. Consequently, for every single fact relating to the campaign we have to go to the French sources. These were, not unnaturally, considerable in number and volume, but however fair and truthful they may have tried to be, a certain amount of bias cannot have been avoided. It is, therefore, all the more remarkable that they show a singular unanimity and emphasis, amounting almost to enthusiasm, regarding the prowess and achievements of the "English Achilles", as the earl of Shrewsbury was dubbed by them. Whereas they seldom mention the names of the French commanders, that of Talbot is forever on their lips. This reverence for their great opponent has extended even to modern times. In *La Conquête de Guyenne*, by Henri Ribadien, the French author provides but a single illustration; it is not, as might have been expected, of some French commander, such as Jean Bureau, but of Talbot the Englishman. As I say, the amount of bias is small and, as their accounts contradict one another but little, we can reconstruct the story with some assurance.

*   *   *

THE BATTLE

The earl of Shrewsbury, once having made up his mind acted with lightning speed. No doubt his troops had already been warned to expect a rapid move at short notice. Certainly they got little notice now. Parading his army in the early hours of

July 16, Talbot marched out of the city at the head of his mounted men, the dismounted troops following as fast as they could. After a gruelling march of nearly 20 miles at the height of the Gascon hot weather, the army reached Libourne on the river Dordogne by sun-down. But there was little rest in store for them. Talbot had decided upon a night march, and not only a night march but one by unfrequented tracks through the forest along the high ground to the north of the Dordogne valley, instead of by the direct and easier road which led up the valley. A few hours' rest was therefore allowed, during which the veteran earl himself obtained a little sleep. On again at about midnight they went, the mounted troops still leading, with the foot soldiers plodding miles behind. This mounted force was tiny in size, a mere 500 men-at-arms and 800 archers, according to Aeneas Piccolomini. The route would take them through St. Emilion, that delectable centre of a famous wine district; after which it would follow the crest of the ridge to the north of the valley.

As dawn broke on the 17th the advanced-guard reached the woods to the immediate north of the Priory of St. Lorent, without encountering any hostile patrols. The presence of the French archers in the priory had been reported to Talbot, and his night march was no doubt undertaken with the object of surprising this force, for until it was accounted for the main French army could not be attacked. The garrison of the priory may be supposed to have had sentries out on the main road facing west, but they would hardly suspect the presence of the enemy in the almost trackless woods at daybreak without any previous intimating of their approach. Talbot would be aware of this, and his decision to make a bold and sudden attack from the woods, which at this point reached almost down to the priory, was a natural one and was in accordance with the English tradition built up during the Hundred Years War. It met with rapid and complete success. The luckless French archers, taken unawares, many of them being still in their beds, put up but a feeble resistance, and such as were not cut down fled to the refuge of the

French camp. While the fight lasted, the main French army made no attempt to send aid to the priory. This is not surprising; there was little time, even if they had been aware of the attack, which they probably were not, for they were out of sight of the priory, which was distant from the camp about a mile, and no cannons took part in the engagement.

It was a brilliant little affair, and must have "put up the tails" of the attackers. The driving power of the aged leader in this headlong advance, and his sure grip and skill in arriving at precisely the right place at the right time, despite the difficulties of a night march through 12 miles of unmapped woodland, compel our admiration and must have proved to his troops that age had not dimmed his prowess. The whole operation was similar to, and probably based on, Talbot's own night march and attack on the French at Pontoise 16 years before. It showed a nice judgement on his part, and it is noteworthy that Frenchmen of his time described him as a man of good judgement. But the very success of this affair was to have the most unexpected and sinister results, as we shall shortly see.

Some men-at-arms pursued the fleeing archers right up to the French camp and came back with useful reports as to its position and nature. The question for Talbot was now whether to push straight on to the attack, striking while the iron was hot, or to await the arrival of his infantry who were still some miles in rear. He decided on the latter course: the enemy in the camp had been aroused, surprise was now out of the question; his own men were fatigued with a 30-mile march on empty stomachs, followed by a fight; the French archers had left plenty of food and drink in the priory, and so the earl ordered some of this food to be issued to the troops, after which they were to get what rest they could. He also sent forward Sir Thomas Evringham to make a careful reconnaissance of the camp. It would be hard to criticize this course of action.

Talbot now ordered his chaplain to prepare a celebration of the Mass for himself, while his men were breaking their fast. But just before it was ready, a messenger dashed in from the town

stating breathlessly that the French were in full retreat; their
horsemen could be seen from the town walls hastily quitting
their camp, and leaving a trail of dust behind them. What was to
be done? Cancel the previous orders and put in an improvised
attack? Allow the enemy to retreat if he wished to? Or await
the arrival of the infantry and then, if not too late, attack? The
last course was urged upon him by Sir Thomas and others, but
it was not in the nature of the old warrior to let go a chance of
this sort. The enemy was in retreat, he should be scattered to
the winds! Swearing to his chaplain that he would not hear Mass
until he had beaten the French, he gave orders for an instant
attack and pursuit. Calling for his charger he mounted and led
his army out of the priory. He must have been a striking figure,
on his white cob, his white locks surmounted by a purple velvet
cap–for he wore no armour. (When released after his second
captivity in 1450, he had–so it is said–sworn to the French
king never again to wear armour against him. This vow he was
now keeping to the letter.)

And now was seen the true subtlety of the siting of Bureau's
camp. If attacked from the north the assailant would be confronted by the river and steep bank; if from the west–the direct
line of approach–the frontage presented would be only 200
yards, insufficient for full deployment of the attacking army; if
from the south, the assailants would have to pass across the front
of the camp at a short distance from it, since the Dordogne
flowed only 600 yards south of the camp, and moreover the
English would have to fight with their backs to a broad swift-
flowing river.

Despite these disadvantages, Talbot decided to attack from
the south. To do this his army had to ford the little river Lidoire
600 yards short of the camp. This was successfully done, and the
advance was continued towards the hostile camp. But a dread-
ful surprise was in store for the Anglo-Gascon army. Instead of
being in full flight, the French were standing their ground,
their guns almost wheel to wheel, their infantry manning the
parapets, motionless and ready. What had gone wrong? Simply

this; when the fleeing archers took refuge in the camp which
was already uncomfortably crowded, in order to make room

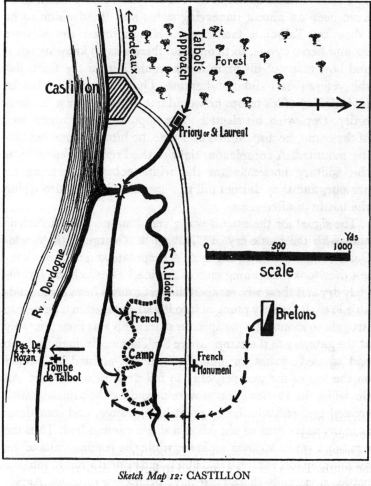

Sketch Map 12: CASTILLON

➤ English movements

➤ French movements

for them the horses, or a portion of them, had to be turned
out; it was the sight of the varlets riding these horses away at a
gallop that had misled the Gascon watchers into supposing that

the whole army was in retreat. Thus the surprise and flight of the archers had led to their victors themselves being surprised. The serried ranks of the French army ranged in position must have been an almost unnerving sight; and the decision to be taken by Talbot a fateful one. His mounted troops were outnumbered by over six to one, and there was no knowing when and how many of his main army would join in the fight. But the veteran earl did not hesitate. Quietly confident in the invincibility of his troops he would not deign to give a counter-order. Deploying his slender force opposite the southern face of the camp, he dismounted everyone, he himself alone remaining mounted. A conspicuous sight to the French defenders was this solitary horseman on the white cob and wearing no armour, and they did not fail to remark on it when describing the battle in after-years.

The signal for the assault was given, banners were unfurled[1] and, with the battle-cry of "Talbot! St. George!", the Anglo-Gascons advanced and engaged. A desperate and confused contest then took place along most of the line.[2] The ditch was fortunately dry and those who escaped the first rounds from the formidable French artillery plunged into it and engaged in a desperate struggle to mount the parapet. In places this was done; notably at the gateway to the camp, where Sir Thomas Evringham (who had advised against an immediate attack) planted his banner on the top of the parapet, only to fall dead next moment. All the while the French cannon were pounding the attackers with crossed and enfilade fire at point-blank range, and sometimes as many as six men would fall to a single cannon-ball. Thus the struggle swayed for over an hour, while the leading units of the dismounted force arrived in driblets and rushed straight into the battle. Eventually there must have been close on 4,000 Anglo-Gascons present on the field. Even so, the attackers were badly outnumbered, and were also deprived of the support of their own guns, none of which arrived in time for the battle.

[1] Some of these banners—if we are to believe Jean Chartier, were inscribed with rude remarks about the claims of Charles to be the legitimate king of France.
[2] "Un grant et terrible assault" (*Chartier*).

In spite of all these disadvantages encountered by the English army, French chroniclers admit that the issue remained in doubt till the sudden appearance on the field of the Bretons. It will be remembered that they had been stationed in the woods to the north of the camp. Swooping down from the heights and crossing the Lidoire, on the east side of the camp, a party of these men, all picked troops, made an unexpected inroad into the exposed right flank of the already hard-pressed attackers. Talbot drew off some of his men to oppose the new foe. Noticing this partial withdrawal the garrison of the camp, reinforced by the remainder of the Bretons, left their defences and with all forces combined drove their enemy back towards the river Dordogne.

The English army scattered in flight, the majority falling back direct to the rear. Thus the main body of fugitives found themselves on the bank of the river Dordogne. By the natural process of trial and error, and after a number had been drowned,[1] they discovered a practicable ford. This ford is now called the Pas de Rozan and has been used at exceptionally low water within living memory. Here the earl of Shrewsbury, who had been swept along in the retreat, tried no doubt to organize a defensive line covering the ford, actively supported by his son, the Lord de Lisle. But the pressure of the enemy grew ever greater, and eventually a chance cannon-ball struck the famous white palfrey which fell, bringing the old earl with it to the ground and pinning him underneath. In this defenceless posture a Frenchman named Michael Perunin was able to deal him the death blow with a battle-axe on his unprotected skull. His son, Lord de Lisle, died with him. That was the end of the battle, the Anglo-Gascon army dispersed, and Gascony was lost to England for ever.

The body of the earl of Shrewsbury was found next day, with great difficulty, and only recognized by a missing tooth. According to one account he was buried where he fell. Whether this is

[1] In 1954 a spear-head was found in the river bed near the ford—no doubt dropped by a drowning English man at arms. An iron cannon ball, 5 inches in diameter, was found near the same spot.

true or not, the body was removed shortly afterwards to Falaise, where it was reburied, the skull being taken to England and buried in the parish church at Whitchurch, Salop. In about 1493 Sir Gilbert Talbot removed the body to the same resting place. The grave was opened in 1860 and "the true cause of death was seen to be a blow from a battle-axe on the skull".

So died the English Achilles, and after the battle a monument was raised to him by the victorious French generals. It was called Notre Dame de Talbot. The spot came to be known as La Tombe de Talbot, and it is still marked on the map as Monument de Talbot. The chapel was destroyed during the revolution, but a modern cross has since been erected on the spot. It originally had no inscription on it, but I was told that Talbot's name did appear on the old one. On the 500th anniversary of the battle a plaque, presented by the local commune was unveiled.[1]

Of the many tributes paid to the dead warrior by contemporary French chroniclers, I will quote but one, that of Matthew d'Escoucy:

"Such was the end of this famous and renowned English leader who for so long had been one of the most formidable thorns in the side of the French, who regarded him with terror and dismay."

One is forcibly reminded of the saying, "A prophet is not without honour, save in his own country".

With the loss of the battle, the English Dominion of Gascony was lost and on October 10, 1453, the reluctant Bordelaise received once more in their midst the French conquerors. The Hundred Years War was at last over.

APPENDIX

SOURCES

There are no English sources for the battle. The main French sources are as follows (the length of time in years after the battle being given in brackets):

---

[1] The author was privileged to be present at this ceremony, and now possesses the unveiling flag.

1. A letter from Angoulême, written two days after the battle, giving a second-hand account of it. (Printed in *Bibliothèque de l'École des Chartes*, 1846.)

2. A short letter from Charles VII, written six days after the battle and based on the above.

3. The official account, written by Berry the Herald, last printed by the *Société de l'Histoire de France* 1863. (One year.)

4. *Histoire de Charles VII* by Jean Chartier, edited by Vallet de Viriville in 1863. (A few years.)

5. *Chronique de Matthieu d'Escoucy* in *Société de l'Histoire de France*, 1863. (About 12 years.)

6. *Les Vigiles*, a poem by Martial d'Aubergne, last printed in 1724. (Not cited by Ramsay.)

7. *Histoire de Gaston IV* by Lesuer, printed in 1826. (Also not cited by Ramsay.) (23 years.)

8. *Histoire de France* by Thomas Basin, last printed in 1944. (24 years.)

Of modern works none exists in the English language. The classical French account is in *La Conquête de la Guyenne* by Henri Ribadieu (1866).

THE FRENCH CAMP

The claim made in the text that the lines of the French camp are still visible (though not in their totality) requires some justification. A sentence in a scarce French book written in 1866 that the lines could then be traced, caught my eye and attention. On investigating the subject I found that in the 17th century, the lines were reported to be still visible. I further found the statement made in 1863 by Leo Drouyn in *La Guyenne Anglaise* that they were still visible but that in 25 years they would have completely disappeared. This statement was repeated three years later by Henri Ribadieu in his *La Conquête de la Guyenne*. I found a copy of Drouyn's book in the British Museum, and to my satisfaction it contained a large-scale plan of the camp. I made a tracing of it and took it out to Castillon in 1948. As there had been no reference in any book that I could find, referring to the existence of the lines during the last 82 years I was not hopeful. However I had no difficulty in finding the lines, exactly as depicted on Drouyn's map. My delight was unbounded. The existing lines take the form of a continuous ditch, on the average now one foot deep and about two yards wide. They are the easier to trace since they for the most part have been utilized by the farmers to form field boundaries (in one case a farm boundary). I did not however succeed in locating the supposed grave-pits possibly because the grass was long in that area, and about to be mown. I think there is little doubt that the very indentated trace (it measures nearly 1,600 yards) was in order to provide enfilade fire for the guns, and also to find room in a single line for the great number of guns present. I reckon that 250 guns could at a pinch have been placed in position along the east, south and west sides.

THE NUMBERS

Anglo-Gascons. The earl of Shrewsbury took out with him 3,000 troops. Reinforcements brought by his son, Lord de Lisle, brought this up to about 5,500. But we do not know, (1) the wastage, (2) the proportion put into the field, (3) the number of Gascons engaged. One thing is clear: Talbot set out at short notice taking with him only troops already concentrated at Bordeaux, and without the possibility of picking up more than a handful en route. I should suppose that the resulting number of English troops available could hardly exceed 4,000; if we add as an outside figure 2,000 Gascons it makes the "ceiling" 6,000. Now Jean Chartier gives the figures 5,000 to 6,000, and Professor Lot accepts this. So do I.

French. M. Lot gives the accepted strength of the French army as 9,000, but he adds that the French camp would not be large enough to hold this number and he concludes:

"The most probable thing is that the forces present were approximately equal in number–6,000 men."

This is rather a lame and inconsequential assessment, and one would like to know the basis on which the professor has come to this conclusion. In any case his argument leaves out of account the archers in the priory of St. Lorent and the Bretons in the woods, each 1,000 strong. This would leave only 4,000 to garrison the camp. The horses should only take up one sixth to one quarter of the space. The men would have no tents, it being high summer. To man the perimeter at one man per yard would consume over 2,000 men and the remainder would not require much sleeping space. In short, I consider the camp large enough for the numbers stated, and that the French army was approximately 9,000 strong. As to how many of the 6,000 Anglo-Gascons ever reached the field of battle history is silent.

RETROSPECT

IT is easy to become cynical about the Hundred Years War, and especially about this latter part of it, which for convenience I have called the Agincourt War. For, after 115 years of intermittent strife, England had lost all her traditional possessions in France, and the only asset she could show for all her efforts was a harbour in the extreme north–Calais. Moreover she only relinquished a war on the Continent to become engaged in a fresh one at home. And she had yet to learn that civil strife is the worse evil of the two, for the latter is founded upon envy and and ambition (disguised as "the better government of the realm"), whereas the foreign war can–as this one did–unite a country's inhabitants in a common task.

On the credit side of the account, the Hundred Years War produced a breed of mighty men and illustrious leaders such as can stand comparison with those of any other century in our history. The Crecy War produced a galaxy of great men whose names should in our flowing cups be remembered–Edward III, the Black Prince, Henry of Lancaster, Sir John Chandos, Sir Thomas Dagworth, and many others. The Agincourt War, though not quite so prolific, brought to the fore great leaders such as Henry V, Bedford, Salisbury, and the peerless John Talbot. The country had basked in the sun of their greatness and waxed prosperous in the process, despite taxation for the war. A strong national spirit had been born, one that a generation of civil strife was to prove powerless to eradicate.

France, on the other hand, found herself after the war in a weaker state than that in which she had entered upon it. In the words of Edouard Perroy, "France emerged weakened and worn, and incapable for centuries of resuming her former position." On the other hand, the war had provided her with a band of national heroes, Duguesclin, Dunois, Richemont, La Hire and of course Joan of Arc, and in a specialist sphere Jean Bureau, the greatest artilleryman of his day. The bone of contention – the homage – that had embittered the relations of the two countries for exactly 300 years had been dropped, and for 60 years they were to be at peace with one another.

Yet the long war had ended on an ironical note that was to puzzle the international jurists for another 350 years. (It was not till 1803 that the *fleur de lys* disappeared off the national flag of England.) No treaty of peace was signed, the English claim to the throne of France was not dropped (for England would not consider herself defeated) and the question of the homage lapsed simply because no fief remained in English possession on which it could be claimed. Juridically, I suppose, the war has not yet ended.

INDEX